Campion's Career

Acknowledgements

I wish to thank Joyce Allingham, who gave me permission to quote freely from her sister's work and considerable help in the achievement of the checklist; and Allen J. Hubin, who showed his faith in much of what follows by a serialization in *The Armchair Detective*.

Copyright   1987 by Bowling Green State University Popular Press

Library of Congress Catalogue Card No.: 86-72912

ISBN: 978-0-87972-380-4

Contents

Chapter 1
Before Albert—and Without Him

Margery Allingham was something of an Infant Phenomenon, earning her first professional fee as a writer at the age of eight, and seeing her first novel in print when she was nineteen. Her childhood home was effectively a literary workshop for her parents and their writer friends, and Margery lost no time in joining in. The dust-wrapper of *The Tiger in the Smoke* records her early start and its effect on the exasperated new housemaid who once snatched away her ragged exercise-book, exclaiming "Master, Missus and three strangers all sitting in different rooms writing down lies, and now you startin!" The 'lies' came naturally in a family which 'regarded writing as the only reasonable way of passing the time, let alone earning a living'.

Allinghams had been writers for some generations before Margery so notably crowned the family tradition. One of her forebears wrote transpontine melodramas, some of which survive in the British Library. Her grandfather owned a nonconformist weekly called *The Christian Globe*, and her great-uncle used the pseudonym 'Ralph Rollington' for his stories in boys' comics. Her father was H. J. Allingham, who gave up the editorship of her grandfather's journal to become a prolific and successful pulp writer. Her mother wrote for women's magazines and her aunt was founder and editor of *Picture Show*.

Margery grew to admire her father's professionalism and in later years was proud to sign herself 'his industrious apprentice'. She came to regard herself as 'the last of the professional writers', schooled from childhood in an honorable and demanding tradition. She wrote steadily through her schooldays, 'trying vainly to get into print for nine years whilst handicapped severely by life at a boarding school.' At least four plays were written in her early years, one produced at her school in Cambridge and another at the Regent Street Polytechnic, where she was a student. Another was submitted to Shaw, who offered constructive criticism, and a one-act piece called *Water in a Sieve* was published by Samuel French in 1925, as the author's second book.

For some years Margery Allingham was herself a journeyman writer, producing stories and serials to order, to make a living and buy time for her novels, which were 'not then all that profitable.' She invariably distinguished between 'right hand writing' of the kind that she really wished to do, and the 'left hand writing' imposed on her by economic necessity. One of her earliest chores was to provide a succession of stories for a weekly magazine run by her aunt: based on the plots of current films, these ran to 10,000 words and were dictated to her husband, usually in 'a single twelve-hour sitting'. She also wrote pulp fiction for Lord Northcliffe's popular presses, under the strict supervision of his editors. Youngman Carter recalled 'an epic serial dealing with the adventures of The Society Millgirl and the Seven Wicked Millionaires'. There was some 'left-hand' crime writing, too, like the long story written for an edition of *The Thriller* in 1933 and three books issued under the pseudonym 'Maxwell March.'

As time progressed and her novels gained a hold, Miss Allingham's 'left hand' work became increasingly sophisticated and satisfying. She reviewed novels and wrote the occasional light essay for *Time and Tide*; and she became a regular contributor to *The Strand Magazine*, with the stylish series of stories collected in the two editions of *Mr. Campion and Others*. These are supremely graceful pendants to the major novels that were being written at the same time. Their knight errant is Albert Campion, who is usually involved in rescuing some glossy young woman from the consequences of her follies. Oddly, in view of the quality of her work, the name of Margery Allingham seldom appeared on the magazine's cover (though Agatha Christie's, Dorothy L. Sayers' and Carter Dickson's did). But at least they gave her a good illustrator, Jack M. Faulks, whose drawings are always suave and engaging: his view of Campion is exactly right.

The first book was *Blackkerchief Dick*, a historical adventure novel published by Hodder & Stoughton and Doubleday in 1923, when its author was nineteen. It derives from a series of seances held in August 1921 at an Allingham house on Mersea Island. What emerged from the seances gave Margery her novel, which was publicized as a fictional version of events relayed from the seventeenth century by certain pirates and smugglers. On publication it proved more attractive as a romance than convincing as evidence of occult communication: *The Bookman* for October 1923 welcomed 'a thrilling novel of smuggling days' with 'an exciting and cleverly handled plot of love and stirring adventure': but felt that 'spiritualistic investigators will probably regret that the experiences of the seances were not set forth in an ungarnished manner'. (There was to be nothing 'ungarnished' about Margery Allingham's fictions at any stage of her career). Long afterwards, Youngman Carter claimed that the occult transmissions were probably 'entirely the product of Margery's dynamic imagination'. Whatever the truth of the matter, the book effectively established its young author's competence.

Of the twenty-three novels that followed only two were outside the mystery genre: an early work about youth in the twenties, which remained unpublished, and a wartime family chronicle called *Dance of the Years*, set in the past, like *Blackkerchief Dick*, and based this time on the author's own family history. The unpublished prentice novel gave her considerable trouble, so that she was happy when the time came to 'escape into the Mystery,' the form that drew out her talents and brought them to maturity. Her need for a pattern to work to was answered by the formal disciplines of detective fiction. She saw the mystery as a box with four sides — 'a Killing, a Mystery, an Enquiry and a Conclusion with an Element of Satisfaction in it.' The box gave her 'sanctuary,' restricting without inhibiting her, 'at once a prison and a refuge': she could build on a secure foundation, yet embellish to her heart's content.

She showed her form immediately with *The White Cottage Mystery*, first published as a 'Daily Express' serial in 1927, when she was still only twenty-three. According to Youngman Carter, it was 'wildly mutilated' in the process, so that its book publication the following year must have been doubly gratifying. Despite Miss Allingham's refusal to allow its republication in later years, it remains an attractive book, vividly imagined and confidently achieved. The victim is properly hated by his entire acquaintance and the least likely person proves to be the killer. The investigator is a distinguished Yard inspector called W.T. Challoner, whose son acts as his collaborator. The action moves from rural Kent to Paris and Mentone, where it reaches an unexpected climax when the inspector abandons the case (not because he has not solved it, but because he has). Only after seven more years have passed does he name the killer and explain his delay in doing so.

Because Miss Allingham had not yet invented him, Albert Campion does not appear in *The White Cottage Mystery*. He is deliberately excluded from the later *Black Plumes*, despite its setting in characteristic Allingham territory, close to his home ground. It's the last of the 'thirties' novels, published in 1940, but firmly rooted in a complacent pre-war world, enclosed and cosseted, and even a little preposterous in its serene self-importance. In Campion's stead, a canny old Scots policeman investigates, primly but implacably haunting the scene and not easily to be deflected. He's an engaging character, sinister yet genial, unnerving but somehow deeply reassuring. Despite his shrewdness and the complex pattern he assembles, a bold and brilliant climax finds him not quite a match for a cunning and vengeful killer. For all its preciosity, the narrative achieves a genuine eerie force that distinguishes the book and sets it rather apart. The atmosphere is dark and oppressive, the action concentrated and continually menacing. Only the murderer's motive evokes a wider, bleaker world, austere and remote, and in vivid contrast to the enclave of privilege we are shown.

Something of the same atmosphere persists into the group of four novellas that also stand rather apart from Miss Allingham's more characteristic work: *Wanted: Someone Innocent* and *Last Act*, joined as *Deadly Duo* or *Take Two at Bedtime*, and *The Patient at Peacocks Hall* and *Safer Than Love*, together forming *No Love Lost*. All four are love stories as well as mysteries, in the vein that served Patricia Wentworth so well for so many years. Three are female first-person narratives and all end with the obligatory embrace between the lovers (implicit rather than actual in one case). The dedication of *Deadly Duo* implies a commission from Doubleday, so that it may be legitimate to regard this volume at least as 'left-hand' work, but Margery Allingham was always—and in all senses—a romantic, and it may be that she welcomed the chance to exploit an overt vein of sentiment and, indeed, to test her skill in a relatively unfamiliar field.

The mysteries are effectively shaped and neatly resolved, but the hand of the author is most readily seen in the characterization, whether of a dependable Irish nurse with an accent 'as broad as her beam,' or an elderly char with a keen 'histrionic' instinct for the drama latent in all aspects of life. She does not so much describe people as reveal them to us, with sympathy and humor, insight and zest: the foppish old doctor who drives a vast, high car embellished with 'as much brass as a band'; the 'coarse, kindly' Pimlico landlady in a 'straining gown,' with 'dark red curls' and a 'festoon of chins'; the vivid octogenarian actress who has only to sit on a bed for it to seem 'a throne'; the outspoken small-town lady who gives the arm of a new acquaintance 'a squeeze that would have startled a bear'; and the voluble impresario with 'plump hands dipping and swooping' as he talks, 'like seagulls over the dome of his grey waistcoat.'

In *Safer Than Love* we have our first view of Superintendent Fred South, the unnerving rural policeman who features with Campion and Charlie Luke in *The Beckoning Lady*. As befits a 'legendary personality', he proves elusive and enigmatic, a living presence long before his delayed first appearance. At once smiling and sinister, his manner seems to embody both comfort and threat, like the inspector from *Black Plumes* (and yet significantly, even essentially, unlike him). He is 'Uncle' to everyone, a plump, jocular, 'amusingly ugly' man, with a face that 'could have been designed by Disney' and 'bright little eyes which danced and twinkled and seemed ever stretched to their widest.' His step is light and buoyant, so that his first entry is silent and sudden, like that of 'an amiable demon in a children's play.'

At the start of an interview, he waits for his reassuring appearance to make its effect as a necessary preliminary to the unsettling sequel: 'You think he's your father and mother rolled into one and then—crash!' His habit of smiling broadly persists even when he is 'condoling with the bereaved or giving evidence in court.' On the telephone he sounds 'friendly but sly, like an uncle asking trick questions'; face to face, the dancing eyes seem suddenly 'bright with secret entertainment.' There is 'something sinister in that knowing twinkle with its undercurrent of irrepressible gaiety', and in no time at all the narrator finds she has 'grown to fear' its power to disturb. Even the cooked dinner his wife sends to each temporary base reflects the man's essential ambivalence: is she acting from devotion or subjection?

Chapter 2
Plumpuddings

Albert Campion makes his first appearance at the Black Dudley dinner-table, one murky evening, by candlelight, an uninvited guest at what rapidly whips up into an eventful weekend party. Described in general terms by a fellow-guest as "a lunatic...just a silly ass" (a catchphrase that links him with Bertie Wooster and even facets of Lord Peter Wimsey), the initial account of his appearance bears out this impression. He is "fresh-faced... with tow-colored hair," "foolish, pale-blue eyes behind tortoiseshell-rimmed spectacles," a "slightly receding chin," and a "mouth...unnecessarily full of teeth," through which he speaks in an "absurd falsetto drawl." Although Miss Allingham does not in later novels insist on the receding chin, or the protruding teeth and falsetto voice, Campion's features do not in essentials change over the years: rather, they are modified as she takes him increasingly seriously.

In the same way, although his persona is decidedly comic at first, there is yet implicit in the absurdity something of the seriousness of his later self. Such a question as "Who would dream of the cunning criminal brain that lurks beneath my inoffensive exterior?" is, in fact, a flippant foreshadowing of Campion's essential attitude, that of the guileless-looking nonentity whom it is almost obligatory to understimate. (In the first book, it is Chris Kennedy, the beefy young rugger blue, who makes the mistake: ' "You stand by,' said Kennedy, with something suspiciously like a sneer on his face...'And by the way, I think you're the man to stay with the girls.' There was no mistaking his inference.") When Miss Allingham tells us that "Mr. Campion's personality was a difficult one to take seriously," she is establishing an image of him that persists at least as far as *Flowers for the Judge* in 1936 (where Miss Curley takes some minutes to realize that he is different from the many "consciously funny young men, most of them ill-mannered nincompoops" of her acquaintance, and that his particular "flow of nonsense" cloaks "more than poverty of intelligence.")

Campion's eccentricities save him, in this first book, at least, from the danger of conventionality. There is, after all, nothing exceptional about his heroics at Black Dudley; the courage, the resilience, the resource, constitute the stock-in-trade of the most standard model of fictional adventurer. The special interest of Campion is that we do not at first know how to take him—that he proves, for instance, to have an "agility and strength altogether surprising in one of such a languid appearance": and it is this capacity for "surprising" that makes him, from the first, an intriguing figure with very real possibilities for development.

In this introductory adventure, Campion is very much a man of mystery, quite apart from the uncertainty engendered by his dual personality as harmless clown and man of action. George Abbershaw, the book's amateur detective, is at first unable to "place" him, although convinced that they have met before; and when he does call to mind the circumstances of their previous encounter, which are never specified, he identifies him, not as Albert Campion, but as "Mornington Dodd" (the first of several noms-de-guerre that enliven the earlier novels). Here, too, is the first reference to Campion's real identity, that of the younger son of a noble house: ' " Campion...is your name, I suppose?' 'Well—er—no,' said the irrepressible young man. 'But...my own is rather aristocratic and I never use it in my business.' "

So alarmed is Abbershaw by his earlier knowledge of Campion, and his reflections on the irregular nature of his profession, that he suspects him for a time of the Black Dudley murder; but his conduct is increasingly reassuring, and his apologia sufficiently disarming to remove any serious doubts, for the reader at any rate: "I live, like all intelligent people, by my wits, and although I've often done things that mother wouldn't like, I have remembered her parting words and have never been vulgar... I do almost anything within reason...but nothing sordid or vulgar—quite definitely nothing vulgar." Elsewhere, we have his additional assurance that most of his commissions "are more secret than shady."

This first novel sets the tone for the four "adventure" stories that form a distinctive group at the beginning of Miss Allingham's oeuvre. Although there is a definite murder mystery, which seems of central relevance, but is in fact no more than incidental, it is rather as a novel of action and atmosphere that *The Crime at Black Dudley* (U.S. title: *The Black Dudley Murder*) continues to make its effect. The book is dominated by Black Dudley itself, a "great tomb of a house," "bare and ugly as a fortress," set on the Suffolk coast in "miles of neglected parkland." Within, it is "magnificent," with "a certain dusty majesty," the candlelight sending "great shadows like enormous ghostly hands, creeping up to the oak-beamed ceiling." Here is a fit setting for the Black Dudley dagger, a "long 15th century Italian" weapon of "unmistakably sinister appearance," that seems to "shine out of the dark background like a living and malignant thing," and for the unnerving ritual that attends it, in which it is passed from hand to hand in darkness, to run with blood if handled by a killer.

It is during the ritual that Colonel Gordon Coombe, the owner of Black Dudley, suddenly dies, and a precious document concealed in a wallet disappears, thus establishing the two lines of the action (and, incidentally, a kind of basic pattern for all four "adventure" novels, in each of which a violent death occurs on the periphery of the action, while the main business of those concerned is to retain or gain possession of a precious object). There is much coming and going by way of trapdoors, secret panels, wardrobes and chimneys, and the central action culminates in a spectacular appearance by the Monewdon Hunt, led with impressive panache by Guffy Randall, an old school-friend of Campion's who reappears in *Sweet Danger*.

The narrative is enhanced by the author's characteristic felicity of detail, already much in evidence. The principal villain, "the most dangerous and notorious criminal of modern times" is, incongruously, "the living image of those little busts of Beethoven which are sold at music shops"; the Colonel's vintage car, "one of the pioneers of motor traffic," proves to be set mysteriously "upon the chassis and engine of the latest...Rolls-Royce"; Chris Kennedy attempts a bold break for freedom by filling his drained petrol-tank with high-class Scotch; and, imprisoned in a room upstairs, a vengeful old besom called Mrs. Meade anticipates with confidence the coming Wednesday, when her son,"a rare fighter," will come to exact vengeance on those who have dared to shut her up against her will.

With the departure from Black Dudley, and the disappearance of Campion ("through the portals of one of the most famous and exclusive clubs in the world,") the real impetus goes out of the book, and the closing chapters constitute a rather disappointing coda to the main action. There is an abortive chase after one of the villains for a time suspected of the murder, but the real killer, his motive, and the evidence that betrays him, are not revealed until the last chapter. Miss Allingham was to become more scrupulous in this respect.

Published in 1930, *Mystery Mile*, in which the violent death is a suicide, dispenses with the "whodunit" element altogether. Rather, it is a "whoisit"—who is Simister? the celebrated master-criminal, who was Campion's shadowy employer in *Black Dudley*, and who is very nearly his murderer on this occasion. There are not many candidates for the role, so that the revelation is hardly unexpected; but the clue to his identity is very beguiling, although we do not have sufficient information to read it aright until the author is prepared to elaborate. (Incidentally, Simister's alter ego is revealed in passing in *Traitor's Purse*.)

This second book is less openly melodramatic than *Black Dudley* and there is a slight but perceptible advance in sophistication. The setting is idyllic, a remote village on the Suffolk coast, linked to the mainland by a single strip of land (an attractive map, the first of several, is provided). The Manor is a "long, low, many-gabled building, probably built around 1500", hidden in a "thick belt of elms" sheltering "rose-trees under its eaves," and boasting in the grounds a maze, much overgrown. The Rectory is "ivy-covered," and the locals are interbred, close-knit and feudal to a man (except for the postmaster, a "foreigner" from Yarmouth, and arguably the novel's least successful feature).

Although the story is basically pure adventure—Biddy Paget disappears, and six chapters are devoted to getting her back—there are a number of intriguing questions to be answered, so that the element of mystery is stronger and more rewarding than in the previous book. Why does the Rector of Mystery Mile shoot himself after a visit from a sinister society fortune-teller? Why does he send Campion a red knight from a chess-set as a farewell message? Why must this cryptic message be such a closely-guarded secret? What is the significance of a suitcase full of children's books? The answers to these and other questions are invariably neat and satisfying, as Miss Allingham's answers almost always are, throughout her career.

The object of the villain's fell designs is human on this occasion, the only time in the four "adventure" novels that this is so. Judge Crowdy Lobbett is thought to know more than is good for him, and is accordingly in recurrent danger of sudden death. His preservation is therefore the main preoccupation of his family and friends, and the principal business of the book. Attendant on the action are a number of agreeably comic figures, including George and Anry Willsmore, heading the army of local rustics; Thos. T. Knapp, an unsavory eavesdropper on telephone conversations, whose methods, though deplorable, produce undeniably useful results (he reappears, incidentally, in *More Work for the Undertaker* and *The Mind Readers*); his appalling mother, "a vast florid person" with "scrawny reddish hair" and a face "chiefly remarkable for some three or four attempts at a beard which grew out of large brown moles scattered over her many chins;" the exuberant Ali Fergusson Barber, a loquacious, ubiquitous, long-suffering Turk, drawn with immense bravura; and, in a first sketch already hinting at the richness of things to come, one of Miss Allingham's most engaging and enduring characters, Campion's manservant, Magersfontein Lugg.

For addicts, that it features Lugg for the first time must be the chief distinction of *Mystery Mile*, just as, later, *Sweet Danger* is above all the novel that introduces Amanda. Lugg is first brought to our notice as a "thick and totally unexpected voice" on the telephone, huskily announcing himself as the "Aphrodite Glue Works" and thereby much alarming Marlowe Lobbett on the other end of the line. His actual appearance is delayed until the return to town in search of information, when he is revealed as "the largest and most lugubrious individual Marlowe had ever seen...a hillock of a man, with a big pallid face which reminded one irresistibly of a bull-terrier." He is "practically bald" and conveys an "all-pervading impression of melancholy." His criminal antecedents are delicately hinted at—he wears "what looked remarkably like a convict's tunic"—and the special nature of his relation with Campion—mutual derision veiling the deepest affection and trust—is defined in the first of many entertaining dialogues.

Also in attendance, and again for the first time, is Stanislaus Oates, for something like forty years a principal prop of the C.I.D. in Margery Allingham's stories. It is interesting to note that he is already "the *old* detective," although he has plainly just become a father—and presumably for the first time, since the new tooth of his "son and heir", Campion's godson, forms the opening topic of their initial conversation (also, coincidentally, over the phone). A detective-inspector at this preliminary stage of the acquaintance, he is no more than an outline of the definite character he was to become in later years, a pipe-smoker, a family man, informative and affable, but standing as yet only on the sidelines of the action.

Campion himself is much as before, "a pale young man...trying to hide behind his enormous spectacles," his "natural expression" one of "vacant fatuity," his voice "slightly falsetto." The "silly ass" element is still well to the fore, so much so that a fellow passenger on board the Elephantine wonders if he has "inadvertently stumbled on a mental case," and Marlowe is later prompted to ask, as Campion "rambled on inconsequentially," 'I say...do you always talk like this?' (Lugg's view is refreshingly different: when Campion says "I'm serious," he replies, "That's un'ealthy for a start.")

A revealing phone call establishes that Campion's true Christian name is Rudolph, and that his exalted brother—owner of a Bentley and a chauffeur named Wootton—is called Herbert. Elsewhere we hear that his surname begins with a K (and that is all we ever do learn on the subject), and that, conversely, his list of aliases includes "Tootles Ash" (on the telephone to Oates), and "Hewes" (in conversation with "old W.T."). Supporting evidence of the variety of Campion's noms-de-guerre comes from Giles Paget's account of an extraordinary progress down Regent Street in his company, when they encounter a number of distinguished persons, "every single one" of whom "called him by a different name."

Revealing in a different way is our first glimpse of Campion as lover, albeit an unsuccessful one. For the hand and heart of Biddy Paget, he finds himself in competition with Marlowe Lobbett, a conventional maiden's dream, and for once his eccentric looks and

demeanor do prove a real handicap. But however difficult it is for
Biddy to take him seriously as a lover—and one can see her difficulty—
the reader is clearly expected to do so. In this respect, at least, Campion
is vulnerable, and Miss Allingham in earnest.

Here, too, is our first acquaintance with the flat over the police
station in Bottle Street, off Piccadilly, with its Girtin water-color, its
Rembrandt etching, its "remarkable collection of trophies," including
the Black Dudley dagger, and its distinctive "tradesman's entrance,"
the service lift connecting Campion's dining-room with a cupboard
at the rear óf Rodriguez's restaurant, invaluable in an emergency.
The full address of the flat—No. 17 (becoming 17A in *Police at the
Funeral*)—is not specified until the next book, *Look to the Lady*.

First published in 1931, *Look to the Lady* (U.S. title: *The Gyrth
Chalice Mystery*) is a splendid affair, gay and exciting, and brimming
with imaginative detail, from the opening sequence where Val Gyrth
catches sight of his own name on a cast-off envelope lying amid the
litter of a London square, to the final conversation between Campion
and Professor Cairey regarding the exact nature of the guardian of
the Gyrth Chalice.

The setting is Sanctuary, another of Miss Allingham's charming
Suffolk villages, "one of those staggering pieces of beauty that made
Morland paint in spite of all the noggins of rum in the world." This
time, there are two maps, one of the village with the Tower and Tye
Hall, and the other of the gypsy encampment and the stables on
Heronhoe Heath. The Tower is conventionally "attractive and even
majestic," but an interesting touch of realism enters with the account
of Peck's cottage as "one of those picturesque, insanitary thatched
lath and plaster dwellings which stir admiration and envy in the hearts
of all those who do not have to live in them."

The Gyrth Chalice is coveted by a member of "the most powerful
and...wealthy ring in the world," and the Gyrth family, supported
by Campion, Lugg, a tribe of gypsies and, ultimately and most
effectively, by the fabled guardian of the treasure, find themselves
ranged against "The Daisy," the agent for the covetous villains, whose
identity is confirmed two-thirds of the way through the action. The
chalice is more than ordinarily precious and the Gyrths' guardianship

of it is in the nature of a sacred trust. It is invested with an aura of ceremonial and mystery, and Val regards his aunt's folly in allowing it to be photographed for a glossy magazine as sacrilegious. There is a ritual revelation to the heir on his 25th birthday, of a kind that leaves its mark, and proves to be truly awe-inspiring: the secret in which Campion is finally privileged to share is indeed one "of no ordinary magnitude."

Not only at the Tower is there an atmosphere of mystery and superstition: there is also a resident witch in the village, and a haunted wood nearby. So terrifying is the nameless horror that haunts the wood that Val's aunt, the foolish Lady Pethwick, is literally shocked to death by it, and even Lugg is so unnerved as to "bellow the place down...and generally carry on like an hysterical calf elephant." The evocation of the blood-curdling atmosphere of Pharisees' Clearing as the appalling creature approaches provokes something like an authentic shiver: Campion's is not the only scalp to tingle with sheer nervous apprehension. Nor is the explanation an anti-climax: if anything, it enhances the eerie effect of what has gone before.

The witch is a "venomous old party" named Mrs. Munsey, with "red-rimmed eyes" and a hairless head, living in unspeakable squalor with her idiot son, and commanding a "wealth of archaic invective" that is hair-raising in its intensity, and delivered with a "concentrated hatred" at the object of her displeasure.

Combining with her to add to the color and verve of the narrative and to help justify the title are two other distinctive women—Mrs. Dick Shannon, a noisy, intrepid horsewoman, and Mrs. Sarah, the Gypsy Queen. Mrs. Shannon is an "evident...personage," a mannish, commanding woman with "an eye like a hawk," a "high strident voice" and a "wrist like flexed steel." People are "impelled by the force of her vigorous personality" to do what they would prefer not to do, and she reveals a positive genius for embarrassing her acquaintances in company. One is forced, however, to concede her a reluctant admiration: her superb self-possession quite literally never deserts her, not even in the most fantastically daunting circumstances.

Mrs. Sarah's authority is less abrasive, but no less positive in its quiet way. A much be-ringed, "monstrously fat old woman," who looks like a "figure of Hotei...all wrapped up in colored print," she makes a single decisive appearance, and proves a very ready help when the call comes.

Campion is at his boldest, outsmarting the enemy by devious maneuvers; invoking two aliases at need ("Christopher Twelvetrees" at the City house of Mr. Israel Melchizadek, and "Orlando" to secure the gypsies); decoying the horror of Pharisee's Clearing into the stacknet; and finally braving the lion in its den, and being almost trampled to death by a frenzied mare as a result (a near-death that is only marginally less spectacular than the villain's actual end). Still very much the conscious clown, he makes his first appearance at the door of his flat trailing a pink balloon on a string, considerably startling Val Gyrth, who has never met him before. The flow of badinage is usually agreeable and occasionally witty as when he swears by "the bones of my Aunt Joanna and her box," or reflects philosophically that "All these things are ordained, as the old lady said at the Church Congress." At moments of drama, the "inane expression upon his face" still appears, if anything,"more strongly marked than ever," and his assertion at a time of maximum danger that "Manly courage, intelligence and resource are my strong points" maintains the casual irony of his customary stance.

Oates is on hand as occasional consultant, and Lugg is happily much in evidence, emerging strongly as a personality in his own right. His nervous collapse after his night of horrors in the wood is one of the most engaging episodes in his entire career: "The room was darkened, and there was a muffled wail from a bed in the far corner... [Campion] turned to face the cowering object who peered at him wildly from beneath the bed quilt...Mr. Lugg pulled himself together. The sight of his master seemed to revive those sparks of truculence still left in his nature. 'I've resigned,' he said at length.

' " I should hope so,' said Campion bitterly. 'The sooner you clear out and stop disgracing me the better I shall like it.'

"Mr. Lugg sat up in bed. 'Gawd, I 'ave 'ad a night,' he said weakly. 'I nearly lost me reason for yer, and this is 'ow yer treat me... You spend the night in the wood and I'll take you to Colney 'Atch in the morning. That thing killed Lady Pethwick... And she wasn't no weakling, let me tell yer. She was a strong-minded woman. A weak-minded one would 'ave burst.' "

His final appearance is equally characteristic: "Coming across the lawn towards them, sedate, and about as graceful as a circus elephant, was Mr. Lugg. As he came nearer they saw that his immense white face wore an almost reverent expression.

"'Ere,' he said huskily as he approached his master, see 'oo's come? Orders are for you to nip into the 'ouse and report in the library. Lumme,' he added, 'you in flannels, too. I believe there's an 'ole comin' in the sole of them shoes.' "

These and similar "picturesque remarks" from Campion's incomparable henchman punctuate and enliven the novel, contributing richly to one of the author's most spirited achievements.

Last and best of the four "adventure" novels is *Sweet Danger*, (U.S. title: *The Kingdom of Death*) published in 1933, the book that introduces Amanda and gives Mr. Campion's "lighter side" its final uninhibited fling, including an improbable transvestite stint in some of Amanda's aunt's old clothes. Even his first appearance is more than usually startling, and Guffy Randall may be forgiven for misjudging his welcome when he blunders cheerfully into his presence at the Hotel Beauregard in Mentone. With Johnathan Eager-Wright and Dicky Farquharson in solemn attendance, Campion is holding court as the Hereditary Paladin of Averna, which accounts for Guffy's decidedly chilly reception: it is, after all, hardly correct procedure to greet even a minor royal personage with the words, "What ho, your Highness!"

Averna, a minute Dalmatian state of hitherto minimal significance, has been rendered "a natural harbor with natural fuel" by a recent earthquake, and is now ripe for exploitation. It belongs both by right of conquest and subsequent purchase to the noble but depleted Pontisbright family, now represented by Amanda Fitton and her brother and sister; and it is Campion's concern to trace the proofs of their ownership before Brett Savanake, a bold, bad baron of commerce, can lay unscrupulous hands on them.

Specifically, both men are after the Pontisbright crown and its attendant documents, the charter granted by Henry IV, and Metternich's receipt for the purchase-money in 1815. The chase involves them in "a fine old-fashioned treasure hunt with clues complete"—

a cryptic account of the crown from a MS in the British Museum, and a teasing verse octet carved on "a huge cross-section of an oak-bole." Campion's ingenuity is fully equal to all this: he locates the charter by running a drum to earth in a Norwich museum; recognizes the crown in the more humbly decorative role to which time has reduced it; and, with Amanda's technical guidance, contrives a prodigious device for revealing the whereabouts of the Metternich receipt.

Pontisbright appears, if anything, even more idyllic than Mystery Mile or Sanctuary. The air seems characteristically "warm and flower – scented", and the village looks unalterably tranquil in "the last rays of the sun." The mill in its setting represents the "real rustic loveliness of Suffolk at its best," and the mill-house is revealed as "amazingly attractive," a "nearly perfect example of late 15th century architecture," with a "certain drowsy elegance...very soothing and comforting in a madly gyrating world."

And yet this is not, after all, cloud-cuckoo-land. Our introduction to the vicinity is by way of a sign chalked on a gatepost— a cross surmounted by a cedilla—which Campion interprets as the primitive "God-help-us" mark, "probably the most ancient symbol in the world"; and it soon becomes apparent, from the innkeeper's patent terror of "the powers of darkness," and Lugg's discovery, laid out on the heath, of a corpse which subsequently disappears, that the village is in the grip of a superstitious dread so pervasive that not even Amanda is untouched by it.

This subsidiary mystery of the stricken atmosphere of the valley deeply involves the local doctor, whose explanation, of a curse afflicting the inhabitants in the form of a terrible disease, is rejected by Campion on at least two counts. But it is not until his primary concern is approaching its climax and demanding all his attention, that he realizes the full extent of the doctor's involvement, and the true nature of his "unusual practice," so that the two lines of the action finally converge in a vivid total denouement of gratifying splendor.

The Fittons, and their downright, dependable aunt, Miss Huntingforest, have a "family gift for making friends," and their charm is a potent force to which the visitors succumb to such an extent that Eager-Wright, during the initial interview with Amanda, is unable to "take his eyes off her face," and Guffy and Mary are engaged within the week. Mary, in the words of her lover, is "sweet...and womanly. Gentle, discreet, and all that sort of thing," and Hal, too, is sober, with a "grave courtesy which was his chief characteristic." At sixteen, the youngest of the three, he is endearingly solemn and middle-aged in manner, very much on his dignity as head of his diminished house, and deeply shocked by Amanda's questionable goings-on. Distinguished, like his sisters, by the flaming Pontisbright hair, he looks, in the innkeeper's memorable phrase, "like the burning bush coming along."

Amanda is at first a voice in the gloom, greeting her prospective paying guests in near-darkness, and establishing that they don't mind "tears in the furniture" before allowing any light to enter the threadbare room. But amid the vanished glories of her setting, "the girl herself" glows with youth and health and beauty. She is almost eighteen, with "big honey-brown eyes," "an extraordinary mop of hair so red that it was remarkable in itself," and a "wholly disarming" smile which "opened her mouth into a triangle, and revealed very small white even teeth." The author stresses her rarity: she is "at a stage of physical perfection seldom attained at any age," and her Pontisbright hair is of "a blazing, flaming and yet subtle color which is as rare as it is beautiful."

She proves a splendid ally, distinguished especially by electrical skills uncommon in one of her age and sex. Her gifts are renowned locally—the landlord marvels at her offer to write his name in lights— and her proudest possessions are her dynamo and "an extremely ancient but unmistakable electric brougham," which cost her a pound, but is limited to a maximum of five miles at a time, two-and-a-half there and two-and-a-half back: "then the batteries have to be recharged." It is her technical expertise that enables Campion to bring the third and most testing part of the hunt to a successful conclusion, and it is typical of Amanda, no believer in half-measures, that the device she achieves is so phenomenal as to become "one of the wonders of Suffolk for many years to come."

She is compact of all the virtues—candid, intelligent, loyal, resourceful and resilient, with a natural gaiety and, at the desperate climax to the adventure, uncommon courage. Even her willfulness, the truculence with Hal, is endearing, so that one is inclined to agree with Guffy's reflection "that the Fitton family had a charm that made even their quarrelling delightful." Her spirit is indomitable, whether she is staggering to her feet, "stiff and breathless and quivering with rage" after the "visitation" by Savanake's minions, or displaying, the morning after, "a light of triumph in her eye, and an even more pronounced jauntiness than before, . . . her spirit . . . strengthened rather than diminished" by what she has been through. At the moment of greatest danger, when everything appears to depend on her and, for all she knows, Campion is drowned in the mill-pool, "her courage, which had temporarily deserted her," returns with the realization that there "was something definite to be done."

At the end, Campion finds himself strangely moved by her as she lies in bed recovering from her ordeal—and by no means solely because she has saved his life. Earlier, he has gone "out after Savanake with the intent to kill," "because of something which he would not have explained even if he could, and which was definitely to do with Amanda"; and now, in assent to her request to be allowed to put him "on the top" of her "list," when the six years she needs to become "ready" for him are up, he holds out his hand "with sudden eagerness." He stands finally, "looking down very tenderly at this odd little person who had come crashing through one of the most harrowing adventures he had ever known and with unerring instinct had torn open old scars, revived old fires which he had believed extinct." As a love-scene it is decidedly unorthodox, though highly characteristic of the two people involved in it; and by concluding the first phase of Mr. Campion's career with an authentic emotional experience, Miss Allingham points decisively towards the time of greater responsibility and maturity that is now upon him.

Chapter 3
Growing Up

He has in fact already had his first taste of more serious commitments, in *Police at the Funeral*, published in 1931, two years before *Sweet Danger*. It is interesting, here, to note Margery Allingham's own distinction (in a brief preface to *Death of a Ghost*) between those adventures of Campion's "which have been frankly picaresque," and those in which he "comes up against less highly colored but even more grave difficulties." Of this latter group, *Police at the Funeral* is the first and one of the best.

Campion, as is fitting, is presented in a more sober light, and though he continues to prattle inconsequentially, causing both Uncle William and Joyce Blount to doubt him (Joyce, "who had no experience of Mr. Campion's vagaries, shot him a quick, dubious glance;" and Uncle William's "dubiousness concerning that young man's possible use in...an emergency was as apparent as though he had spoken it"), his accomplished handling of a difficult case is ample vindication. For the first time, Campion feels called upon seriously to justify himself, putting Joyce's doubts into words: "Am I a serious practitioner or someone playing the fool?"; and going on to assure her that he is "deadly serious... My amiable idiocy is mainly natural, but it's also my stock-in-trade" (a more open acknowledgement of the standpoint indicated by the flippant question in *Black Dudley*). Campion's actual answer to Joyce's question, "Don't you find your manner a ... detriment in your business?" is a characteristically light evasion: "Can a leopard change his spots? I am as I am"; but the implicit answer is a rousing negative: if anything, his "faint inconsequential air" and facility for appearing "almost imbecile" at times are natural advantages of inestimable value.

Police at the Funeral marks the author's artistic maturity: it is a novel of palpable distinction, with an atmosphere at once leisurely and menacing, writing of wit and perception, and an intricate, teasing action. Campion is summoned to Cambridge on the disappearance of Andrew Seeley, disagreeable uncle of Joyce, who is the fiancee of a friend. The setting is Socrates Close, home of Mrs. Caroline Faraday, relict (the mere word "widow" seems inadequate) of the celebrated Dr. Faraday, Master of Ignatius, and, almost certainly, "the last household in England of its kind" (at one point the company sits down to "Mrs. Beeton's complete Friday menu for April in non-Catholic households"). The old lady's word is law, and in their middle age her two daughters, her son and her nephew are subjected to the rigorous disciplines of children in a Victorian household: "that atmosphere of restraint which is so racking in adolescence was here applied to age:" Campion's friend Marcus defines the specific dangers inherent in the situation: "There's rank evil there," he went on unexpectedly... "There they are, a family forty years out of date, all vigorous, energetic people by temperament, all, save for the old lady, without their fair share of brains, and herded together in that great mausoleum of a house, tyrannized over by one of the most astounding personalities I've ever encountered...there are stricter rules in that house than you or I were ever forced to keep at our schools. And there is no escape...no vent to the suppressed hatreds, petty jealousies, desires and impulses of any living soul under that roof."

Not surprisingly, things start to happen. Andrew is found dead in the river and Julia Faraday poisoned in bed; a clock-weight, a window-cord and a revolver are discovered to have vanished; a curious sign appears on the library window, with a monstrous naked footprint beneath it; Uncle William, in the small hours, suffers a savage cut on the hand from an unexplained source; Campion hears sinister repetitive whispers outside his bedroom window — and so it goes on, in gorgeous profusion, the stuff of which really first-rate detective stories are made, the mystery intensifying with every further revelation, and, at the end, an explanatory conjuring trick that is both meticulous and plausible.

Dominating the action, as she dominates her household, is Great-Aunt Caroline, "a prodigious old Hecuba," "like Queen Elizabeth and the Pope rolled into one," physically frail, but with a proud and steely spirit, melting into genuine graciousness to those who find her favor, but daunting and remote to those who do not (even Campion, from the first one of the favored, experiences "one terrible moment" when he fears he might have offended her). Unlike Oates, who is ill-at-ease in her presence, Campion is utterly charmed by her, responding to her in the manner born. In private, she addresses him as "Rudolph," revealing an intimate knowledge of his family and a steady faith in his ability to act for her, both derived, it appears, from a correspondence of 45 years' standing with "Emily, the dowager," Mr. Campion's grandmother. Her addiction to lace is much in evidence, and the variations in her dress are lovingly recorded: clearly, Miss Allingham, like Campion himself, "had an eye for such things." Not even she is immune from suspicion, however: if the crimes are beyond her physically, might she nonetheless be the brain behind them, using for her purpose the "strength, courage and blind trust" in herself of her powerful personal maid, Alice? In such a context of suspicion, her remark "I don't know how I should get on without Alice" assumes an ominous overtone that sets Campion wondering.

Her son, William, for some time a more definite suspect, is the most engaging figure in the book, a full-scale characterization of sustained comic force. A "shortish, tubby individual" of "about 55," he has a "pink face, bright greedy little blue eyes," a would-be military moustache, and a "smug personality." He shares with Falstaff the supreme gift of endearing himself in spite of his shortcomings, and his life follows a pattern of small-scale subterfuge repeatedly subjected to embarrassing exposure. His principal weapon in the face of attack is truculence—"his was not the temperament to accept... reproaches with dignity or even politeness"—and he appears frequently in danger of bursting from an excess of emotion, "his face suffusing with angry color." On his first entry, he blows and fumes "like the proverbial frog," and when he is later accused by his sister of becoming "secretly—inebriated" on occasion, he stands "petrified...a hunted expression in his little blue eyes," glaring "balefully from his flaming face." Not until his "complete suffocation" appears "no longer probable," does he recover his voice "on a note clearly higher and louder than he intended," to bluster anew.

Challenged by Oates to justify his contention that it was a cat that attacked him, he releases a "high-pitched squawk of exasperation," and a subsequent bout of "subterranean rumbling" is "followed by an explosion in a much higher key than he or anyone else had expected." (Uncle William's refusal to budge on the issue of the "cat" is, for the reader, one of his most endearing attitudes, and though one sympathizes with the investigating powers, especially Oates, it is impossible to agree with Campion that he is here "not at his best.") Elsewhere he is peremptory with a charge of having made conflicting statements—"All this insistence on time is very confusing"—and unwilling to provide details of a questionable visit to a Harley Street nerve specialist, "grunting softly to himself like a simmering kettle" before giving in and supplying the exact information. Even his passing claim to an athletic past is no more than incidental humbug—"I don't take a cold tub now. When a man gets to my age he has to look after himself. Penalty of being an old athlete"—and it is small wonder that Marcus, "who knew the sum total of Uncle William's athletic prowess was represented by the silver mug gained at a preparatory school in 1881," should frown "at this unwarrantable assertion."

Most disarming are his persistent, doomed attempts to disguise his fondness for the bottle by accusing his mother of senile delusions on the subject, and referring repeatedly to the alcoholic tendencies of Andrew—"He paused and added with a grotesque droop of a baggy eyelid, 'Drank like a sponge, under the rose' ". When it becomes necessary to admit to drowning his sorrows "now and again" as a relief from "living with a pack of ill-natured fools," he contrives "to convey the impression that he regarded himself as a man confessing to a past peccadillo with a good grace"; and the manly frankness of his undertaking to Campion is altogether admirable: "He laid a heavy hand on the young man's shoulder, peered into his face and spoke with deadly earnestness. 'I'm telling you as one man to another. I'm going to cut out the glass. Not another drink until this business is over.' " (Nor does the irony depend only on "the empty decanter downstairs" and the removal of "the key of the tantalus": the full implications do not emerge until the denouement). In his different way, Uncle William is as much a triumph as Lugg, and it is cause for rejoicing that he reappears in *Dancers in Mourning* and even, posthumously, alas, as late as *The Beckoning Lady.*

The most unexpected member of the family is the black sheep, Cousin George, a seedy and disreputable figure with a "coarse red face, sagging mouth and general air of leering satisfaction." After setting the household briefly but decisively by the ears, he suffers a gratifying fate in the very finest traditions of poetic justice.

But most intriguing of all, in many ways, is the portrait that slowly emerges of the dead Andrew. No one has a good word to say for him, and not even the "de mortuis" tag can protect his deplorable memory for long. To Marcus he was a "petty cantankerous little person" with "a strain of the bounder in him," and Uncle William imagines him "looking up from Hades. . . and laughing at the precious uncomfortable situation he's got us all into." But it is Joyce who really points for Campion the dead man's true nature: "He was a beast" who "moved even the meekest. . .to a sort of frenzy of loathing at times." A host of subtle details go to endorse her view and compose the picture: the photograph of Campion's uncle, the Bishop of Devizes, with its fake inscription; the horrifying small relief of the Laocoon, which Andrew had tried to insist that his cousin Kitty should learn to live with; the devious irony whereby he flattered Kitty into exhibiting on the dining room wall a "patently plebeian" photograph of her late husband; and the "vituperance. . .urge and. . .spitefulness" of his book attacking the memory of his uncle, Dr. Faraday. These and similar touches are assembled with impressive imaginative truth to define a personality of ugly complexity.

Because Joyce's account of Socrates Close decides Campion "that Lugg must be kept out of this," he makes only a token appearance at the beginning of the book—sufficient, however, to allow him to apologize to Joyce for "being in negligee" on entering the room in shirtsleeves (and to return later "resplendent in a grey cardigan"), and to establish that his "pale waste of a face" is now "relieved by an immense pair of black moustaches," a source of evident pride.

Oates, officially in charge of the investigation, is seen in action for the first time. "Lately promoted to the Big Five," he is still the "doting father," whose good temper returns "miraculously. . .at the mention of his son." His contribution to the investigation consists principally in trying to build a case against Uncle William, and despite the author's evident affection for him, and the "admiration" Campion "had always felt for this quiet, grave man with the penetrating grey eyes," it is difficult not to see him as a foil for Campion's superior luck and judgement.

Death of a Ghost, which followed *Sweet Danger* in 1934, confirms the impression that Margery Allingham was now a fully mature artist. One of the most individual of her books, part whodunit, part investigation into the murderer's mind and personality, it appears to be constructed with almost mathematical precision, the action falling neatly into four parts. The first ten chapters, which cover about 2/5ths of the book, create the situation and atmosphere of the classic whodunit. The next section, a further fifth, contains the second killing and Campion's growing conviction that he has recognized the killer, and the third, again roughly a fifth, provides the additional information necessary to clinch the case. But because there is no material evidence, Campion feels obliged to offer himself as a third victim, and the last fifth of the book is a coda to the main action, in which he almost loses the life he is using as bait (under a tube-train), and the murderer comes to a shocking end (but one for which, in a second reading at least, one realizes the author has skillfully prepared us).

The quality of the book declares itself immediately in the brilliance of the opening chapter, where the author sets up with economy and precision an explosive situation involving a number of colorful people. The setting for the first time is London, Little Venice on the eve of the eighth of John Lafcadio's posthumous one-picture shows, when seven of the nine principals in the subsequent drama congregate, with Campion, in the dead artist's studio. Lafcadio has guaranteed himself at least a limited immortality by leaving a number of pictures to be shown, one at a time, annually, from the tenth year after his death. Though not the "ghost" of the title (the subtlety of that point does not emerge for some time), he is very much a "presence" in the novel, and his circle in life continues to revolve around his bravura personality long after his death.

Assembled on the eve of Show Sunday are Lafcadio's widow, Belle; his passionate grand-daughter, Linda; his self-appointed "entrepreneur" and critic, Max Fustian; two of his former models, his sometime "inspiration", Donna Beatrice (nee Harriet Pickering), and the Italian Lisa, once a beauty, but now a "withered, rather terrible old woman"; the woeful, ineffectual Tennyson Potter, who devotes his life to lithography in red sandstone; and Tommy Dacre, a gifted young artist, loved by Linda, whose imminent destiny it is to die and to have all his extant works destroyed by an unknown hand. Introduced later are Rosa-Rosa, the cause of the tension between Tommy and Linda, a naive Italian model, "a John gipsy" with "the face of a fiend"; and a figure of more central importance, Potter's wife Claire, another of Lafcadio's models, "one of those efficient handmaids-of-all-work to the arts," a dowdy, commonly brisk little woman, but now incongruously harried by guilt.

Belle is old and stout—"ample" is the author's kinder word—and creased like the portraits of Rembrandt's mother, but her charm is potent and lasting, and the other women in the book are outclassed by her. Campion's warm affection for her is characterized by the special protective tenderness that distinguishes his relations with older women, whether natural aristocrats like Belle and Great-Aunt Caroline, or game old girls like Renee Roper and Poppy Bellew (whereas Amanda has largely to take his affection as read, at least before they are married).

Contrasting with the genuineness of Belle are the affectations of Donna Beatrice and Fustian, each a victim of the author's cool raillery. Both are practiced poseurs—it is relevant that at one point an unexpected development startles them simultaneously "out of their respective poses"—but Donna Beatrice performs on a necessarily more restricted stage than Max, who is on a grander scale altogether. She has all the forlornness of something that has outlived its period without adapting to change; from being "a lady who had caused a certain amount of flutter in artistic circles in 1900" with an "infinite capacity for sitting still and looking lovely," she is now reduced by time to "a figure of faintly uncomfortable pathos" like "a pressed rose, a little brown about the edges and scarcely even of sentimental value." But she makes a brave and entertaining show, directing the labors of the Guild of Women Workers in Precious Metal, and making "mystic revelations" in a voice "soft and intentionally vibrant"; and though it is possible to disconcert her, it is by no means easy.

Fustian's persona is less uncompromisingly eccentric. His affectations are geared to a wider and more sophisticated sphere, and for all his occasional absurdity, he has impressive moments that mark him as a force to be considered: "his personality, exotic and fantastic as it was...never...overstepped the verge into the ridiculous." A remark of Belle's forewarns us of his extreme egocentricity and prepares us for his first flamboyant entry: "His first book about Johnnie...was called *The Art of John Lafcadio, by one who knew him*. His eighth...came out yesterday. It's called *Max Fustian Looks at Art: a critical survey of the works of John Lafcadio by Europe's foremost critic*.' " He does not so much enter the house as "surge" into it, "irresistibly, and with the same conscious power with which a successful actor-manager makes his first appearance in the first act of a new play": inside, he stands for a moment, "holding the gesture of welcome as one who realizes he has made an entrance." Professionally, he is formidable, his galleries "a fitting tribute to his taste and business acumen," his salesmanship the perfected technique of a master, as witness the "ordeal by innuendo" to which he subjects a hapless prospective buyer. "In his own surroundings" he seems "a more comprehensible person than he appeared in Lafcadio's home," and Campion comes to "regard him with a new interest": Fustian belies his name, in fact, and Campion is led to acknowledge that he is "not merely an empty poseur," but "a most arresting personality" with "a tortuous, subtle brain, unexpectedly mobile and adroit."

In this context, Campion is more subdued than we have ever known him hitherto: gone are the cheerful inanities of the earlier books—instead he is on his best behavior throughout. Even his appearance, though essentially as always, is modified, so that now"the general impression one received of him was that he was well-bred and a trifle absent-minded" (and, of course, by implication, easy to underestimate). Clearly, he has recognized the need to grow up, and one sees why Miss Allingham prefaced the book with a brief apologia.

As a detective, he is here at his most subtle and perceptive, since there is no hard evidence at all, and Oates, his initial suspect cleared by the second killing, is at a loss. Campion feels his way to the killer's identity by an intuitive grasp of an "unmistakable family likeness" between two important features of the action. He becomes "aware that the root of the uncomfortable impression chipping at his mind" lies in "something which his unconscious mind had seized and was fighting to point out to him." When his conscious mind makes the connection, "the idea which had been nibbling at the back of his mind" suddenly becomes clear, and its significance sends "an unaccustomed thrill down his spine": he is "momentarily stricken by what he could only regard as a species of revelation." It is an exciting process, for the reader as for Campion, and its achievement confirms his title to the most serious consideration.

The next novel, *Flowers for the Judge*, published in 1936 stands apart from most of Margery Allingham's work in two ways: it is her nearest approach to a courtroom drama, and the action is centered on a pair of lovers, Gina Brande and Mike Wedgwood. It is arguably the least rewarding of the earlier mature novels, mainly from an excessive sentimentality that envelops the central pair. As the key figures at the trial, Mike in the dock, Gina the victim's widow, they become rather too obvious victims of circumstance, their innocent, unspoken love inflated by odious publicity into a sustained, impassioned adultery, their bruised emotions impossible to escape for long. They fall, too, so palpably within the convention that young lovers are incapable of murder as to reduce by two an already limited number of suspects.

Almost everyone involved is associated with the family firm of Barnabas & Co., "publishers since 1810 at the Sign of the Golden Quiver" in Holborn. Of the three partners, all cousins, Mike is the most junior: Paul, the next in seniority, is Gina's husband, the murder victim, dead before we meet him. Head of the firm is the oldest of the cousins, John Widdowson, "an impressive, interesting-looking person, with his tall, slender figure, little dried-up yellow face and close cropped white hair." Campion's estimate of him as "a spoilt child of his profession," a "little tyrant nurtured" in a "carefully prepared nursery," is very much in keeping with Miss Curley's reflective contempt for her employer's "irascibility, his pomposity and his moments of sheer obstinacy"; and yet, Campion is willing to concede that he has "met his battles" and "fought and won them," and that his face is "by no means a weak" one. His settled attitude to the catastrophic events that overtake the firm is very much that traditionally ascribed to the ostrich, and it takes a totally unexpected body-blow like the verdict against Mike at the coroner's court to shake him out of his bland, indifferent self-containment in the face of disaster.

A fourth cousin, Ritchie Barnabas, holds the position of Reader to the firm. A "tall, loosely-built" man, with big, bony hands, "like some thin and dusty ghost," he has "the emotional outlook of a child and the mind of a schoolboy": the "mainspring of his personality" is a "complete simplicity." He is very much a solitary, spending long hours alone in "a small room at the top of the building," detached by temperament, and, significantly, "out of the circle, leaning back in a chair in the shadows" when we meet the assembled company. His "habit of flitting from subject to subject, linked only by some erratic thought process at which one could only guess" is reflected in staccato, Jingle-like speech and wild, inarticulate gestures; and though not the "romantic and mysterious figure with some secret inner life too delicate or possibly too poetic for general expression" that certain young women had occasionally supposed him to be, subsequent events reveal a sufficient, if ironic truth in this assessment. For all his oddity, he is not without charm: to Gina he is a "sweet person," and in the process of comforting a distraught girl, he reveals "a gentleness...which was very attractive." And yet, in the final analysis, Ritchie is rather less engaging than Miss Allingham clearly intended him to be: he, too, like Mike and Gina, is seen through a sentimental haze that damps one's response to an original conception.

Of the other characters, Miss Curley, whose "benevolent and omniscient intelligence" is "one of the firm's most important assets," makes the most agreeable impression, proving her worth in the crisis and helping to sustain Gina in her ordeal. Yet another Barnabas connection, Cousin Alexander, enters the action to take charge of Mike's defense, and we are given an exhilarating account of his commanding manner: especially rewarding is his emotional reconstruction of Mike's unfortunate walk on the night of the murder, with the regretful conclusion that, because "love is suspicious" in law, he won't be able to use it. Mrs. Austin, Gina's char, torn between genuine solicitude for her employer and ghoulish delight at the sensational turn of events, is another diverting figure: but the disagreeable Mr. Rigget, ferreting furtively on the edges of the action, and grovelling in self-abasement before Campion, is more difficult to accept.

Campion is brought in by an invitation to call after "shop tea," a traditional Sunday-night inquest on the day's papers for the family and Miss Curley. The usual company is assembled, except for Paul, Gina's husband, whose conspicuous absence is also the reason for Mr. Campion's invitation. During the evening Mike goes down to the Barnabas strong-room next door; and it is here that Paul's body, dead for several days and sprawled where no one could miss it, is discovered the following morning. Not unnaturally, suspicion immediately centers on Mike, and he finds himself, with Gina, trapped in the events that culminate in his trial for his cousin's murder.

A unique feature of the book is the protracted treatment of courtroom procedures, in the five chapters devoted to the inquest on Paul and Mike's subsequent trial. Although she never again ventured at such length into the courtroom, Miss Allingham shows herself fully equal to the convention, avoiding the monotony inherent in the formal pattern of question and answer, and alive to its dramatic possibilities.

Campion, of course, plays no part in all this: that officialdom looks to carry the charge against Mike is all the more reason for him to get on with finding the real murderer—and, incidentally, to probe the beguiling subsidiary mystery of the disappearance of Tom Barnabas, brother of Ritchie and cousin and co-partner of John, who vanished into air one morning in May, twenty years earlier. (Miss Curley gives us an intriguing hint as to the manner of his disappearance, should we be perceptive enough to interpret it properly.) Campion solves both problems creditably enough, though not, one feels, inspiringly; fixing the role of the secretary Miss Netley, and her bank-book, and recognizing, with the help of his godfather, Professor Bunney, that one of the firm's greatest treasures, the manuscript of "The Gallivant," an unpublished play by Congreve "set down by his own hand," is not merely an attractive incidental, but an item of central relevance. Having alerted the killer, he very nearly succeeds Paul as second victim, all but hurling himself at the door that opens over a sheer drop of three floors onto "the jagged stone foundations of the house that had been next door."

His first appearance comes as something of a shock to Miss Curley, who knows of him only by repute, and is "therefore quite unprepared" for his "slender, drooping figure" and the "pale, ingenuous face," masked as always by "immense and unusually solid horn-rimmed spectacles". Nor do his opening remarks, in which he appears to have reverted to his earlier manner, at all allay her misgivings: "'No tea? No party? It must be business then,' he chattered on, smiling affably. 'Cheap, clean and trustworthy, fifteen months in last place, and a conviction at the end of it.' " But he has "the grace to look abashed" at finding her eyes fixed "upon him in frozen disapproval," and by the end of the evening has sufficiently made amends for her to summon him at the first available opportunity the following morning.

Lugg is happily restored, if not exactly to prominence, at least to a substantial subsidiary position. His first entry is magnificent: "There was a rumble in the other room as though a minor earthquake had disturbed it, and preceded by the sound of deep breathing, Magersfontein Lugg surged into the room." His principal function is to act as a kind of bodeful Cassandra, whose message, delivered in a "thick, inexpressibly melancholy voice" is that it's "going to be a nasty case" and the best thing Mr. Campion can do is to "keep out of it." He has entered a new phase in his career and, on the strength of Campion's possibly improving chances of becoming a duke has acquired "a black velvet jacket," a "superior" set of drinking companions, and a new air of refinement. "I see in the paper that a certain important relative of yours is not too well, and if anything 'appened to 'im and you were suddenly called to take your place in the world I should like to be prepared." The ringing of the doorbell and the need to appear at his best before the visitor prompt a further show of affection: "Moving across the room, he opened the bottom drawer of a bureau, and took therefrom, to Mr. Campion's horror, a remarkable contraption consisting of a stiff collar with a black bow tie attached. With perfect solemnity and a certain amount of pride, Mr. Lugg fastened this monstrosity round his neck by means of a button at the back, and moved ponderously out of the room, leaving his employer momentarily speechless."

Earlier, he has reluctantly surrendered to pressure and agreed to act as a go-between when Campion wants to establish contact with a shady old key - smith in the purlieus of Camden Town (despite fears of the question "Surely I saw you in Camden Town, Mr. Lugg?" from housemaids in the years ahead). But, once embarked on the enterprise, his spirits perceptibly soar, and Campion becomes convinced that he is "beginning to enjoy himself for the first time...for years." The episode is another of the most rewarding in Lugg's career:

"...they paused in the narrow, dusty little road...while Lugg went through an elaborate pantomime of noticing a small shop some few doors down on the opposite side.

"'Why, there's Mr. Samson's joint!' he said, with theatrical astonishment. 'I wonder if 'e's still alive? I'd better go and look 'im up...' With the nonchalance of a loiterer observing a policeman, Mr. Lugg lounged into the shop, beckoning Mr. Campion to follow him with a jerk of his shoulder.

"...presently a bright young man...sauntered towards them. Mr. Lugg showed surprise.

"'Business changed 'ands?' he asked suspiciously. 'I come reely to enquire after an old friend, Mr. Samson.'

"The young man eyed Lugg...'One of the old brigade aren't yer?' he said cheekily... Mr. Lugg was taken off his balance.

"''Ere, what're you gettin' at?' he said, taking a menacing step forward. 'When I want any lip from two penn'orth of string bag I'll ask for it.' In spite of a certain flabbiness induced by high life, Mr. Lugg was still a formidable opponent, and he was not alone. The young man retreated."

The interview is satisfactory and the old man comes across with the wished-for key; and when Campion returns home battered and bruised after expecting to make use of it but encountering instead the frantic Mr. Rigget, Lugg is predictably tart, the more so because of the hurt he secretly feels at not having been invited to participate.

For habit dies hard, and in the process of self-improvement Lugg has become a battlefield of conflicting emotions. Patching up Mr. Campion after his all-in fight with Rigget, he is clearly "the victim of a two-way complex. His newer self revolted at the unpleasant publicity with which he saw his employer's name surrounded as the trial progressed, while his elder spirit was deeply hurt that Campion should have enjoyed a scrap in which he had not been permitted to take part." Almost our final view of him offers the "spectacle of that mournful figure, clad solely in a pair of trousers, standing upon a bath-mat at seven-thirty in the morning, a minute pair of surgical scissors in one enormous hand, and an even smaller strip of sticking-plaster in the other," engaged in the "patching process" of which he is a "past master." Despite the distinctly censorious tone of his remarks, this is "one of those experiences that Mr. Campion frankly enjoyed," and for which the reader, too is abundantly grateful.

Chapter 4
Fun and Games

The Case of the Late Pig, which followed in 1937, was originally a paperback, and appeared in hard covers in Britain only in 1963, in the first Allingham omnibus, *The Mysterious Mr. Campion*. It is much the shortest novel in the canon, covering 120 pages of the collected edition, as compared with the 197 pages of *Black Plumes*, the next shortest; and it represents for the author a rare venture into the first person, with Campion himself as narrator. This works admirably, and Campion is permitted to establish himself in a crisp, bright style, more in keeping with his earlier than his later self, and blessedly free of facetiousness. Whether consciously or not, the style achieves something of the quality of P.G. Wodehouse, bringing one back to the "silly ass" link between Campion and Bertie Wooster; and the opening paragraph strikes a definite Woosterian note, with Campion's determination "not to let any damned modesty creep in to spoil the story," and his reference to the "harp quintet" he hears whenever he considers the closeness of death, both to Lugg and himself, during the affair.

The narrative abounds in comic phrases of Wodehousean felicity: "He looked...puzzled...like a spaniel which has unexpectedly retrieved a dodo"; "Birkin, I saw, was destined to confine his attentions to dog licences for some time to come"; "the old man bellowed, as he always does when he fancies the subject needs finesse"; "the late Lady Pursuivant liked her furniture gilt and her porcelain by the ton"; "the general effect [of her costume] lay somewhere between Hamlet and Aladdin"; "Janet smouldered at me across the hearthrug"; "He turned and eyed me with a glance which conveyed clearly that he was an old man, an experienced man, and that dust did not affect his eyesight"; and, perhaps best of all, "I remember thinking at the time that he constituted a waste of space."

There is, too, a markedly Wodehousean flavor about the plot development, particularly in the movement of Chapters 6 to 8, each of which rises to a climax that would not be out of place in a Wooster imbroglio, given that Bertie were ever to tangle with a corpse. First, Campion's reconciliation with Janet, who is jealous of Effie Rowlandson, whom Campion claims not to know, is shattered by the butler's announcement that "a Miss Effie Rowlandson had called to see Mr. Campion, and he had put her in the drawing room"; next, Campion and the local inspector accompany Effie to inspect the body, only to find that it has disappeared' and finally, the vicar appears, soaked to the skin, long after he should have been at home and in bed.

But, of course, the resemblance ends on the surface, and what seems the mad logic of a Wodehouse plot becomes very much the grim logic of an Allingham one: Miss Rowlandson has come to identify a corpse, which has been removed by the murderer for a very good reason; and the vicar's drowned appearance is immediately suspicious when it seems the body may have been thrown into the river.

The action moves on an intriguing discrepancy, whereby Campion is summoned, in June, to view the newly dead corpse of a man whose funeral he has attended the previous January. He is first drawn by the announcement of the death of R. I. Peters in "The Times", from which Lugg, in emulation of a colleague with aspirations to gentility, has taken to reading to him, while he breakfasts in bed. Simultaneously, he is puzzling over a newly arrived anonymous letter, a virtual fantasy on the theme of Peters' death, and of a rococo extravagance to guarantee entrancement, both for Campion and for the reader. (In this and the two like effusions that follow, what Campion calls "the nature-note motif" is prominent: and, after we have been exhorted to "consider, o consider the lowly mole," Miss Allingham scrupulously gives us, in two stages, the clue that should clinch the matter for us, some 20 pages before the explanation.)

The Peters of both obituary notice and letter is identified by Campion as the resident bully of his prep-school, who was commonly and deservedly known in those far-off days as "Pig." Campion has vivid memories of Pig Peters, none of them pleasant: "We were boys together...Pig Peters took three inches of skin off my chest with a rusty penknife to show I was his branded slave. He made me weep till I was sick and...held me over an unlighted gas jet until I passed out." As "a major evil" in the life of Campion, Guffy Randall and others at that time, Pig Peters ranked with "Injustice, the Devil, and Latin Prose."

Most recently, as "Oswald Harris," he has been bullying the inhabitants of Kepesake, the "sort of country paradise" where the story is set, another idyllic East Anglian retreat in the line of Mystery Mile and Pontisbright. It is here that Poppy Bellew has retired from the stage, and established, at Halt Knights, the principal mansion, "the finest hotel and country pub in the kingdom"; and it is here, too, among the "gracious shadowy trees...sweet meadows and clear waters," that Pig Peters, having bought out Poppy, has planned to install "a hydro, a dog-track and a cinema dance-hall." Predictably, no one is much surprised when an urn falls from a balcony onto the destroyer's head—and a "hysterical" phone call from Janet, the Chief Constable's daughter, brings Campion back into the affair.

Campion still has some way to go before he has established the motive force behind that urn, and identified the occupant of Pig's premature grave: the rest of the action is a complex, dancing mechanism that ticks over like clockwork, the two major mysteries enhanced and embellished by several minor ones, all impeccably dovetailed in— Poppy's confusion over the stranger called Hayhoe; the appalling cough, supposedly exclusive to Pig Peters, that Campion hears at the man's own funeral; the phone-call from London, from someone who simply sighs and hangs up when Campion answers; and, of course, the anonymous letters.

Campion admits early to drawing the obvious inference about the urn, and to being, at this juncture, "absolutely wrong...about everything." Later, with "the whole case under my nose," he sees "unfortunately...only...half of it," and further miscalculations undermine his own estimate of his performance as "pretty nearly brilliant." Elsewhere, he is more modest, denying any claim to be considered "one of those intellectual sleuths": "My mind does not work like an adding machine, taking the facts in neatly one by one and doing the work as it goes along. I am more like the bloke with the sack and the spiked stick. I collect all the odds and ends I can see and turn out the bag at the lunch hour." Certainly, he has his successes, but to make any stronger claim is to disregard the death of the killer's second victim, and the narrow escapes from death of Lugg and himself, all of which derive from his own errors of judgment. It is also to disregard the part played in the affair by his old schoolfriend Whippet, who moves in a mysterious way on the edges of the action, and ends by saving Campion's life and stealing Janet from under his nose.

Although, "it is about as easy to describe Whippet as it is to describe water or a sound in the night," he makes a lively impression. So do the other main characters, despite the limited compass of the book—Poppy, the ex-actress, one of the author's game old girls; the jealous vicar, Bathwick, a "red-hot innovator," "who'd be quite a good chap if he wasn't so solemn"; the "solid-looking" doctor, Kingston, with his relentless enthusiasm "to play the detective"; and the shrewd and likeable policeman, Pussey.

We get a fuller account of Janet's father, Sir Leo Pursuivant, who is also the Chief Constable. He is doubly "magnificent," both in his appearance ("in his ancient shootin' suit and green flowerpot hat", he is "a fine specimen for anybody's album"), and in his "innocence, which is as devastating as it is blind." The "chief characteristic in a delightful personality" is his "singleness of purpose," which "is not to be diverted by anything less than a covey of Mad Mullahs." Predictably, he views Lugg with "mistrust"—his "ideas of discipline are military and Lugg's are not"—but the full weight of his considerable indignation and scorn is reserved for the "bounders" of this world, that "terrible feller" Harris, and the fantastic Hayhoe, who is "the sort of feller one'd set a dog on instinctively."

Hayhoe himself is another more elaborate figure, "a revolting old fellow" with "little grey curly moustaches," "beady bright eyes," and a "mincing" gait, who arouses in Campion "an extraordinary sensation of dislike" the moment he sees him. Established from the first as a poseur—he adopts at Pig's funeral a "conventional attitude of grief" that is totally "unconvincing," and subsequently greets Leo with a "wave of the panama delivered with one of those shrugs which attempt old world grace, and achieve the slightly sissy"—he is nonetheless capable of directness when it comes to negotiating terms. His macabre end is one of the many small triumphs of the novel.

Chapter 5
Albert in Love

Dancers in the Mourning, like *The Case of the Late Pig* published
in 1937, was the author's finest achievement up to that time, and
it remains a classic of the genre. A superlatively subtle book fraught
with complicated tensions and crowded with insights, it is remarkable
for its sustained emotional force, its adroit social comedy, and its
scrupulous rendering of every development in terms of human
personality. It is at once stylish and clever as a whodunit, and mature
and satisfying as a novel of character.

The action centers on Jimmy Sutane, star of *The Buffer*, a revue
based on the supposed memoirs of Mr. William Faraday. Uncle William
himself sits watching the 300th performance at the Argosy in
Shaftesbury Avenue, Campion at his side, the audience "a great pleased
animal whose vastness filled the theatre." On stage, Sutane sings
effectively, dances superbly, and commands the house by "sheer
personality"; the applause, as always is thunderous.

He is immensely, universally popular. He has "grace and skill,"
and "ease and dignity," and his "sophisticated, amused but utterly
discontented intelligence" makes a "deep appeal" to all kinds of
people—a Sutane show is "a recognized intellectual leveller." Even
a little off-stage dance, a spontaneous release of nervous tension, strikes
Campion as "amusing, stimulating and aesthetically comforting."

Sutane is as much at the center of the novel as at the center of
the stage. The other characters revolve round him much as the people
in *Death of a Ghost* formed a circle around the painter Lafcadio.
He is, in his own words, "an important person—so damned important
I'm terrified whenever I think of it. Three hundred people in this
theatre are dependent on me... There's not another star in London
who could carry it. It depends on me. Then there's White Walls.
Gardeners, Campion. Maids—Linda—Sarah—Eve—Sock—Poyser—

old Finny—the nurse—they're all dependent on me. On my *feet*. Every time I look at this damned theatre I go cold with terror... They're all directly or indirectly supported and held up by me, and I'm just an ordinary poor little bloke who has nothing—God help him—but his feet and his reputation. Nothing must go wrong with me, Campion. I've got nothing to fall back on. A business man has his organization and his firm, but I've got nothing. I'm doing it alone."

Throughout the novel, the pressure on Sutane is intense and unrelieved. Uncle William defines "the life the feller leads" — "overworked, thinks too much, no peace at all, always in the thick of things, always in a hurry." He has the nervous energy of a dynamo: in rehearsal for a new show, "it's only Jimmy who holds 'em all together." "Sunday is more of a breather than any other day," but Sutane "would never realize that a world existed in which time for thought was not only unrationed but as free and bountiful as to have no value at all" (just as the old doctor, Bouverie, cannot conceive of Sutane's loving his daughter, Sarah, but literally having no time to give her). His physical condition is a major preoccupation, and even his eating and drinking are governed by rules.

In addition to the routine stresses of his life, Sutane is now subjected, cruelly, to two more: a vicious persecution campaign, and the recurrence in his life of Chloe Pye. The campaign moves through a whole series of "little tuppeny ha'penny squirts of malice"—a claque in the gallery, a garlic bouquet, a pin in the greasepaint—to a devastating, full-scale "fiasco"—a tea-party for what seems the entire neighborhood, an indiscriminate melee of "county" and "trade," "mixed by a hand that pure ignorance could scarcely have directed" (and to ensure that we appreciate that the maximum damage has been done, Miss Allingham places this after Campion's realization that local designs on Sutane as a captive lion have been frustrated by his inaccessibility: he is cut off from his neighbors by the rigorous disciplines of a life that totally excludes the casual).

Chloe Pye seems at first to represent less serious a threat to Sutane's peace of mind, but she has clearly brought some pressure to bear. The 300th performance of *The Buffer* marks her return to the London stage after "a long colonial tour," and she is so patently outclassed by the rest of the cast that Campion wonders "why...she should have elected, much less been invited, to attempt a comeback in the midst of such strong competition." Her presence at White Walls is equally clearly an embarrassment to the rest of the circle, and her claim that she and Sutane are "old friends" is not borne out by his attitude and subsequent denials. Sutane later concedes that she was an added source of strain: "If you're nervy already that sort of relentless pursuit gets under your skin."

Sutane is appallingly vulnerable to any sort of hold Chloe may have over him, and to the kind of calculated publicity that gradually accumulates round the details of the persecution, intensifying the harm that is being done to him. His entire reputation "depends on goodwill": in Linda's words, "When a man's name is part of his assets he can't afford to do the simplest thing without taking the risk that it will be seized on, twisted and made into an amusing story." Understandably, Sutane is "going to pieces" and in danger of being driven "insane with worry." An interruption provokes "a passionate protest"; his voice goes "sharp with nerves"; his face increasingly resembles "a death's-head"; his eyes are not "merely tired" but "desperately weary," like Lawrence's circus elephants, with the "aeons of weariness" about their eyes.

The pain in the book is very real, the tensions of a kind that demand a sympathetic response, and it is the measure of Miss Allingham's mastery that in no way do they seem inappropriate to a detective story. The persecution, for instance, is genuinely effective as part of a sophisticated mystery, and equally so in human terms, both in its effects on the victim and his circle, and in the revelation of the motivation behind it. Similarly, the unspoken threat that Chloe Pye seems to embody makes its mark on both levels: she is clearly being set up as a deserving murder victim, and yet her behavior is plausibly irritating, even pathetic, and entirely right for the emotional context in which it is set.

Campion himself, for the first time in his life, is seriously "caught up and exalted and hurt" by events, and his personal involvement is of an intensity that affects his entire view of the case, so that only at the eleventh hour does his judgment clear and point out to him the killer of Chloe and the other victims. Emotionally, he goes through the fire: of all the people involved, most of whom experience a desperately worrying time, only Sutane himself suffers more than Campion. At one point, he relapses consciously "into the protective inanity of his early youth," but otherwise we are far from the Campion of younger and lighter days. He is still given to "effacing himself," "as was his custom when his immediate presence was not necessary," but no one doubts for a moment his resource or his intelligence, and he is commended for his "gift of making people talk" and understanding "what they say." To the former policeman, Blest, he looks "less of an ass than he had ever seen him," and Inspector Yeo notices that he is "looking...a good deal more intelligent than his usual, casually elegant self."

But the real difference in Campion goes much deeper than this. His passion for Linda Sutane leads him to abandon "his customary position as an observer in the field" and to step "over the low wall of the impersonal into the maelstrom itself." Alone with her, "his carefully trained powers of observation were temporarily in abeyance" and talking to her, "for what was probably the first time in his life, Campion ceased to think during an interview." "He had ceased to be an onlooker and was taking part."

After ten minutes in her company, he is so moved by her that, on an "insane impulse," "he nearly kissed her"; later, they share an extraordinary complicity of mood: "they paid each other the irresistible compliment of complete comprehension, the most delightful and dangerous quality of mutual stimulation"—and, again, the instinct to kiss her, "completely casual, unpremeditated," is almost beyond his control. Before long, he is fully aware that he is "in love with her and that he would never again be completely comfortable in her presence." Intellectually, he is still capable of an objective assessment of his situation: "He had no doubt that his bitter-sweet preoccupation with her would wear off in a little while" — but, emotionally, he is racked by the conflict in him. He faces squarely the issue as he sees it between himself and the Sutanes: "Regarded dispassionately it resolved itself to a simple enough question. If you are violently and unreasonably attracted to a married woman, to discover immediately afterwards that to the best of your belief her husband has killed, either by accident or design, a previous wife, in order, presumably, to retain his present menage intact, do you involve yourself further in the situation, denouncing him for his crime and walking off with the lady?" The answer, inevitably, is "no," but still the "gnawing, shameful preoccupation with Linda" persists and, as the climax approaches, he is "besieged" by "intolerable temptations" to spare her the pain he fears, wrongly, lies ahead of her. At the end, having given the police the crucial information they need, yet still unaware of the truth, he feels that "his own gamut of sensation" has "been played through... He was emotionally finished and ...strangely at peace."

His regular associates all register the change in him, from Lugg— "You're not quite yourself, are you?"—to Uncle William, to whom "he seemed to have suddenly become a stranger." Campion's contributions to the police investigations (for the second and third murders, these are defined in detail) are decisive but reluctant: "After years of the closest and most friendly cooperation with the authorities he felt his present position on the fence very keenly, and his resentment at the combination of circumstances which had forced him to take it up grew deep." Oates is moved to address him "with unusual formality," and Yeo is frankly surprised at him: "I've never known you like this, Mr. Campion. You're usually so keen."

To us, Yeo is a new policeman, though an "acquaintance...of long standing" to Campion. He is the least developed of the author's three recurrent policemen, comparing poorly with Oates for length of service, and with the later, younger Charlie Luke for color and vitality. A chief-detective-inspector, he is "square and efficient, with a solid bullet head and an insignificant, almost comical face. His snub nose and round eyes had been a serious disadvantage to him all his life, undermining his dignity and earning him friends rather than admirers." His unfortunate face makes him look at times "like a comedian in the midst of his act." but we are assured of his "quite extraordinary ability," and his energy and single - mindedness are certainly impressive.

Oates is as solid and dependable as ever, still "at heart the eager, solemn young countryman whose concentration and tenacity had first earned the commendation of a rural inspector nearly thirty-four years before," but, like Yeo, impressive in his "logical, and conventional" way, and fully determined to find the killer, whom he defines as "a bad, dangerous fellow."

Linda's view of the other members of Sutane's circle puts them in perspective: "...they're all performers, aren't they? All mild exhibitionists. They're so busy putting themselves over that they haven't time to think about anyone else. It's not that they don't like other people; they just never have a moment to consider them." (Uncle William puts it differently, but no less effectively: "We've landed ourselves among a funny crowd, my boy...A damned curious bandarloggy lot.") Later, it occurs to Campion "what a pack of children they were, all of them. Their enthusiasm, their eagerness to escape from...reality, their tendency to make everything more bearable by dramatizing it; it was the very stuff of youth." When he looks at Linda, he sees that "she alone had reacted to the tragedy in a way he fully understood."

Apart from Chloe, who neglects to act only when bad temper forces a genuine if childish response from her, Sutane's understudy, Benny Konrad, is the most overtly theatrical of the circle. Lacking in any suggestion of individual talent, his whole demeanor is a parade (whereas Sutane, who has genius, has no need to display it except in the theatre). He is clearly a young homosexual of the petulant, narcissistic, spiteful kind often inaccurately regarded as typical. Though Miss Allingham is forbidden to be explicit here, Uncle William's scornful allusion of "those fellers"; the association with that "regular old pressed rose," Beaut Siegfried, the ballet master; and Mr. Howard's view of the cycling club of which Konrad is president as "a pack of pansies on bicycles," together with the all male-claque that derives from it, leave one in no doubt. His forehead is "as clear and modelled as a girl's," and his face is "indecently pretty," when made up for the stage. He has "golden curls," too, and a succession of giggles and flounces and bridles and sulks accumulates against him. He is undoubtedly very disagreeable, and yet he has the pathos of the artist who isn't good enough, and this makes him interesting as a person as well as effective as a "villain." Watching him perform, Sutane sighs: "It's not there," he said softly. "I knew it. He knows it, poor beast." And Sutane's sigh, despite "a definite underlying hint of satisfaction," is "an expressive sound, mainly of regret." Even Uncle

William, though with no suggestion of sympathy, recognizes that Konrad is "like a feller in a fine tail-coat without the chest to fill it out."

The other great egotist in the company has talent to match his wayward persona: Squire Mercer, the composer of *The Buffer*. He has an uncomfortable but genuine gift, and there is real feeling in his music: however trivially or, in Campion's word, "horribly" it is expressed, the emotion demands a response in the listener: "That's what makes some of those songs so unbearably embarrassing." Because of his gift, he is "tolerated and encouraged by his friends," and consequently "never considered anyone except himself, not only as a main rule but down to the smallest and most trivial circumstance." Uncle William considers him "a thoughtless chap. Quite extraordinarily selfish," and Linda defines the curious nature of his self-containment: "Mercer has never had to consider anything except his work, and now I don't think he's capable of trying to." So, he continues to strum on the piano, reiterating the same few notes of a "half-finished melody" regardless of the strain this imposes on the other four people in the room; and he reacts to an objection with "unexpected fury" —it is not for him to stop but for others to "go away." He seems wholly unaffected by the tragedy and all it entails for the household; to him, Chloe's death is the germ of an idea for a song. Even a request that he should accommodate two guests for the night he takes "as though the suggestion had been put forward as a measure to spare him any loneliness." Both "callousness" and "irresponsibility" are "typical" of him: and he is so withdrawn from other people, so intensely "lost...in his own private and particular world" that even his speech ignores their convenience; he has "a voice so slovenly that the words were scarcely articulated" and, later, he drawls and mumbles at Campion, "his articulation...maddeningly bad."

Of the other characters, three are particularly interesting: William Faraday, Dr. Bouverie and Miss Finbrough. Uncle William we have met before and it is a joy to renew the acquaintance. He has moved on since *Police at the Funeral*, emancipated from the house in Cambridge by his mother's death, and from the "blameless inactivity" of fifty-eight years by the freak success of his *Memoirs of an Old*

Buffer, on which Sutane's hit musical is based. The book is largely fiction since Uncle William had found "the work of inscribing the history of his life almost as tedious as living it had been" and had begun "to prevaricate a little upon the second page, working up to downright lying on the sixth and subsequent folios." His supposed Indian exploits derive in fact from Kipling and Jules Verne, as he confesses disarmingly to Campion: "Got all my India for my memoirs out of *The Jungle Book* and *Round the World in 80 Days*. Tried *Kim* but couldn't get along with it."

He is fully aware of the joke at his expense implicit in the success of his book: "Funny thing about those memoirs, Campion. If I'd done the decent thing and stuck to the truth no one would have read 'em. As it was, they laughed at me and I made a small fortune. I'm not a chump, you know. I can see how that happened. Better be a clown than a pompous old fool." Nor is this the only instance of Uncle William's shrewdness: he perceives, as no one else apparently does, the mutual attraction of Campion and Linda, and his comments on Squire Mercer are often pungent and original: "He's the kind of feller who ought to be hanging around sleepin' on people's floors, pickin' up scraps of comfort, lookin' after himself like a London pigeon, but, by means of a trick...he's made a fortune out of those footlin' songs of his and it's put the feller out of gear." After his discovery of a love-note in a bird's nest, he even does a little successful detecting on his own account.

Uncle William's portrait is assembled lovingly in a succession of attractive details, from the "small bright eyes" through which he watches the 300th performance of *The Buffer* to the "deep and alcoholic peace" that enfolds him at the end, "faulty but incorruptible, human but honest as the day." The physical account is unfailingly vivid: his "small bear's body" sways to the show's hit tune; he surfaces from a nap and sits "blinking rosily"; he pulls "the large tweed cap he affected for motoring more firmly over his ears"; the shortness of his neck involves him in "a rather complete" movement when he turns in his seat; the downcast angle of his head exposes for a moment "his misty tonsure frilled with yellow-white curls"; he waves a "pudgy" hand and crosses "chubby" feet. He is always with Campion, so that one invariably has the impression of his looking up.

The element of self-betrayal, so marked in *Police at the Funeral*, is again much in evidence. He is given to uttering "disastrous asides" and Campion is more than once disconcerted by his candor. He has "a shy confiding which was almost the whole of his charm." Despite the assumption of worldliness, he admits to being thrilled by the world of the Argosy: "Vie le Boheme, lights, far-off music, smell of the grease-paint, women and so on." After expressing his regret that Slippers lacks sex appeal offstage, he coughs "as if he feared he had betrayed himself"; and he seems for a moment akin to Mrs. Geodrake, Sutane's inquisitive neighbor, when he sounds "a little regretful" that his "first experience of Bohemia" at White Walls has not been more liberating. Reacting with embarrassment to Konrad's initial greeting, he coughs "noisily," responds "fiercely," and mutters "in an all too audible undertone," "I hate those fellers!"

The endearing self-importance and humbug of the earlier portrait are also here; in the unabashed adoption of theatrical jargon, for instance—"he was lookin' for a shop, as we call it." Waiting to introduce Campion to Sutane, he looks "worldly and benign, and somehow bogus, with his watery blue eyes serious and his expression unwontedly important." He writes of himself to Campion as one who has had, in his time, a "light sure hand with a woman"; and he slips with ease into his "Man of the World, circa 1910" persona, "his third happiest role but one which he particularly enjoyed." Perhaps his most astonishing claim, however, is that Campion reminds him "amazin'ly" of himself as a young man.

His formula for dealing with the upset occasioned by "stirrin' times" is characteristic: "...there's only one thing to do...and that's to light a good cigar, take a glass in one's hand and wait until one sees a ray of light shinin' at one through the gloom"; so is the solemn inspection of the sheets on Mercer's beds before he and Campion retire for the night. Other memorable moments are the reminiscence of an exotic visitor to White Walls—"a prince... A Russian feller...kept me awake half the night with tales of wolf-shootin' "; his disparaging dismissal of the concept of wish-fulfillment—"it sounded unhealthy to me and I told him so"; and the bemused assumption that Don Marquis must be a "Spanish feller."

Three other speeches confirm him in our affections: his early attempt to comfort Linda—"A terrible thing. But we're here, you know. Campion and I. Do anything we can. You can rely on us"; the serio-comic appeal to Campion not to desert his post—"...a gentleman's got to meet his engagements. Speakin' man to man now, you understand. Old stuff, I know. Made a lot of fun of these days, but still holds good. Jimmy here is a decent feller in trouble... Your commission is to get him out of it"; and, best of all, his unhappy declaration of loyalty to Sutane at all costs: "I've consulted my heart and made up my mind and I'm stickin' to my decision. It may not be the right way, but battles have been won on it."

Dr. Bouverie is an autocratic old man with the massive dignity of "some great animal...a bison, perhaps." He is a "vast, imposing figure" with a "pugnacious old face," "drooping chaps," "a wise eye" and "many chins." His voice has "authority...of the magisterial variety:" it is "an old voice, slow with the affectations of the educated seventies, the father, as it were, of Uncle William's voice." Hearing him speak to Sarah in "that half-contemptuous tone which yet carried such absolute conviction," Campion is reminded of a belief formulated in his own childhood when similarly addressed—that"That's how God talks."

Arriving to examine Chloe, the old man dominates the scene "like the spirit of rural justice incarnate." His monumental probity is "frankly awe - inspiring" at such a time, and in the face of it the anxieties of Sutane and his manager seem petty, distracted, and devious. With Sutane's servants he is "olympian": the nurse is "an imbecile," the maid a "very silly little girl" whose "family are fools." To summon his own servants he either bellows "at the top of his surprising voice" or claps his hands "with a Sultanic gesture curiously in keeping with his personality"; and he has no hesitation in rousing his gardener from his bed merely to attend him while he shows Campion his roses. In the interests of solving the third murder, he keeps his "sleep-dazed chauffeur" working all night—"Young Dean wanted to give up at one o'clock but I kept him at it"—and "the full force of his astonishing energy" is "loosed upon a reconstruction of the crime with a generous disregard for the hour and his own and everybody else's personal convenience."

And yet he is so far from being a charmless bully that we can respect him and delight in his contribution to the novel. It is for good that he punishes himself and those around him: justice is not an abstraction for him, but something it is worth toiling all day and fighting all night to achieve:"The assurance that a great many people were losing their sleep in a decent public endeavor to clear up the mystery which had smirched his beloved district comforted him considerably." His limitations are those of his class and generation—Campion mentally designates him "a Georgian tough"—and his failure to sympathize with Sutane or understand the reasons for Sarah's neglect must be seen as inevitable. He lives only five miles from Sutane and yet "the brittle world of White Walls and the stage" seems "a long way away."

He has, too, a milder aspect and even, in his passion for roses, a reserve of tenderness: "The Doctor put his blunt fingers under a blossom and tilted it gently.'Isn't she lovely?' he said softly. Good night, my little dear. " The visit to his home has a charmed and haunting quality, and though he is clearly a dictator, he appears a benevolent one, since his servants and his dog are "silent, utterly obedient, and yet friendly and content." Even at White Walls, he has his less awesome moments: in handling the dead Chloe his hands are "exquisitely gentle." With Sarah, he is matter-of-fact but doggedly determined to right what is wrong, "not unkind, but not unduly sympathetic."

Miss Finbrough is Sutane's masseuse and she looks like "a little boiled cart-horse." When he first meets her, Campion thinks he has "never seen anyone more self-possessed." Like the doctor, she is a force to be reckoned with—the "authority in her voice" is "tremendous"—and she dismisses Campion and Uncle William "with a finality which would have daunted a newspaper man" and "had done so, of course, on many occasions." It is small wonder that everyone at the theatre is "terrified of her."

She is "devoted to Sutane" and lives to serve him: "' *He's* working in the hall,' she said, lowering her voice and giving the personal pronoun a particular importance." While acknowledging Sarah's isolation and her need for companionship and freedom in her own home, she sees this, brutally, as the price the child must pay for having "an overworked genius for a father." When Campion remonstrates with her for being callous, her answer is fierce and immediate: "Have you seen him dance?...You can expect *him* to upset his health, filling the place with children." By the end of their brief exchange Sarah becomes even more negligible: "It would run away, just when we were so upset already"—even the dog, earlier, is "He."

In her passionate concern for Sutane's physical well-being Miss Finbrough tends the sun-ray lamp "as though it had been a sacred fire." When Konrad accuses Sutane of having murdered Chloe, she loses control, swooping "down upon him like a Valkyrie," and shaking him in a fury; but when, kindly but firmly, she is rebuked by her employer, she dwindles at once to "a plain middle-aged woman, very red and hot with unaccustomed emotion," sobbing as she stumbles from the room, her passion, as never before, exposed and therefore embarrassing.

Because her devotion to Sutane is so intense and unquestioning, she will do whatever he asks of her: but a theft from Chloe's lodging has an unexpected aftermath and when Campion next meets her he is "startled by the change in her...Now she was turgid-looking and dry-skinned, red with the redness of sandstone. Her strength seemed to have been drawn into itself, as if the muscles of her body had become knotted and hard." For once, Sutane has abused her feeling for him and her strength is wholly undermined. Even Campion misjudges the extent of the havoc wrought in her: he warns Yeo to expect "some difficulty" in persuading her to confess her guilty knowledge but in the event she cracks "at once." Again, as with Chloe and Konrad, the author's development of personality is plausible and arresting while at the same time serving the action.

Two other characters are near the center of events—Sock Petrie, Sutane's publicist and Eve, the star's sister. Sock is an "intensely virile" young man, an obvious contrast to Konrad throughout, "large, raw-boned" and, in appearance, "disreputable" (his clothes were "creased" and "runkled" and his wallet...would have disgraced a lie-about); but with a corresponding "natural ease of manner," and breathing "an atmosphere of worldly common sense." Eve, by contrast, is far removed from any such atmosphere, moving unhappily through the action, sulky, resentful, graceless, and increasingly mysterious. Her behavior is notably picturesque—she drifts around the garden in tears; dances in vengeful triumph on the dead Chloe's discarded skirt; corresponds with an unknown lover by means of desperate notes in a defunct bird's nest; and finally disappears without explanation.

Others occur more briefly: Slippers Bellew (can that ever have been a plausible name?), Sutane's co-star, enchanting onstage but, to Uncle William's regret, with "no sex-appeal off"; Poyser, Sutane's manager, "his small face alive with worry and invention" as his brain attacks the problem of lifting his star property clear of Chloe's death; Sutane's small daughter, Sarah, blossoming from her loneliness and isolation into Lugg's firm friend and pupil in dubious skills; Renee Roper, Chloe's gay and friendly landlady, a sketch for the full portrait drawn in *More Work for the Undertaker* and two striking exemplars of the author's gift for the comedy of social embarrassment—the strident, intrusive neighbor, Mrs. Geodrake, agog for a close-up view of a Bohemian world of erotic abandon, and unshakable in her resolve to extract the maximum of "hard-won" information in the teeth of her reluctant hosts; and Chloe's appalling sister-in-law, "like some monstrous black toadstool," her parade of grief a self-indulgent sham, but her "essential strength of character" apparent in her successful demands on people far more sophisticated than herself.

Lugg is here, too, all "seventeen stone and eight pounds" of him: "there was a minor disturbance which shook the walls a little and Mr. Lugg billowed grandly into the room." Despite the improbability which Campion, Lugg himself and the author acknowledge, he serves Linda nobly as her temporary butler, and establishes instantaneous rapport with the six-year-old Sarah. At first, he resists the move to lend him to Linda, but he capitulates on learning who are to be his new employers—"There's somethin' chick about the stage"—and he takes to White Walls "like a duck in water." Sarah takes to Lugg in the same way, and their extraordinary relationship develops as between "two persons whose minds were singularly of an age" (and it is echoed much later in the canon when Lugg enters with the children in *The Tiger in the Smoke*). At one point, Lugg, "vast and impressive in a cutaway coat and posed ridiculously in a flower bed" indicates "suitable blooms for Sarah to cut for the drawing-room bowl," and elsewhere they mount a joint attack on the housework, at dawn. Sarah learns how to pick a lock and is nearing perfection in the three-card trick when the idyll ends: Campion's announcement of their departure prompts "a moment of great sadness," and even in his grim mood of terminal resolution Lugg's employer feels a "sudden sympathy" for him.

Miss Allingham miscalculates with two subsidiary men, Peter Brome, Chloe's last love, and Mr. Howard, the secretary of the cycling club of which Konrad is president. Peter Brome is twenty-two and convinced that his love for Chloe was "tremendous... the only thing that matters." The author is alive to his absurdity and yet she knows that what he utters is "emotional truth"—it's a difficult balance to achieve and the result is purple patchwork: "His voice wavered and was silent, and the face he lifted to the London stars was angry and, in its extraordinary beauty, rather terrible." And yet the very next sentence shows that Miss Allingham knows essentially what she is about.

The brash Mr. Howard is spoilt by an ill-assimilated element of caricature: did anyone ever talk of a cycling enthusiast as a "wheel lover" or rejoice in the opportunity to "see things awheel"?

But these — and the author's misuse of "infer"—are tiny jolts from a machine that in the main runs beautifully—from the opening evocation of the appeal of the theatre to mind, eye and heart, to the final dramatic irony of Sutane's appeal to Campion: "'How could I, old boy?' he said."

Chapter 6
The High Style

Like *Dancers in Mourning*, the next book, *The Fashion in Shrouds*(1938), focuses on a small circle of "top people," whose glossy lives are jolted by odd and menacing events that culminate in murder. They are successful competitors at the highest level in their respective fields, and they lead super-sophisticated lives against a background of fashion houses, modish clubs and restaurants, and long running West End plays—the names of which, like points on a map of fashion, punctuate the narrative: Papendeik, Lelong, Leonard Loke; the Tulip, the Poire d'Or, the White Empress; "The Little Sacrifice," "The Lover."

Against this elegant backcloth moves an army of minor figures who, by serving the fashion best serve themselves. Some are characterized in a few pungent lines, like the doctor Juxton-Coltness, with his "colossal fees and his magnificent manner," "his cold eyes cautious in spite of his general air of contented omnipotence," his "deep voice...thick with sad conviction," "his entire scheme of life...to be obliging to the right people"; and "the lean Ulysse," head waiter at the Tulip, who "received them with all that wealth of unspoken satisfaction which was his principal professional asset and conducted them to a small but not ill-paced table which he swore he had been keeping up his sleeve for just such an eventuality. The worst of the cabaret was over, he confided with that carefully cultivated contempt for everything that interfered with beautiful food, which was another of his more valuable affectations." Many others, names merely, flit past like prestigious ghosts—Jules Parroquet, "whose golden rule for the exploitation of a successful restaurant and nightclub was simple—a new name and orchestra to every two changes of paint";

Reynarde, who transformed Maud Perowne's park Lane mansion for Lady Papendeik; Colin Greenleaf, who photographed the result for "all the more expensive illustrated periodicals"; and the resounding line-up for Caesar's Court: "The chef from the Virginia, Teddy Quiot's band, Andy Bullard in charge of the golf course, the Crannis woman doing the swimming, and Waugh the tennis," not to mention Mirabeau, "the beauty king," and Ditte, "his coiffeuse," who "designed" Lady Papendeik's hair, as she herself reverently informs us.

This aspect of the novel is exhilaratingly well done; the author enjoys evoking the extravagances and absurdities, the affectations and inspirations of her beau monde. She gives a buoyant account of Caesar's Court, the inordinately expensive luxury hotel just outside London in which most of her principals have sunk much of their money, relishing such details as the "pink and apple-green curtains" that billow in the "dark eyes" of "pompous windows," or the transformation of "a grim box with a black and white squared floor" by "a set of red chessmen painted on the stones," or the enlivening of "an alcove with a red glass lobster in place of the seventh Earl's bust of Cicero." The Tulip, too, is attractively individualized, with its "ceiling of flowers...still noticed and admired" after seven months, and "the silly little striped canvas canopies...as fresh and piquant as when they had first been erected."

Perhaps because the action opens in a women's fashion house, and certainly because its two dominant figures are women, the book has an obsessively feminine quality that sets it apart. Each of the principal women is at the top of her profession: Georgia Wells is a star emotional actress, and Valentine Ferris, Mr. Campion's sister, a major fashion designer. Both are important to the mystery, Val as its victim for a time, and Georgia as its "raison d'etre," but the author is at least as interested in them as formidably successful career women. In particular, she is occupied by the conflict between their worldly success and what she sees as their essential dependence as women.

Throughout the novel, lightly at first, but with increasing seriousness as the action develops, the differences between men and women are emphasized. We no sooner meet Val than we are made aware of her intense femininity. She is out to captivate Alan Dell, whose aeroplanes provide the clients of Caesar's Court with the ultimate in expensive toys, and when Campion observes that she is "dressed up to look like a female," she exults in being, consciously, as "female as a cartload of monkeys." The impression is reinforced by the contrast between her highly stylized "burgundy-red suit" and the sober, "mercifully uninspired" product of Messrs. Jamieson & Fellowes that Campion is wearing: just as, later, their cars are contrasted—Campion's is simply "the Lagonda," but Val's is "her famous grey Daimler with the special body," its "soft grey-quilted depths...like a powder-closet...shut away from the chauffeur and as exquisitely feminine as a sedan-chair."

But his sister's radiant assurance somehow disconcerts Campion, and before long he is "glad to note" in her "sufficient feminine weakness" to make her "thoroughly inferior on the whole." Despite her success, which he regards as "astonishing," "she could always be relied upon to make him feel comfortingly superior"; and even when, in conversation, she makes him feel "that she was older than he was," he is able to discount this effect as having been achieved "for all her femininity" or, more bluntly, in spite of it. Later, when Val speaks with considerable perception, Campion looks at her "with one of those sharp glances which betrayed his surprise. Her insight was always astonishing him. It was misleading, he reminded himself hastily; a sort of inspired guesswork or, rather, an intermittent contact with truth"; again, he instinctively downgrades her achievement.

The author's clear conviction that men and women have radically different thought processes is frequently shown. This is done reflectively, as in Campion's musings at the memorial service for Georgia's husband, Sir Raymond Ramillies: "Val, he knew, was beside her, and the thought of her reminded him of the uncanny accuracy of her guesses. Most women are alarming in that way, he reflected again. They muddled through to truth in the most dangerous and infuriating fashion. All the same they were not quite so clever as they thought they were, which was as it should be, of course, but odd considering their remarkable penetration in most other practical matters. It was astonishing how the simple, direct reactions of the ordinary male eluded them." It's also done dramatically in the long exchange between Campion and his sister where Val "placidly" persists in regarding a post-mortem on Ramillies as something that won't occur, despite all Campion's attempts to reason her into some sort of alarm. "His masculine mind revolted from this "in touch with the stars' attitude" and he deplores her "feminine inability to adjust the viewpoint." He pleads with her to use her intelligence, to formulate reasonably the threats inherent in the situation, but she remains unconcerned, exasperating him with her "damned silly introspective rot" and "getting him muddled with her intuitive convictions and airy statements."

Details setting women apart from men accumulate and words like "terrifying," "alarming," "dangerous," and "shocking," reinforce the wedge the author drives between the sexes. Campion observes that "easily the most terrifying thing about women was their practical realism"; and he recalls some advice given him by Belle Lafcadio: "Women are terribly shocking to men... Don't understand them. Like them. It saves such a lot of hurting one way and the other." Twice, the author remarks on the lack in women of a discipline of centuries that she believes has been instilled into men—when Val says to Campion, of herself and Georgia, "our feeling is twice as strong as our heads and we haven't been trained for thousands of years. We're feminine, you fool!"; and when Campion damns Georgia for the "filthy tale" about Val that she has irresponsibly set in motion: "That's what comes of emancipating the wrong type of female. For a thousand years they breed a species to need a keeper and then they let it off the chain and expect it to behave." After a swinging emotional irruption by Val into his well-bred, well-ordered thought processes, Campion is left ruefully contemplating the cat-like "ruthless, hag-ridden" nature of women, beside whom men are, by contrast, dog-like, "gentle, conservative...rather pathetic" and "defenseless."

And yet the novel defines, equally, the vulnerability and essential dependence of women, however gifted, however successful. Lady Papendeik early advances the doctrine that the sexes are not "separate," that the only "human entity...is a man and woman"; and for Val and Georgia, at least, this is patently true. When Alan Dell expresses the need "we all feel at times...to vanish, to abandon the great rattling caravan we're driving and walk off down the road with nothing but our own weight to carry," Val disagrees—"Women don't feel like that," she said. "Not alone."

Miss Allingham reserves her most explicit statement of this theme for a passage of external commentary on Val and Georgia, placing them exactly in the "fine modern world" they inhabit with such distinction: "They were two fine ladies of a fine modern world, in which their status had been raised until they stood as equals with their former protectors. Their several responsibilities were far heavier than most men's and their abilities greater. Their freedom was limitless... They were both mistress and master...and yet, since they had not relinquished their femininity, within them, touching the very core and fountain of their strength, was the dreadful primitive weakness of the female of any species. Byron... once threw off the whole shameful truth about the sex, and, like most staggeringly enlightening remarks, it degenerated into a truism and became discountenanced when it was no longer witty."

As if in direct response to Byron's famous lines, Alan Dell's masterful proposal to Val ("You would be my care, my mate as in plumber, my possession if you like") assumes that their marriage would mean "the other half of my life to me, but the whole of yours to you" — exactly the "woman's whole existence" that the poet postulates.

To the very moment of Dell's proposal, Val is unsure of herself. Earlier, she has confided to Campion her difficulty in loving: "Female women love so abjectly that a reasonable hard-working mind becomes a responsibility... I'd rather die than have to face it that he was neither better nor even more intelligent than I am!... I've so constructed myself that I've either got to ask too much or go maternal"; and even now "she still shrank from investigating him... The risk was too great to take. Her own exacting intelligence, her own insufferable responsible importance, weighted her down like a pack. She was desperately aware that she wanted something from him that was neither physical nor even mental, but rather a vague moral quality whose very nature escaped her. It was something of which she stood in great need and her fear was not only that he did not possess it but that no-one did." But Dell's proposal, which is nothing if not unambiguous, instantly shows her what she wants: "Authority. The simple nature of her desire from him took her breath away with its very obviousness and in the back of her mind she caught a glimpse of its root. She was a clever woman who would not or could not relinquish her femininity, and femininity unpossessed is femininity unprotected from itself, a weakness and not a charm." She laughs "in that sudden freedom which lies in getting exactly what one needs to make the world that place in which one's own particular temperament may thrive," not only content to resign her place as "one of the most important business-women in Europe" to become a man's dependent wife, but unable to conceive of any other course. Miss Allingham leaves us in no doubt of her total endorsement both of the proposal and its unconditional acceptance.

Val is undoubtedly very tiresome at times and it is no longer possible to sympathize wholly with her instant abandonment of her career (if for no other reason than the suppression of her creative gift that it must entail) —but she experiences real emotion and suffers real hurt, and to that extent one is concerned and ultimately glad for her. But it is hard to sympathize at all with Georgia, and despite the author's defense that she has an "odd streak of realism that made her lovable," one shares Campion's "impulse to take her by the shoulders and shake her till her teeth rattled." Amanda's view is typically direct —"I'm afraid that Georgia woman's a sweep"; and Val, all things considered her principal victim, admits to having had the thought that her "beastly, predatory vulgarity" deserves to be silenced forever. Where she doesn't actually repel she at least disconcerts. Campion considers her "as wanton and unexpected as a rudderless steamboat in a gale," and he reflects at Ramillies' funeral that Dell is probably recalling "every little offensive trick of mind which she has betrayed." She is even further down the scale of reason than Val—according to Campion her mind is "like a demented eel," and Val herself says of her that "She doesn't actually think at all. She goes entirely by feel." Her vulgarity, to Campion, is "staggering... the overpowering, insufferable vulgarity to which nothing is sacred"; and that she should adopt her "Little Sacrifice" pose and maintain the pretense that Ramillies is going to regain consciousness, when she knows perfectly well that he is dead, is "horrible" to him, and he is understandably "sickened" by "the complete insincerity of the entire scene."

Georgia acts repeatedly with what seems instinctive mischief, creating difficulties and embarrassments for her friends so that one feels it is hardly overstating the case for Val to call her "fundamentally sadistic." Attracted instantly to Dell, she immediately puts Val in a position in which, however, "unjustly," she is "forced" to apologize, and then creates in Dell "a conviction that there had been a general disinclination to present him." Her treatment of Dell is monstrous and the wonder is that the uncompromising "possessor" of the proposal to Val can become so humiliatingly Georgia's slave. At the "hangover" party for Ramillies, she behaves abominably. After her "blatantly triumphant" entry and "naive delight in her captive," her decision to sit "beside Val with an arm round her shoulders" is no less than refined cruelty. By a covert yet public allusion to their intimacy, she causes Dell to blush violently, and in the high-handed, hectoring obtuseness of her objections to the Quentin Clear medallion (a distinction exclusive to "about three men in the world"), she appears at her absolute worst: "My dear man, you can't go about like that. You look like a darts champion." Her parting shot to Val— "I must fly. He's waiting for me like a little dog on the step, the sweetie"— is enough to have justified Val had she indeed put "a good dose of cyanide" into the headache powder she gives her.

When it transpires that this "cachet blanc" was in fact administered to Ramillies, Georgia, true to her tendency to "say any mortal thing that comes into her head," implies that Val may have intended to poison her— and not all her pantomime of laughing and covering her face with her hands, and looking "startled" by her own innuendo, can convince us that she could ever have kept it to herself; and, indeed, she spoils her "denial a moment afterwards by allowing an ill-timed flicker of mischief to pass over her face. "After all, my pet, why should you want to get rid of me?" Predictably, "the trouble was made"; a postmortem is now inevitable, and the damage to Val is only beginning.

Val's introductory view of Georgia—"She's witty, beautiful, predatory, intrinsically vulgar and utterly charming"—makes two claims that the narrative fails to substantiate. Her beauty is undeniable — she is lovely on the grand scale, a "Spanish galleon" of a woman, with a "broad, beautiful face," "designed by nature as a poster rather than a pen drawing" — and both her predatoriness and her vulgarity are much in evidence; but nowhere is there any indication of wit in Georgia, and though we are aware of what Val means by her charm, and indeed we see it in action, its effect is so calculated, and its purpose so selfish, that it loses conviction as a genuine force.

Unlike Val, Georgia doesn't go very deep: temperamentally, as well as professionally, she is an actress, and her personality is aptly described as "magnificent" but "fraudulent." No sooner does she become aware of Dell's intense admiration for her performance in "The Little Sacrifice" than she begins, subtly and gradually, to introduce "touches of the character...into her voice, into her helpless little gestures, into her very attitude of mind." In the course of the novel, she expresses many emotions, but though she may at the moment of their expression believe them to be genuine, few of them, in any true sense, are. When she tells Campion of her distress at the discovery after three years of the bones of Richard Portland-Smith, whom she had loved, she appears to Campion "perfectly sincere... For the moment at any rate Georgia Wells was genuine in her despair." But before long a doubt is raised—Georgia's cry came from the heart, or seemed to do so"—and "the next instant" she has sighted Dell, loosened her grip on Campion's arm, and demanded "in an entirely different tone," who the stranger is. It is impossible for long to take such "despair" at anything like Georgia's own valuation.

Typically, she discharges a "warmth of friendliness" towards Val, immediately after she has become aware of Dell, and immediately before putting Val in the wrong; and she shows her "gift of utter directness" at what is in fact a highly - charged and complex moment. Again, when "The Trumpet" wants her on the phone, "Georgia's hunted expression would have been entirely convincing if it had not been so much what one might have expected." She is openly "seen through" by Campion and Amanda: she embraces Amanda at the Tulip with "a sort of fine, generous spirituality which made Mr. Campion think of Britannia in the cartoons of Sir Bernard Patridge"; and her "charming exhibition of wifely devotion" to Ramillies two hours before his take-off to Ulangi seems to Amanda "comfortingly obvious." Her apology to Val for the "cachet blanc" incident is perhaps in a class of its own: "Georgia put her arm round Val. It was a long, slow movement, and, laying her dark head gently against the apple-green dress, she allowed two tears, and only two, to roll slowly down her cheeks. It was exquisite, the most abject and charming apology Campion had ever seen. Georgia seemed to think it was pretty good, too, for she brightened perceptibly for an instant before resuming her mood."

In love with Dell she's "like a house on fire" and for as long as it lasts even Val admits her to be "riotously, deliriously, ecstatically in love." Amanda, however, gives short shrift to such sentimentality, and when Campion, too, subscribes to the idea that Georgia is "genuinely very much in love at the moment," her refutation is emphatic and convincing: "She's not," said Amanda. "If you're in love with a man the one you're frightened of is doing him any harm. That's the whole principle of the thing. She's not thinking of A. D. at all. She's using him to make herself feel emotional and that means there are at least two or three hundred other men who would do just as well." Later, Georgia herself confesses that her loves don't last: "I really love them. My whole life is controlled by them. I see everything from their point of view...I want to *be* them. I want to get into their lives... At the same time I'm terribly, desperately hurt. I can't stop it. I'm just the same as any little servant girl helplessly in love for the first time, but *it wears off.*" And yet, even here, where she is telling the truth so far as she is able, we can see that this doesn't apply to her feeling for Alan: to tell a man wearing an almost unique decoration that he looks like a darts champion is not seeing everything from his point of view — and if anyone gets hurt by their liaison, it is Alan, not Georgia.

But Georgia's confessional is largely true of her love for Portland-Smith and Ramillies, and an ultimate consequence of her relations with them is that both men die. Miss Allingham's most striking achievement in this novel is arguably the use she makes of Georgia's passions. They are, in fact, the pivot on which the entire double action turns, and the exhaustive account of Georgia's temperament is finally seen as serving the novel in both its aspects, as a mystery and as an inquiry into the nature of women. Had she not fallen for Alan, Val would have married him sooner and been spared much hurt: had she not loved Portland-Smith and Ramillies, neither would have died as he did.

Amanda holds blessedly free of the rather suffocating female intensity that emanates from Val and Georgia. "Traces of femininity in Amanda were rare" and she has a straight-from-the-shoulder directness that might appear masculine in anyone less likely to resemble "a Botticelli angel" on her wedding day; certainly, it is refreshing after the excesses of the other two women. On arrival, she announces herself in military terms, reminiscent of *Sweet Danger*: "The lieut. has come to report," and when Lady Papendeik asks how she keeps her stockings up, Campion replies: "Two magnets and a dry-battery, if I know her, or perhaps something complicated on the grid system." Her home is described as "rational," and her brother, Hal, chooses her clothes; and at the Tulip she quickly suppresses her distress at the exhibition Dell is making of himself, setting herself "to be entertaining... Her manners were irreproachable. Amanda was, as always, the perfect gent." She is lovely, of course, and wears her Lelong evening dress with a natural grace that wins the approval of so stern a judge as Lady Papendeik: but of the "fragrance and flutter" that characterize Val there is mercifully not a trace.

She is now a valuable member of the Alandel aeronautics team—Dell himself says "We shall feel the draught without her"—and her enthusiasm for her work is boundless: everyone is "fanatically keen...It's such a wizard show. We're all behind him, you see. We'd do anything for the work, absolutely anything." Her enthusiasm is the essence of Amanda: it is "infectious and comforting" and it occurs to Campion that "she would retain it all days. It was part of her make-up and sprang from a passionate and friendly interest in all the many and exciting surfaces of life."

If "the years between eighteen and twenty-four had not robbed Amanda of her pep," those between her twenty-four and his thirty-eight make Campion "aware of a chill" at his distance from the "idiotic, exasperating but tremendously exciting world" of young ideals and endeavors. He has long emerged from the high-fantastical world of *Sweet Danger* and we have seen, as Amanda has not, the maturing process of time and experience: now she calls him "a poor old gent" and makes "dispiriting remarks" about his "bleached" look and loss of elan: "'I hope you're not getting old,' said Amanda dubiously." But Campion has the doubtful satisfaction of knowing that he is not alone in decrepitude: when Georgia makes her triumphant entry to the hangover party, with Dell in tow, Campion catches Amanda "regarding them speculatively... He was startled. She was thinking they were poor old things."

Amanda's distinction between the "cake-love" that Val and Georgia and Alan experience, and the much more comfortable "bread and butter kind" provides an interesting gloss on the author's handling of the love between her and Campion. Their unorthodox yet tender love-scene at the end of *Sweet Danger* is followed now by a spurious engagement that "ends" spectacularly: and when next we meet them, in *Traitor's Purse*, they are really engaged, but Campion is amnesiac and uncertain what their relationship is! Lady Papendeik observes that Campion loves Amanda "so comfortably" and without "unhappy excitement," believing of course that their engagement is genuine; and yet only in *Traitor's Purse* are we given any indication that they are capable of loving each other other than "comfortably," and then only obliquely in the pain that Campion involuntarily causes Amanda. But Campion has experienced "cake-love" — as Linda's yellow button reminds us—and he does warn Amanda neither to forget that it exists, nor to think herself immune to it; and Miss Allingham places the warning at the end of the book, with perhaps a hint that its imminence will not catch them entirely unawares.

Lady Papendeik, as befits the head of a great fashion house, has many formidable qualities: a keen intelligence, a sharp tongue, a shrewd business head, and a stylish, dignified presence. In addition, "a certain phoenix quality" has ensured her survival. Haute couture is her element: "Lady Papendeik at work was a very different person from Tante Marthe in Val's office. She appeared to be a good two inches taller, for one thing, and she achieved a curious sailing motion which was as far removed from ordinary walking as is the goose-step in an exactly opposite direction." The theft of a design is a serious matter to her:" "Lady Papendeik rose. 'My dear,' she said, 'my dear.' Her voice was not very loud or even particularly severe, but instantly all the humour went out of the situation"; and she loves beautiful clothes, admitting to having "burst into tears" at the sight of a particularly lovely gown, and, at the showing of "the great dress for the third act of *The Lover*," "sitting back... her eyes half- closed and an outrageous expression of fainting ecstasy on her face." She herself, though "ugly" with "a little lizard head," "a lifted face," and "narrow black eyes," has "the gift of making a grace of every fold she wore," and she sweeps by at the Tulip "looking like a famous elderly ballerina in her severe black gown, her head crowned by a ridiculous little beaded turban which only Val could have devised." The author's account of Lady Papendeik's "evolution" suggests the source for her view of men and women as complementary and indispensable to each other. "The man is the silhouette and the woman is the detail. The one often spoils or makes the other." She "had been an acute French business woman, hard and brittle as glass and volatile as ether"; and Roland Papendeik "had taken her ... and had created from her something quite unique and individual to himself." As if conscious that she has become more "mellow" and has gained added enjoyment from life as she has grown older, she confesses to Campion: "I nearly died of old age when I was 33, yet look at me now."

Although there is nothing cosy about her, she is not without a certain warmth. Campion appears especially favored—he invariably calls her Tante Marthe—and she is charming to Amanda, delighted by the "engagement," and honestly looking forward to gossiping about it: "This is only a secret, isn't it?...I can tell it in confidence?" Unexpectedly, she tells Val to "enjoy" her misery over the loss of her lover, looking "down at her hands with the little brown mottles on them. 'There's a great deal to be said for feeling anything,' she remarked.'I don't.' "

The mischievous Caroline Adamson flickers in the background, central to two moments of crisis and privy to much of the book's secret action; and yet she is oddly elusive, at once ubiquitous and evanescent, and finally brutally expendable. Anna Fitch is deliberately drab, the kind of woman who merges with her background, and frankly more functional than interesting: though her very unexpectedness as the mistress of Georgia's flamboyant manager is intriguing, and both the disarming effect of her sense of humor and her ultimate attachment to her jewels arouse curiosity.

Our introduction to Ferdie Paul, Georgia's manager, comes by way of a sharp remark from Lady Papendeik, prompted by a stop press paragraph on the finding of Portland-Smith's remains: "It will be interesting to see Ferdie Paul turn it into good publicity." When we meet him, we don't doubt that he will. He is a theatre and club owner, with fingers in numerous pies and irons in various fires. Georgia is his star property, but he is also the man behind Caesar's Court. Physically, he is "baroque and Byronic," his "plumpish face with its rococo curves and contours" and "proud, curling mouth" making him look, in a marvelous phrase, "like a pretty bull."

Despite his manifest abilities, Campion detects in him "a peculiar uncertainty of power, like pinking in a car engine"; and the director of Caesar's Court, Georgy Laminoff, thinks him "brilliant" but "born tired": "If only he weren't so lazy he'd be a force, a power... He never does anything at all if he can get someone to do it for him." The truth of this remark is strikingly shown by his generalship at the Tulip when, to avert a social disaster for Georgia, he presses into service a fellow impresario, "the Tulip's most promising gigolo," a waiter "with a card on a salver," and Lady Papendeik. When he does exert himself he is extraordinarily forceful: to quell rebellion in Georgia, he virtually hypnotizes her into submission to his will, and elsewhere he enters on "a great wave of nervous energy" or propagates "an atmosphere of nervous excitement."

Georgy Laminoff, too, is "a person of resource" and it is not his fault that the author's decision to have everyone call him "Gaiogi... with the g's hard" is a constant irritant. He is a Russian prince who makes a "life study" of "the art of being delightful," with conspicuous success, as his introduction to Campion makes clear: "He took Mr. Campion's hand with a murmur of apology which came from his soul. It was an intrusion, he insisted, an abominable and disgusting thing, but Val has assured him that it would be forgiven and he was happy to note from the very amiability of his host's expression that it was indeed miraculously so. He seated himself when bidden, conveying without saying so that the chair was incomparably comfortable and that he knew and appreciated the superb quality of the sherry which had been offered him."

Caesar's Court is his "kingdom": "He's a prince with a point to him and he's hysterically happy." Val pays tribute to his understanding of "organisation as well as magnificence" and evidence of his gifts abounds at Caesar's Court: the "rosy building had retained the dignity of a great private palace, but had miraculously lost its pomposity": Gaiogi has "added gaiety" and the great house now exudes "a party atmosphere." Ferdie Paul claims that if "Gaiogi feels like it, he can put his hands on anyone in London within 24 hours" and Campion himself appreciates this aspect of his "celebrated diplomacy" when, at the hangover party, he suddenly realizes that "every member of the party had a definite reason for being present" (and finds the realization "for some obscure psychological reason faintly disturbing, as if one had accidentally discovered that the floor was laid over a well").

The couturier Rex observes that Gaiogi will "do anything" to ensure ease, delicacy, and elegance: "When the Poire d'Or was actually smashing, he wouldn't give up the orchid on each table"; and a late decision to install canaries in golden cages over the tables in his smaller dining room at once dispels Gaiogi's depression. At Ramillies' funeral, he has "the dignity of a sorrowing emperor," prompting Ferdie's waspish reference to "Czar Gaiogi, representing Caesar's Court."

Rex seems at first almost a caricature fashion-house homosexual, and his appearance "in a costume in which Campion recognized at once Val's conception of the term 'inspired'," his "little coy exuberances," his nearness to tears over a minor crisis, and Tante Marthe's "filthy remark" (that "he's not quite a lady") all contribute to this image. But the author seems later almost to regret the imputation of effeminacy. Rex is still "ladylike," still giggling "coyly"; but his watch is specifically described as "very delicate without being at all womanish," and we learn that he fought in France for three years in the First World War. Campion suddenly sees him "objectively," as "a natty, demure little soul, only effeminate insomuch as sex shocked him for its ugliness and interested him because it shocked him" (and even if it is by no means certain what Miss Allingham meant by this, the intention somewhat to 'vindicate' Rex is nonetheless clear).

Sir Raymond Ramillies, Governor of Ulangi, has "a flat, staccato voice," a "dazzling, childlike smile," and a "quick-eyed charm which was ingratiating." He also has a determination to have his own way whatever the cost, a remarkably violent temper, a tendency to sulk "with a watch-what-I'm-going-to-do air about him," and a "disturbing air of active irresponsibility." As a schoolboy, he had left "a banner of legend behind him" and he has since become the subject of "fantastic and rather horrible rumours." The alarm he inspires seems to be general: Val dislikes "having him in the house" lest he be struck by a thunderbolt, and Gaiogi sees him as having an "impious challenge" and thinks "he should be exorcised"; Ferdie, too, has a vivid phrase for him: "He was the 'scatty beaver' breed: you know, half-built dams in every square foot of stream." Campion's first thought on meeting him is "that he would be a particularly nasty drunk," and he recalls a young man who had spent "a month at the Ulangi Residency and who had been strangely loath to discuss his adventures there on his return." Lugg shows virtuous horror at Val's acquaintance with such a man, pronouncing his name "with such a wealth of disgust that his employer's interest was aroused in spite of himself"; and his account of an escapade in Hampstead confirms the impression of a violent, undisciplined, crackbrained temperament, arrogant, jealous and secretive, and capable of outrages inconceivable to more ordinary minds.

By dressing Caroline Adamson in a complete replica of his wife's outfit and taking her to the Tulip where Alan is already entertaining Georgia, he provokes a spectacular contretemps and achieves "an ultimate degree of outrage — the quintessence of going a bit too far." Nor does his death disappoint us: "They found Ramillies cramped in the back seat. His tweed ulster billowed around him, and beneath it, strapped to his body, were the dismantled parts of the Filmer 5A [a gun he has coveted] together with 200 rounds of ammunition."

And yet, just as responsibility is essentially adult, so Ramillies' irresponsibility has something childlike about it. Georgia observes that "There's something so vital about him, like a child"; and Campion recognizes a "naive," even a "wistful" quality behind what seems a thoroughly offensive question. Even at the Tulip, having memorably outraged decency, he loses the initiative and, as Ferdie's minions move into action, he turns "in his chair like an unnoticed child." His stepson, Sinclair, recalls that "He used to go a bit kiddish and earnest at times," and explains that, in a singular reversal of roles, he used to keep an eye on his stepfather and talk him into "doing what Georgia wanted": he had to "follow him around the whole time and play up to him and coax him into being reasonable."

It is not surprising that the quality of Sinclair's "resignation" suggests "a much older person" to Campion and that, later, resembling "some little old gentleman in his old-fashioned ease," he not only recalls his stepfather's "kiddish" qualities, but offers a confident and mature analysis of his unexpected weakness. He is Georgia's son by an earlier husband, an actor who insisted the boy be christened "Sonny" in case he should wish to go on the stage. Unfortunately, not only is he a very conventional child, but he has ambitions towards the Diplomatic Service, so that understandably he prefers to be called by his surname.

He suffers from the dating of his slang: he avoids Amanda's "wizard," but regrettably utters "blub," "cat," "stinkingly mouldy," "squirt," and "snoop" as an adjective. He is, unexpectedly, "Ramillies' chief mourner," and when Campion comes upon him crying in the shrubbery he realizes for the first time "the use of Raymond Ramillies ...as a stepfather he must have been a rock." The boy hints vividly at his sufferings at school from the social unreliability of his parents, and we see that Ramillies has at least given him a certain stability here, however much of a liability he was in other ways.

Lugg is in cracking form and as ever infinitely quotable. Still bent on self-improvement, the current objects of his disapproval are braces, sex, and Sir Raymond Ramillies: "Braces is low, except when worn with a white waistcoat for billiards"; sex is "pitch" and Campion is exhorted to "remember that setout we 'ad down in the country"; and Ramillies is "a ruddy awful chap. 'Ide your wife in a ditch rather than let 'im set eyes on 'er. 'E's a proper blot." His affectations are on the increase: announcing Val and Gaiogi, he speaks "in a voice so affected in tone and quality" as to be "barely comprehensible"; and there is a fascinating recurrence of what Amanda calls his "mother-instinct": "Lugg surged to the door. 'I've laid them eggs there and I want to see 'em when I come back', he said warningly."

When the need arises to be "ready for outside work," he re -
enters the arena gamely, though fearful lest word of his "mud-rollin"
should reach Mr. Tuke, his mentor at "the club." Two exchanges
are especially reminiscent of the old days: "'Have you tried Miss King?'
'I 'ave. Just got out alive' "; and "'Ollie is the man you want. Ollie
Dawson of Old Compton Street. Take him a bottle of Kummel.' 'Is
it Kummel? I thought 'is fancy was dressed crab. I'll take both'.'"
   Best of all is the use to which he puts his newly-acquired book
of quotations:

> Mr. Lugg let down the flap of the cocktail cabinet with elaborate care...
> "Silence is like sleep," he observed with unnatural solemnity. "It refreshes wisdom."
> "Eh?" said Mr. Campion.
> A slow, smug smile passed over the great white face and Mr. Lugg coughed.
> "That give you something to think about," he said with satisfaction. "D'you
> know 'oo thought of it? Walter Plato."
> "Really?" Mr. Campion was gratified. "And who was he?"
> "A bloke." The scholar did not seem anxious to pursue the matter further,
> but afterwards, unwilling to lessen any impression he might have made he spurred
> himself to a further flight. "'Im what give 'is name to the term 'platitude'." He
> threw the piece of information over his shoulder with all the nonchalance of
> the finest academic tradition and peered round to see the effect.
> He was rewarded. Mr. Campion appeared to have been stricken dumb.

At one point, to deflate his obvious enjoyment of his status as
a "character," Campion tells him that "A lot my friends think you're
overrated"—but only the infamous Barzun and Taylor could ever agree.
   Campion becomes involved in the affairs of Georgia Wells after
"months of careful investigation" on behalf of Sir Henry Portland-
Smith, the father of Georgia's Richard. The day before his lunch with
Val and Alan, he has discovered the bones of Sir Henry's son: now
he wants to talk to Georgia. As always, he makes an art of observation,
and there is much to reward him. When, as one man, both Ramillies
and Ferdie Paul forbid Georgia to answer the "Trumpet's" call to
discuss Portland-Smith, Campion becomes "aware for the first time
that the undercurrent which he had been trying to define throughout
the afternoon was an unusual and, in the circumstances,
incomprehensible, combination of alarm and excitement"; and when
the "explosion" over the theft and duplication of Val's dress design

occurs, he suspects that it may be acting as "a safety-valve, seized upon gratefully because it was a legitimate excuse for excitement actually engendered by something less politic to talk about." He wonders, too, why Georgia should be *angry* to learn that Portland-Smith committed suicide, and subsequently refuse to accept that this is so.

After the inquest on Portland-Smith, he agrees to keep an eye open on Sir Henry's behalf, but weeks pass before the affair enters its second phase, with Ramillies about to fly to Ulangi, and both Val and Amanda anxious for Dell; Val because she fears Ramillies may turn nasty, and Amanda because she wants Dell back at work. At Caesar's Court, Ramillies dies inexplicably and before long Campion receives "the key to the entire story. At the time he did not recognise it, but afterwards, when he looked back, he saw that it was then that the shadowy wards were formed and spread out for him to recognise."

When he realizes that the doctor conveniently on hand will sign a death certificate with no questions asked "another little detail in the key of the problem flickered under his nose"; but when he finds himself unable to protest, and becomes aware that not only Juxton-Coltness but he himself has been "sized up accurately" in the exact context of Ramillies' death, "his sense of personal outrage" grows: "The 'plaything of fate' sensation was bad enough, but he had an uncomfortable feeling that the fate in question had a human brain behind it, and there was insult as well as inconvenience to counter."

Now, in turn, Val, Sinclair and Amanda voice the same idea — of "organised machinations of fate" surrounding Georgia. Val sees Georgia as immune from harm: "There's no danger of a row because danger has been carefully eliminated. It's all working out. There's a superstition in the Theatre that everything works out for Georgia. You must never cross Georgia. If you go with her you're on wheels." Sinclair, too, has noticed this phenomenon: "Things do work, don't they?" he said. "Things happen and link up rather peculiarly. Haven't you noticed it? They do round Georgia and me, anyway. Don't they do it everywhere?" Amanda's conviction that she can "hear machinery" seems conclusive, and Campion feels "for the first time that old swift trickle down the spine." The impression of an apparent cyclic elimination of Georgia's men is inescapable: "It's fishy that Portland-Smith should have been driven to suicide just as Georgia met Ramillies, and fishier still that Ramillies should have looked up his ancestors just as Georgia fell for Dell."

A further echo of the idea of organized fate comes surprisingly from Stanislas Oates, ordinarily the least fanciful of men, when Caroline Adamson is found dead of a very distinctive knife-wound: the "inhuman quality" of the killing suggests to him "a machine or the hand of Fate" and even "Nemesis" itself. But Campion feels that the "pseudo-Nemesis had slipped up at last. The hand of Providence so seldom has a knife in it"; and Inspector Pullen agrees with him: "He's a two-legged Nemesis if you ask me, and if he has two legs the chances are he also has a neck."

Nonetheless, it's a more elaborate statement of the organized fate motif that gives Campion the impetus he needs to solve the case, and the hard evidence of the knife proves surprisingly intractable. But, because Lugg's unexpected quotation from Sterne ("Providence, having the advantage of knowing both the strengths and the weaknesses of men, has a facility for unostentatious organisation undreamed of by our generals") is essentially a variation on the hand-of-fate theme, and also because Campion has witnessed and been fully aware of the exceptional deployment of forces on several occasions, we cannot but feel that he might have seen the killer's "wheels go round" rather earlier than he does.

But, despite this reservation, Campion makes an impressive showing here, and the few reminders of his earlier self are agreeable echoes rather than unflattering disadvantages: the self-effacement—"It was never Mr. Campion's custom to make an entrance"; the vacant look—"Mr. Campion preserved his famous half-witted expression"; and the failure to be taken seriously—"I thought you were three parts fool, but I take it back." On the trail of the brothers who moved Caroline Adamson's body from Soho to Coaching Cross, his energy, resource and knowledge of the stews of London are prodigious, and the chapter that incorporates this pursuit is among the most sheerly exciting that Miss Allingham wrote, ending, in Campion's message to Oates—"Ask him if one of his fat suspects had curly hair"—with an authentic, thumping thrill. His speech at the "end of engagement" party fairly crackles with threat and sting and challenge—he is at his most impressive here, "vigorous, deeply intelligent, and by no means unhandsome in his passionate sincerity"—and his subsequent handling of the killer is bold and shrewd and properly reciprocal. There is a hair-raising moment when, as he is driving in the dark, he becomes aware of a "movement so close to him, so warm, so familiar and yet so horrible in its very intimacy," and realizes that someone is "breathing on his neck"; and another, equally chilling, as he loses consciousness soon after: "This is why the knife went in at the right angle. This is why Caroline Adamson lay so still."

The achievement, then, demonstrably, is dazzling and distinguished, and the book is secure near the top of its genre. But, that said, one must concede that it suffers from a certain self-conscious cleverness, a pretentiousness, even, afflicting the author's style. On the second page, Val fears that the dress she has designed for herself might be "a bit 'intelligent,' " and, except that the author's doubts about her creation were delayed for 30 years, the incident might be stretched to serve as a metaphor for her own creative situation: like Val, she is almost too clever. Even the epigraph that she chose for the book ("...there reigned throughout their whole world a special sort of snobbism and a conscious striving for effect which were the very parents of Fashion") is doubly apposite, both to the world of the novel and to the author's presentation of it.

The kind of preciosity inherent in the style of the novel is delightful when it succeeds: the picture of Lady Papendeik "at her little writing-table making great illegible characters with a ridiculous pen" is a case in point. So is the view of Val as she moves "across the room purposefully...like the Revenge sailing resolutely into battle with pennant flying"—until the phrase "with her little yellow coxcomb held high" strikes a false note. The recovery is immediate, with the image of Georgia as a galleon creating the context for the brief but devastating observation: "Georgia put about"; but the narrative lapses again when Georgia greets Val with the invincibly soppy phrase "My pretty." As an obvious indication of Georgia's extreme affectation and insincerity, the phrase might be said to justify itself—it is meant to ring false: but it doesn't ring false convincingly, and what H.R.F. Keating once called the "Ugh factor" vitiates it utterly. Val's irritating habit of calling Campion her "good ape," and Campion's own reference to his sister as a "dear little bloody" are comparable miscalculations.

A further example of this kind of embarrassing excess is Val's "idiotic refrain" as she gives way for a moment to her misery over Dell: "My dear, oh my dear, my dear, my love, oh sweet, sweet, oh my dear." It is simply no use for Miss Allingham to attempt to get this past the reader by acknowledging it as "idiotic"—it is that, and much more besides.

The narrative has too many "elegances" of style that fail in their intended effect—"Georgia threw the bagatelle over her shoulder happily" — and "perceptive" remarks that emerge as muddled or pretentious, like the comment on Rex's sexual nature quoted earlier. One can just accept that Gaiogi's eye sockets are "as arched and sombre as Norman gateways," but not that Georgia's eyes are "as grey as tweed suiting and rather like it"; nor that Val's voice, for Campion, is "so unlike his own in tone and colour that it gave him a sense of acquisition whenever he heard it"; nor that "Half Gaiogi's secret lay in his naivete and the rest was deep understanding of important fun." Elsewhere, the spirit of Barbara Cartland hovers—in the titles of Georgia's plays, one of which has a heroine called Jacynth, and in a detail of Dell's proposal to Val: "He pulled her towards him and her shoulders were slim and soft under his hands" (the soft shoulder as opposed to the cold?).

Miss Allingham herself came to think the book overwritten and she trimmed it considerably for inclusion in the 1965 omnibus *Mr. Campion's Lady*, achieving a drastic simplification that unfortunately goes too far in the other direction. There is a difference between felicity and preciosity of style, and by striking out everything that seemed to her inessential to the narrative, the author diminished its affectation, but also its elegance. In the first chapter alone she dispenses, properly, with two vaporous opening paragraphs, some expendable brother and sister badinage, an exaggerated comment on the noise from the Papendeik workshop, a "good ape" from Val, an observation that it is Val's *mouth* that is smiling (as if we might suppose it to be another of her features), and Dell's elaboration of the need one occasionally feels to "walk out," with its slightly bogus "great rattling caravan." But we also lose a graceful account of Val's distinctive air of celebrity, the masculine-feminine contrast between what she and Campion are wearing, Campion's observations about feminine weakness, the remark that Georgia is "fundamentally sadistic," the manner of Val's husband's death ("in a burnt-out motor-car with which, in a fit of alcoholic exuberance, he had attempted to fell a tree"), and a good small joke ("Did you see her little black pages downstairs?" "The objects in the turbans? Are they recent?" "Almost temporary."). Interestingly, the "thematic" elements—the contrast in clothes, Campion's conviction of superiority to Val, Dell's elaborate statement of abandonment of responsibility—are either removed or reduced to essentials in the edited version, as if Miss Allingham's interest in this aspect of the novel had diminished with time.

Happily, the two versions co-exist—literally, in that both continue to be re-printed. Each has its compensating virtues, but the ideal version must lie somewhere in between.

Chapter 7
Albert Amnesiac

Campion is absent from the next novel, *Black Plumes*, the last of the 'pre-war' books, published in 1940. When he reappears, the following year, in *Traitor's Purse*, there is a war on: municipal improvements are 'temporarily suspended,' the hospital is empty, wives and children have been evacuated, and Lugg is careful with the black-out. There is a sense of national emergency, of threat, not to any individual, but to the country as a whole. The government is about to launch a "gigantic and drastic project... virtually...putting the British empire on a company footing"; and Campion is stirred by an inner rallying-cry, of a kind to stiffen the sinews and summon up the blood, and such as surfaces only at times of dire national distress: 'something new had appeared on his emotional horizon...a spiritual and romantic faith...a deep and lovely passion for his home, his soil, his blessed England, his principles, his breed, his Amanda and Amanda's children. That was the force which was driving him.'

England is under threat and the enemy is within the gates. Oates writes a 'really alarming' letter in an untypically 'hysterical' vein: 'If you fail, for my part I shall wait quietly until the balloon actually does go up and then swim quietly out to sea... If this thing happens it is the END and I mean that. I'm not a religious chap...but I'm praying now.' Sir Henry Bull puts it more picturesquely, but with no less force: 'At this particular point in history everything hangs on Britain's faith. Europe is conquered; the New World is not yet prepared. So, should this thing happen, it means that there will come once again the Dark Ages which followed Attila... It could happen; that is the lesson of this generation. World barbarism is still possible. The Beast is not dead. It has not even slept. All these years it has been lying there watching with lidless eyes. To a man of my age that is the most awful discovery that could ever have been made.'

Sir Henry is the senior of the Masters of Bridge, the governors of the Bridge Institute, a high-powered research center, 'a living brain factory' in which 'there's more real work done...than in any other place in the country.' The Masters are enormously wealthy, and their wealth gives them power—for good, according to Sir Henry, who defines their 'main function' as 'the welfare of our country': 'The Masters of Bridge are the nation...they're typical of the best of it.' And yet it is at Bridge that the threat looms largest: the Secretary to the Masters is murdered; the town is awash with dubious money; assorted thugs infest the locality; and Campion quite literally finds himself the man on whom the future of Britain depends.

That he does not already know himself to be Britain's last hope is owing to a knock-out blow that has given him amnesia. He wakes in a hospital bed, having forgotten not only what he is doing, but even who he is. Thus, he has literally to find himself, as well as the true nature of the threat to the nation's stability. His amnesia shapes the action, giving it an odd, unnerving, even at times a painful extra dimension. The mystery of Bridge interlocks with the mystery of his own life and personality, and as he pieces together both the plan to destroy Britain and an image of his habitual self, he is continually aware of 'his conscious needy present' and 'the secret forgotten part of himself.'

We are reminded constantly of Campion's double burden—the enormous weight of responsibility on him and the fog of numbing ignorance that shrouds his brain. The imagery of Campion's amnesia is threaded through the narrative, forcing us to experience continually with him the desperate bewilderment of his situation, the 'cold waves' of fear, the 'misery of ignorance,' the 'familiar nightmare...like one of those trick films wherein familiar objects are photographed from an unfamiliar angle,' and 'strange shadows' making 'vast secret shapes, forming a horror where there is none and, worse still, concealing a horror where horror lies.' He feels 'like a man in a stone maze,' or helpless in the face of 'the old dark anxiety' that 'swept down on him, strangling him like a garrotter's scarf.' Revelations come, 'not as a raising of the curtain of darkness which hung between the front and the back of his mind, but as a sudden rent in it which flashed a whole scene from the brightness within, only to close again a moment later as the folds resettled'; or as 'shadowy outlines of facts...coming up on the blank surfaces of his mind' like 'a rubbing of an old brass.'

Through all these terrors of the mind, Campion is haunted by the panic of a race against time, and the increasing realization of the magnitude and the isolation of his responsibility. Oates' letter is 'truly frightful': 'Forced to rely on you only now. Every other line has gone slack and the time is so short.' Later, he is led to the very heart of Bridge and exhorted to 'get whatever you have to do done as soon as possible': 'There was something he had to do here ...and there was no knowing what stupendous matters hung upon his success.' A phone-call from Yeo intensifies both the awesomeness of the responsibility and the fear that he alone can discharge it: '...then it's you alone now, sir. You're the only one now who can do anything.' It is useless to turn to others: Oates has disappeared, and Amanda, Yeo, and Lugg in turn confirm that no one else knows 'the full strength.' 'The thing he had to avert was enormous and catastrophic'— and only he holds 'all the cards.'

One memory from before the waterside brawl that knocked him into oblivion does remain: 'that awful half-recollected responsibility about fifteen,' which 'towered over the rest of his difficulties, a great dim spirit of disaster.' The number's significance has gone, but not the sense of it as 'both urgent and vital.' Fate throws the number in his way: a number 15 bus buckets past him in the darkness; just before his death the secretary, Anscombe, talks in his agitation of 'fifteen miles,' when he means 'five miles, of course'; Oates in his letter claims that 'the figures 15 turn my belly whenever I see or hear them'; Campion's attention is drawn in odd circumstances to the number fifteen on Anscombe's gate-post; and, having penetrated the secret fastness of the Masters, he finds under the heading 'Main Business of the evening,' the 'haunting figures 15' on their agenda. Finally, he is shown the diary of the dead secretary, and a hope emerges that 15 will take a more definite shape: it is 'still a mystery' and 'might mean anything,' but at least the diary directs him to the man who can explain it.

Once he has re-established the significance of 15, his detective powers come fully into play and he at last achieves a synthesis: 'He was shaking with suppressed excitement. All the facts he had stumbled on in the last thirty—six hours were blazingly vivid in his mind...Fifteen...was the pivot. That was fact number one. All round it, gyrating like swing-boats round a tower, were the others. He went over them in his mind... It was all there in his hand. He held it without knowing what it was. In his blindness he had discovered his objective. In his miserable ignorance he could not identify it.' Even in extremis his brain is true, his perceptions acute and relevant. In a total vacuum he achieves a clear, firm outline, and 'for the first time he felt he had a chance.'

Unaware of his career and past achievements, he nonetheless thinks like a detective and acts like a man of action. No sooner does he overhear a conversation between a nurse and a constable, from which it appears that he has killed a policeman, than he is out of bed, and rooting around for something to wear over his pajamas. Through the glass of a fire-cupboard, he sees some oilskins, and it is the work of a moment to pick the lock with a providential hairpin. When the fire alarm erupts in a 'monstrous cacophony of alarum,' he dashes for the door shouting 'Fire!' and drives away in the first car that comes to hand. In danger of immediate arrest, he simply knocks out his guide to the secrets of Bridge, the unfortunate Superintendent Hutch; and his escape via the roof from the siege at the White Hart recalls the carefree days of *Mystery Mile* (an impression enhanced by the fact that the opposition includes former employees of Simister).

It has always been Campion's propensity to surprise others: here, he surprises himself. The discovery of his own physical prowess exhilarates him. Cornered by Hutch, he hits out instinctively: 'His fist possessed a cunning which he did not anticipate. It was a beautiful, expert's blow, which rippled from his left shoulder with the entire weight of his body behind it.' On the roof of the hotel, his 'instinctive efficiency' is astonishing: 'Good Lord, he could climb like a cat! His own skill astounded him.' He finds that he is 'in perfect training,' moving 'like a whippet, easily, gracefully, and so lightly that his feet scarcely sounded upon the tarmac.'

His perceptions are more vulnerable to the cloud over his brain, and sometimes his very vigilance leads him astray: as when the 'greeting of a familiar' and 'a reassuring hand on his shoulder' mislead him into taking for an old friend a man he has met only three days earlier. With Supt. Hutch, he is entirely at sea, convinced that the man suspects him of murder, and seeing only suspicion in the looks of complicity and 'familiar half-smile' that tacitly acknowledge Campion's authority. When Campion smiles, and Hutch, 'catching his expression,' grins back at him, he seems to do so 'secretly, alarmingly': and when the Supt. grins again at the question as to how Anscombe died, Campion is momentarily 'paralysed' by 'the terrifying secret leer which spread over his face.'

Again, when, through force of unconscious habit, he states that 'We're in the hands of the doctor,' he 'could have bitten his tongue out for using that 'we'.' But Hutch, of course, does not even notice it: a man of Campion's experience and standing would naturally range himself with the investigating strength. As the questioning proceeds, a 'trick of the light' gives the Superintendent's face 'a menace which it did not normally possess,' and his attempts to create an opening for a fuller understanding between them become ludicrously distorted in Campion's brain into an 'inhumanly effective' 'cat and mouse game.'

Other bewilderments accumulate. His name is easily assimilated — Anscombe soon calls him 'Campion,' and Amanda, 'Albert'—but the intricacies of his personal situation are less easily interpreted. There is much that appears inexplicable: that 'the man in the paper shop simply whispered "hospital," ' for instance; or why it 'looked odd when he had been found with a lot of money on him'; or Amanda's expecting him to be dressed as a tramp under his oilskins, and her having a change of clothes ready for him in a suitcase.

The wider situation also has its bemusements. Why does the Supt. lead him into the Masters' council chamber in the small hours? What is the significance of the discoveries he makes further into the heart of Bridge, the first seeming 'hardly credible,' and the second 'so unexpected that he almost dropped the torch' that was guiding him? And why does the odd name 'Weaver Bea' click into place in his mind at sight of a white face briefly illumined in the darkness?

Much of the fascination of *Traitor's Purse* lies in Campion's gradual discovery of himself: his past literally catches up with him. It is essential for him to escape from the hospital policeman with his gallows-talk, but, nonetheless, 'it seemed to him that he had known policemen very well and had liked them.' Expertly picking the lock of the fire-cupboard, he has 'no time to speculate on his own peculiar accomplishment.' Looking down on the dead Anscombe, he experiences 'that sense of the familiar' already evoked by a procedural formula uttered by the Supt.: 'Ever since he had first seen the body he had felt less lost and more sure of himself...he knew perfectly well how the man had been killed and what the weapon was which had murdered him... Campion could see the thing quite distinctly in his mind, a long thin murderous bludgeon bound with bicycle tape as like as not.' Assuming command during his nocturnal escapade with Hutch, it occurs to him 'that it was odd that he should issue orders so naturally and should be so certain that they would be unquestionably obeyed.'

There are discoveries of a more personal nature, too. Once, he suspects that his 'new mood of reckless determination' is 'completely foreign to his nature,' and elsewhere he sees his former self, not without some truth, as 'a damned superior young man...always laughingly tolerant, gloriously sure of himself.' When Amanda says, 'I don't want to fuss you—I know how you hate it,' he feels another 'piece of his own character slipping into place. He was one of those men with a horror of being fussed, was he? Yes, that was right; he felt he might be like that.'

The bulk of his self-discoveries are made through Amanda. His amnesia distances him from his relationship with her, enabling him to absorb the fact and suffer the consequences of his earlier emotional detachment with a new and pained awareness. He is given the chance to see Amanda as if for the first time, and to undergo the process of falling in love with her, something he has formerly been far too civilized to do. From the moment he sees, in his flight from the hospital, 'a heart shaped face and disconcertingly intelligent brown eyes,' she leaves 'an uncomfortable doubt in his mind': even with his mind cut off from his past, the fleeting ghost of an emotional commitment touches his consciousness.

In the car en route to the Institute, he experiences sudden delight at the 'conviction that she was his wife': she is all that is fine, intelligent and courageous, resourceful and appealing, 'an astonishing young person, as practical and energetic as a child, and utterly without affectation...her voice...the coolest and most comforting sound he had ever heard.' Her effect on him is 'extraordinary,' and his recognition of her as she climbs the stairs is 'the first real and familiar thing to emerge in the terrifying darkness of his mind': she seems 'suddenly well known and inexpressibly dear to him.'

Already, he had been 'wondering a little at himself,' when she fails to notice a loving gesture: 'it occurred to him that he did not usually exhibit such open affection.' When he calls her 'my darling,' he is puzzled by 'the faint flicker of astonishment in her expression...until he realized that it was the heartfelt, grateful endearment which had surprised her. That was a revelation which brought him up with a jerk and his sudden sense of desolation was not lightened by the conviction that he deserved it.' On learning that they have been casually engaged for eight years without ever in that time having 'had a love affair,' he is blankly incredulous; and when she tells him that she wants to end the engagement, he is 'appalled to discover how much love there was to be reckoned with. They seemed somehow to have achieved the mutual confidence of marriage without it, and now at a stroke it was destroyed.'

Amanda compounds the irony by expressing relief at his undemonstrative nature—'Isn't it a mercy that you've never...I mean that you're a bit sensible and ...er...well, not exactly cold, but...' — and she later curtails a discussion with him of her increasing attraction to their host at Bridge, out of consideration for his distaste for emotional confidences: 'Let's not discuss it. It's not a bit in your line.' However decorously, she at least responds positively, as female to male, to her new admirer, something she has never had the chance to do with Campion. Lugg's assessment of the situation appears substantially correct: 'Courting a woman's like cooking something. There comes a time when it's done. After that you had ought to eat it. If you don't, and keep it simmering on the side so to speak, you're apt to forget it and when you do come to look for it all the goodness is gone away and you're left with nothing but a bit o'skin. And it annoys the young woman too. It doesn't do her any good.'

Ironically, Campion's tenderness towards Amanda now blossoms, and he even comes to wish 'she would kiss him': and yet the desire of a man for a woman is oddly absent. When he experiences 'desire,' it is 'a great surge of desire for comfort from her' that breaks over him. Much of his feeling for her seems to stem from her capacity to soothe, and it is as a mother—substitute that she functions most effectively, 'looking after him like a mother' in the car, and later holding his hand while he sleeps. Reflecting that he has 'probably lost her for ever,' he tightens 'his grip on her hand childishly.' Again, he is 'childishly content and happy to find her. He wished to God that she would take his head on her heart and let him go to sleep'—and how that word 'heart' evades the question of a man's physical need for a woman! As if to enforce the idea of childish dependence, Campion is allowed to feel 'completely adult' only at the end of the novel.

Even the terms in which he expresses to himself his longing for Amanda—as his 'blessed smiling sweet,' his 'sensible, clear-eyed, unembarrassed beloved'—signally fail to convey passion; and one is forced to the conclusion that Miss Allingham was shy about facing the issue of physicality between her lovers. This would not matter so much had she given the relationship less prominence, but as it is central to her purpose, it is impossible not to regret her reticence.

Despite this limitation, we are clearly intended to see Campion's emotional liberation as one effect of his amnesia. But in another of its aspects it is inhibiting, resulting in what would now be called a 'hang-up' in Campion's complex sexual nature. He dreads Amanda's pity 'as he dreaded insufferable pain': her pity is 'the pitfall,' to be avoided at whatever emotional cost: 'To reveal his helplessness at this juncture would be both to plead weakness and to appeal to her pity, and to appeal to pity is very loathsome in love.' He reflects wretchedly that 'Once she knew the truth about him, she'd stick to him with all that eager generosity which was her mainspring. She'd be so kind, so sorry. Pity, filthy humiliating weakening pity! Nauseating compassion! His soul retched at it—the ultimate concentrated essence of second-best.' (The reflection that 'To have forced her into fidelity might have been admissible and even pleasurable' passes interestingly through his mind but is not, alas, developed.)

As if this were not sufficient to restrain him, Miss Allingham makes doubly sure that Campion does not declare himself, providing Amanda with her separate emotional attachment, and later causing Campion to dredge up from 'the darkness in his mind' the fear that she might believe him guilty of murder if she knew the whole truth of his situation: the 'candid trust' with which she regards him in 'the most precious thing about her,' and he dares not risk its undermining.

When spontaneous emotion is generated between them, its effect is destructive. To his own surprise, an instinctively jealous reaction prompts him to mockery of his rival's languishing looks at Amanda, provoking her to box his ears: 'There was no smile on her face now and no animation...He felt himself cracking hopelessly, shamefully, before her eyes.' Within minutes, he has wounded her more deeply still, failing to supply the second line of a couplet that has obviously become a cherished joke between them: 'His mind remained obstinately blank. He could not remember ever having heard the melodramatic doggerel before. Amanda was waiting confidently, all her glorious natural friendliness ready to go back to him. He could snub and hurt her, or explain... It would be so easy to explain and so pleasant... She would be so sorry, so abominably, dutifully sorry... He laughed. 'I've forgotten my cue...' he said. The last thing he saw of her was the smile fading out of her eyes.'

Even when he recovers his memory, this particular betrayal haunts him: 'he saw Amanda in his mind's eye as if she stood before him...looking at him with a sort of stricken astonishment and reciting the first line of that silly old tag they had found together in the 'Gentleman's Magazine' for 1860... The hallucination was so vivid, the pain in his side so acute, and the sense of self—disgust so strong that it brought him to his feet.'

But with his restored awareness, all his doubts and hesitations re assert themselves, and he begins to think of her again in the old way: 'A dear kid, Amanda. So young. Too young for him? Sometimes he was very much afraid so... One got so beastly self-sufficient as one grew older and there was the girl to think of. He'd hate to imprison him into total recollection of 'the three-dimensional truth,' and his 'two minds and personalities' finally merge, that the emotional certainty of the new Campion overrides the hesitancy of the old, making him for the first time fully 'aware of his loss and its magnitude.' He thinks of the 'new Campion's' discoveries as 'witless' from the cloud over his brain when he made them, but if the word is admissible at all, it is so only in relation to the crisis at Bridge: in the emotional field, he is the richer for his hardwon 'certain knowledge.'

As he looks at Amanda, 'sitting placidly beside him,' he reflects that he 'must have taken her for granted for years now.' He has 'the full recollection of a long and sophisticated bachelor life behind him,' and he recalls having 'been in love...many times.' But what he now feels for Amanda is 'not much like it. To say that he was in love with Amanda seemed futile and rather cheap.' Finally, his uncertainties resolved, he simply claims her: 'For the first time in his life he felt completely adult. His hesitancy, his qualms, his intellectual doubts seemed suddenly the stuff of childhood.' The second line of the couplet is accompanied by a kiss.

To some extent, Miss Allingham's preoccupation with Albert and Amanda reduces the impact of her other characters. Even Lugg, deprived of his characteristic derisive stance, is somewhat subdued, though he rises nobly to the crisis of his employer's debility, and flashes out from time to time with something of his old spirit: 'Lugg's dreadful directness was irrepressible. The words came into his head and he said them. : 'He gathered up the cash on the table and rolled back the cloth. 'Wicked to waste it,' he remarked virtuously.'; and 'Lugg came tiptoeing in, bouncing a little like a descending balloon. 'Watch out,' he said. 'They're on the doorstep... You got a hornet's nest on your tail and no mistake. Anyone'd think you was a classic race meeting.'

Lee Aubrey, the Principal of the Institute and Amanda's temporary swain, is a curiously elusive figure, despite an elaborate introductory statement and the subsequent scrupulous assembly of careful insights designed to establish him in depth as a person and a personality. Even Amanda, who is not easily impressed, thinks him 'a great man,' and there is no lack of tributes to his intellectual magnitude, his 'breadth of vision,' and his capacity to inspire scientific achievement 'breadth of vision,' and his capacity to inspire scientific achievement at the highest level. To Anscombe, he is 'one of the big men of our time,' and Sir Henry considers him at least in part a 'genius.'

Aubrey himself would have resented the qualification in Sir Henry's assessment: his consciousness of his own powers is serene and unassailable. Part of the denouement of the novel has him, typically, 'lecturing' a very distinguished company 'from what he clearly felt to be an infinite height of intellectual superiority.'

Faced with the problem of presenting such a figure plausibly, Miss Allingham attempts, interestingly, to show him as largely unable to cope with lesser minds: 'the most striking thing about him was that he could not...provide any stretch of common ground on which to walk with normal men. There was no suggestion of equality in his bearing but rather an exaggerated humility, as if he were in the habit of going down on mental all-fours to conduct any simple conversation.' Consequently, his 'efforts to relax' are 'clumsy'; he is 'self-conscious and uncomfortably gauche like an adolescent'; and he is at once grand and rather absurd: 'His greeting was gravely commiserating, as though he knew that lesser men had weaknesses and he could be tolerant and even a little envious of them.' In conversation with Campion, he chooses, 'his words carefully, as though talking to a child,' and he dismisses a visitor—'Fyshe from the War House'—as an 'extraordinarily inferior mind.' He thinks 'quite openly,' with an 'obvious, almost pantomimic' intensity, and even the expression of annoyance is a 'physical thing' with him, 'as if his personal magnetism had been switched off and on again.'

His remoteness from mere people is emphasized by his excuse for failure to discharge a formal duty to the dead Anscombe: 'Once one gets behind this wall one passes into another world...The mind simply settles down to consider ideas and their technical development. Poor old Anscombe...in here and at the moment he's absolutely remote.' His reaction to police disruption of his dinner party is simple annoyance, and Campion is impressed by 'such magnificent aloofness from the ordinary point of view': if Aubrey betrays a weakness it is inevitably 'a somewhat godlike one.'

Oddly, Miss Allingham makes rather more of a lesser figure, the 'jaunty...bouncing' Pyne, a man of 'shining composure,' as befits the director of Surveys Limited, with his 'ten thousand agents all over England.' He has 'a distinctively ugly face and impudent eyes beneath brows as fierce and tufted as an Aberdeen's'; his voice is high-pitched and confident; and his air is that of 'a man who did not believe in ghosts.' Campion's rashly claiming him as an old friend prompts a metamorphosis from almost back-thumping bonhomie, through 'suppressed anxiety and a touch of antagonism,' to dangerous hostility. No longer brisk, with a 'pleasant, open' laugh, he becomes a 'dreadful little creature with the cruel predatory eyes of a bird.'

Superintendent Hutch, too, is most effective as an ominous presence in Campion's amnesiac doubts and fears, despite comforting elements of both Oates and Yeo—he has Oates' solidity and 'horse-sense,' and Yeo's 'comic country face.' During the enquiry into Anscombe's death, he assumes nightmare dimensions, but, later, as Campion's companionable guide to Bridge, he shares a dream-like progress through the moonlit town, becoming unexpectedly 'friendly' and 'obliging,' and, like a figure in a dream, 'more comprehensible at every step.'

When, in the moonlight, he conjures up the legend of the Nag's Head and the romantic salvation of Bridge, he implants in us the desire for a comparable denouement, pointing what he sees as the 'moral to the tale': 'that the Nag looks after Bridge.' Undeniably, the Nag does look after Bridge, playing a crucial part in the destruction of the enemy, but it does so in a far from dream-like way; and to this extent, perhaps, Miss Allingham fails to answer expectation.

Chapter 8
Survivors

The central figure of the next Campion novel, *Coroner's Pidgin*, (U.S. title: *Pearls Before Swine)* (1945), is also "an inspiring figure with the power to draw brains around him"—like Lee Aubrey, except that his main distinction derives from patronage of the arts rather than the sciences: he has "financed the Czesca Ballet,...established the Museum of Wine, ...put the Pastel Society on its feet,...given Zolly his first half—dozen concerts in London, and ...rebuilt the Sicilian Hall." He is Johnny Carados, an improbably gifted and cultured nobleman—a Marquess, no less—who dominates, in typical Allingham fashion, a gay, glamorous, and tight-knit group, "an odd, interesting outfit, the members all of an age and all highly intelligent...one of the most closely knit of all the little gangs which had characterised the social life of pre-war London." Clearly, they had inhabited the same world as Val and Georgia and Ferdie Paul; and such a reference as that to "the Carados mansion which George Quellett had decorated in his Bakst period" could have come from *The Fashion in Shrouds.*

But things are not what they were, and though the war is all but won, this is London after the Blitz, and the darkness and devastation persist. The city at night is "pitch-dark and taxi-less" and unexpectedly full of "vast open spaces wherein one set of footsteps" rings out "loudly in the silence." By daylight, it is seen that "many of the familiar landmarks" have "vanished, to leave new squares and avenues of neatly tidied nothingness," and that whole roads have been tidied...into little mounds of assorted rubble" by demolition squads. Bedbridge Row in Holborn is now "a half-ruined cul-de-sac"; and Campion, shanghaied by a rogue taxi-driver, finds himself dumped at "Number 27 Goldhawk Mews, North One...practically the only building with a roof for a mile." Even George Quellett's celebrated Music Room in Carados Square has fallen a victim, "its Indian red hangings, its gilt and its green" reduced by German bombs to "a mass of blackened spars"; and Campion has a nostalgic "sudden picture" of the "graceful houses" in the square, "with their slender windows and arched porticos," as they were before the Blitz, standing "like guardsmen round the delicate green of one of the city's finest gardens."

No more potent image of the city's devastation than this occurs, and if the novel makes a statement about war it does so partly in elegiac terms, as a lament for the destruction of beauty and civilization. Miss Allingham even has time to notice, and regret, the passing of the railings in Carados Square, "their slender grace long since sacrificed to salvage." The grim aftermath of London at war is seen less in terms of human suffering than of the destruction of beauty, and specifically of an elegant environment.

This is not to say that Miss Allingham's people are unaffected by the war, but it's very much a question of sophisticates adapting. They discuss intelligently the problems of living in "utterly different worlds," and acknowledge ruefully that they are "not quite the gay don't-cares" they used to be. A casual question transports them suddenly into "that other world before the war when little affairs were fashionable, and no one seemed to have very much to do"; and the diners at the Minoan, a Frith Street restaurant, sit, in "their uniforms and their new gravity," "taking their food seriously and their wine with nostalgic sadness." Miss Allingham approves the Minoan's attempts at "elegant make-do," its "improvised grandeur" and "temporary tastefulness"; and she invents for Evangeline Snow, her revue star, a hit number called "Momma's Utility Baby Gets a Riveter's Lullaby." When a rather portentous wine-tasting is arranged, Carados is deprecatory: "how small peace-time affectations seem these days... What fools we all were." But Campion's reply is instructive: "It all depends on how you look at it," said Mr. Campion cautiously. "I don't know if our present occupation is very bright, fireworks and death." Wine, as a refinement of civilized living, is, after all, not to be despised; and, in the same way, George Quellett's music room was a genuine manifestation of civilization, and its destruction is to be deplored: "it had been worth doing, even for so short a life."

Though the contrast between a bright and carefree past and the "dust and rubble of the present" is a recurrent motif, echoes of the pre-war Allingham world also chime comfortingly in our ears, as if to reassure us. Old Lady Laradine has survived (from *Mr. Campion and Others*) to supervise the exhumation of "some glorious dresses which belonged to her great-grandmother"; and the disreputable Mr. Knapp receives an unexpectedly honorable mention for "pulling his weight" in Italy, "a crook, but not a traitor." We learn that the Museum of Wine was established in Holborn, in a "little house in Jockey's Fields, near Barnabas the publisher," and that, of all things, the Gyrth Chalice was one of its principal treasures (however incongruously in so secular a setting). The sight of "the uniquely horrible bronze group depicting Wealth succouring Innocence squatting unscathed against the bland face of the M.O.L.E. Insurance Building" convinces Mr. Campion that wherever the driver of his taxi is taking him, it is certainly not Euston.

Campion's first reaction to the London of 1945 typifies, in fact, the feeling prevalent in the novel, that whatever has happened, it could have been worse: "He had been back in London exactly one hour and ten minutes, and as yet had had no time to form any real impression of the changes in the great city. But already it had spread its ancient charm about him and he knew from the very smell of it that it was still safe, still firmly respectable, still obdurately matter of fact. He was immeasurably relieved: from the tales he had heard abroad, he had expected worse." Later, as he comes "through the city" with Oates, the feeling intensifies: "It was a moist, grey and yellow morning with a hint of sun behind the mist and great, round drops of moisture dripping silently from the plane trees. The river was busy and warm, and the hollow bellows from the tugs sounded sadly through the traffic's noise...there was work to be done...he was home again." When, soon after, he walks in "on Johnny Carados' reassembled household," he feels, despite "the fact that half the house was down, the famous eau-de-nil drawing room full of unexpected furniture from other rooms, and no one looked in the least bored," that "nothing very fundamental had changed."

There is, nonetheless, an "atmosphere of tension" in the room, arising not from the pressures of war, but from two more immediate threats to the stability of their circle: Johnny's imminent marriage to a strange young woman, for an implausible reason; and the discovery, two days before the wedding, of a dead woman, wearing a black nightdress, in his bed. Of the two, the dead woman constitutes the greater threat, since the fact of her presence in Johnny's bed effectively crushes the wedding: and it is soon established that they know her—less as an old flame of Johnny's than a brief flicker — and that she did not kill herself.

Reactions within Johnny's circle to his engagement have been extreme, and it seems reasonable to suppose that the murder, so suggestive both in its timing and its placing, is simply the most extreme of all. Miss Allingham exploits the tensions resulting from this supposition for all they are worth, assembling suspicion around the entire Carados menage—Gwenda Onyer, hitherto "the mistress of the house"; her husband, Peter, Carados' financial adviser; "the silent Captain Gold who ruled the servants and did the housekeeping"; Ricky Silva, "who existed solely to do the flowers, as far as anyone knew"; Dolly Chivers, the social secretary; and Evangeline Snow, Johnny's long-time love. Gwenda has sought out a handsome young American as a distraction for Johnny's fiancee, and Eve has brought them together. Eve is said to have "hated" the dead woman, and Gwenda to have "got rid of" her. Ricky has "wept and howled like a baby" in dread that "there'd be no place" for him if Johnny married. Peter and Gwenda have seen the marriage as "the end of everything" and are said to be "quite capable of staging this perfectly revolting thing" to prevent it. Ricky reveals that they were all in London at the time of the murder, which is not what Johnny has been led to believe.

Only the brisk and downright Dolly Chivers seems at all detached, able to talk of the engagement as seeming "like the end of the world" "for some of them"; and she cheerfully admits that any of them, herself included, could have sent the paper rose and false pearls that so incense Carados when they are unwrapped. Yet even she is capable of a "vehemence" which surprises Campion, when she hints at "emotional undercurrents" dominating "the life of the famous household," and assesses the group as "a clever, hypersensitive crowd...all living together round one big personality," their "little jealousies and little affections" inevitably taking on "enormous proportions." (One is reminded on Campion's momentary feeling in *Dancers in Mourning* that he and Linda alone among those present are truly adult.) Dolly's view is echoed and intensified by Carados himself: "When sophisticated people do crack, they crack to pieces...I'm beginning to believe that one of us has gone mad."

Campion gives all this its due and chases each hare assiduously, but increasingly, one feels, without much conviction and with a sense of groping in the dark. Oates has suggested near the beginning that the murder may be "a most unpleasant, difficult incident in one of the most extraordinary crimes" in his experience, but no true indication of the "larger, darker" picture beyond it is vouchsafed us or Campion until the novel is more than half over. Carados later has a cryptic remark about "Lives, and treasure, and something rather more important," which confirms Campion in his suspicion that "whatever might be the precise nature of the nightmare which had overtaken him so suddenly the previous evening, it was no simple story of theft and murder. He felt like an actor who had stepped onto the stage half way through some considerable drama."

He has already repeatedly experienced the sense of more-in- this-than-meets-the-eye: when Yeo talks of the murder as fitting in "with the other matter"; when Oates suggests that the spell of amnesia documented in *Traitor's Purse* may have done him "a permanent injury"—"It occurred to him very forcibly that something very odd indeed must be up to make Oates take up this line"; when he surprises Oates and Carados apparently in conference; when he becomes aware in Carados of "some far greater trouble than the one which appeared on the surface"; when Carados seems to attach more importance than is due to the sudden appearance of three cases of a mysterious Burgundy they are to sample that evening; and when Eve reveals her fear that Carados is haunted by more than just a suspicion that his friends are intriguing to prevent his wedding: "'Did you think there might be something else?' he asked ... 'I wondered,' she said."

It is easy for us to sympathize with Campion's sense of grievance at Oates' withholding the full story for so long, since we too are deliberately kept in the dark: and when, "more angry than he had been for years," Campion rounds on Yeo immediately after a second murder has only just been averted, we feel it is about time and enjoy the Superintendent's discomfiture: "While you people don't trust me I prefer not to know you... You waste my time playing silly beggars in the dark. I have not the slightest glimmer of a night thought what you may think you're up to...I've got nothing...not even the confidence of the police."

Oates' anxiety over Campion's former amnesia is dramatically essential to justify his delay in explaining what it's all about; and as soon as he has "come clean," the action moves directly to a spectacular denouement, with the murderer's shocking death as its climax. The earlier mystifications are attractive and absorbing largely because we don't know "the full strength": when we do learn it, the novel takes on a larger excitement, grander altogether than the limited local tensions of the opening stages.

When Oates decides to spill the beans, Campion is on the point of walking out finally, as he has been trying to do from the start. This is one murder investigation he wants no part of: "It's the Coroner's pidgin and yours. Not mine, thank God." After "three years...at large on two warring continents employed on a mission...so secret that he had never found out quite what it was," he is at last heading for home. "Six weeks leave was due, and he was prepared to enjoy it in a leafy peace which yet promised a gentle excitement of its own." Even when faced with the corpse, transferred by Lugg and Carados' mother from Johnny's bed to his own, he determines to duck all responsibility for it: "I'm just going, anyway. I only dropped in for a bath between trains. You just go on as if I weren't here."

When Dolly Chivers appears with Carados, he is "for once...delighted to see" her: "this was one of the few occasions which merited her sort of treatment, the sooner the better, too; after all he had his train to catch." And after a farewell exhortation to the assembled company to confide everything to the police, he actually gets as far as embarking for the station in a taxi. Even when he comes to in a derelict house in N.I. to be unsympathetically questioned by Oates and Yeo, who don't want to know what he has to tell them, he is still bent on catching his train—indeed, Oates complains that he is "obsessed" by the idea; and only when he learns that Lugg has disappeared does he consciously suspend his departure.

Later, he tries again to escape to Amanda: "This was the end of them all, as far as he was concerned." Once assured of Lugg's safety, "he'd wash his hands of them." But habit dies hard, and however much he tries "to put the whole business out of his mind" it is "not so easy. After long years of practice he had developed a routine, and now, despite his inclinations, his brain persisted in carrying on quietly with the investigation. Every scrap of information which he had gathered in the twenty-four hours revolved before his inward eye, trying to slip into the pattern which was already forming."

Earlier, we have watched him at work, his questing instincts alert and secure even when he is "damnably tired" and longing to get home. "He had changed little in the last three years: the sun had bleached his fair hair to whiteness, lending him a physical distinction he had never before possessed. There were new lines in his over-thin face and with their appearance some of his misleading vacancy of expression had vanished. But nothing had altered the upward drift of his mouth, nor the engaging astonishment which so often and so falsely appeared in his pale eyes." He is still the most subtle and delicate of detectives, glancing "curiously," considering "with interest," venturing "a casual question," looking down "sharply" or up with surprise, his eyes widening, or his expression the "old" one of "vacant bewilderment." He still asks the right questions—"What you don't seem to have asked him is why she called" (Yeo having failed to enquire the reason for the dead woman's last visit to her husband)—and even, during a bizarre conversation with Carados, experiences "the half-forgotten trickle...down his spine" that gives the lie to those "times of late when he had thought that he was getting old and that there were no more thrills, no more surprises in the bag for him."

If one were to draw up a balance-sheet, Campion's performance here might appear undistinguished. The killer is forced into the open by chance, operating through the action of an eccentric old woman. Campion identifies the murderer only when he actually witnesses a last-ditch attempt at a further killing. He fears almost to the end that Carados must be guilty of betraying his country on a vast scale, realizing his error only when Ricky Silva reveals the link between the murderer and the true traitor, and when it appears too late to save Carados himself.

In his defense it may be objected that his prompt and accurate action prevents a second murder; that Miss Allingham keeps him too long on a diet of slops and small beer; that he is hamstrung throughout by Oates' embargo; and that the personality of the traitor does not loom large enough for suspicion in advance of the hard evidence that emerges only at the end.

The birth of Campion's son and the deaths of his mother and his uncle are all belatedly reported during *Coroner's Pidgin.* Lady K—'s demise is established by a reference to the resentment she nourished against her brother-in-law "in her lifetime"; and Herbert's is implied in passing when Campion is named as "the only nephew," during a discussion as to the well-being of the Bishop of Devizes' port. His Grace was reported as ailing as far back as *Flowers for the Judge,* when Lugg was expecting Campion to succeed to his title. Since Campion has obviously not become a Duke in the intervening years, we may assume that Herbert sired an heir before dying.

Rupert's birth can be dated to the middle of the war, since he is a nameless "person not yet three" when we encounter him on the last page of the novel. In an engaging end-piece to the action proper, Amanda introduces him to his astounded and embarrassed father as her "war-work," but only in the British edition: *Pearls Before Swine* has a different closing sentence.

Amanda does not feature in the novel, but the heavy brigade of Lugg, Yeo, and Oates is present in force. Lugg, in cracking form throughout, is making a dual contribution to the war effort, as a pigkeeper and as a "stalwart" of the Heavy Rescue squad. In terms of active participation in events, his role is decisive but quickly over; as the story opens, he is climbing the stairs to Campion's flat, transferring the dead woman found in Carados' bed to the imagined safety of Campion's, with the Dowager Lady Carados at the other end of the corpse. When events move rather more quickly than he had anticipated, he makes a "strategic withdrawal" to a bombed cottage near Carados Square, from which he makes sorties after dark to feed his pig.

Lady Carados has impressed Lugg from the first—"All through the Blitz she ran a Voluntary canteen...a real old sport, she is. Not a nerve in 'er body. Me and' 'er always ave got on very polite"— and it needs only his weakness for a title to ensure his full co-operation, however bizarre her demands. He is confident, at first, of a simple suicide—"It's nothing fishy...You know me by this time. I wouldn't mix myself up with nothing dangerous"—and when it appears that Lady Carados might herself have killed the woman he feels betrayed, both by "the old girl" and by "the bee in his bonnet about the aristocracy": "'I fell for it, there's no 'iding that. I took it in like a goldfish. I might 'ave known...but it cast a spell over me, it always does, these days. I can't 'elp it.' 'What does?' enquired Mr. Campion, taken aback. 'Ler Hote Mond,' said the deep voice in the darkness."

Within a surprisingly brief compass, Lugg runs a gratifying gamut of moods and reactions: by turns he is tolerant of the ignorance of the returned traveller: "You're out of touch," he explained magnanimously. "But you'll pick it up."; awed by the prospect of assisting at the wedding: "'I'm going to 'and round at the reception,' he added shyly"; aggressive under attack: "A gleam from a truculent eye reached him through the dusk"; reproachful at a failure of sympathy: "You've got slightly common out at the war, 'aven't yer? Where's yer feeling?"; expressing "sly pride" at the "bijou" nature of his bomb-scarred retreat; put out by Campion's mockery at a moment of emotion:

He turned back to the sty. "Pore old lady," he said. "I'm goin' to leave yer, ducks."

"Perhaps you'd like me to wait in the square," suggested Campion.

"I 'ate yer in this mood." Lugg was embarrassed. "I've got fond of 'er that's all."; and still trying to impose a polite code of conduct within the home: "Do you want to eat yer breakfast in the bedroom? he enquired.

"No, of course not. Bung it on the table in the sitting-room. I'll be in."

There was a moment's disapproving silence. "Goin' to eat where you slep'? That's not quite the thing, is it?"

For one sublime moment, Campion actually mistakes him in the darkness for a shed roof, and since this is also the occasion when we are privileged to overhear him talking to the pig, it is worth quoting at length:

> As he approached, his spirits rose. He heard the sound of voices. To be exact, only one of these was making any intelligible communication; the other punctuated the remarks of the first with a series of acquiescing snorts.
>
> "You're goin' on nicely, old dear. You're a picture now; real class about you. Did they give you a bit o'grub tea-time?" The murmur, tender and solicitous as a lover's, reached Mr. Campion happily through the gloom. "'Oo give it to yer?" it continued. "Old Warty Warden? You like 'im, don't yer, old lady? 'E's all right in is way. I like 'im too, but 'e'll never be the pal I've been to yer. Never go runnin' away wiv that idea. Don't you go trying anything funny. I'll come and see yer nights. I'm wiv yer, though you can't see me, see? You are a fat old devil. Wot yer got round yer chops? Wrinkles? Fat, that is; fat and crackling. You've got 'air on yer ears, d'you know that?"
>
> In the darkness Campion edged nearer to the barrier. He could see nothing whatever in the evil-smelling pit below him, but the black hillock which he had hitherto mistaken for a shed roof now heaved itself and disappeared further into the shade.
>
> "Call that a neck?" said the voice, now considerably nearer ground level.
>
> Mr. Campion could bear it no longer. "Has she got your eyes?" he enquired.
>
> The hillock changed shape abruptly, and Mr. Lugg swore in the dark.
>
> "You might 'ave startled 'er," he said reproachfully.

The portrait of Yeo is rounded considerably beyond the rather limited view of him we had in *Dancers in Mourning*. He is seen throughout with a shrewd but affectionate eye, from the moment when Campion's "sense of homecoming" is "made acute by the sight of that square, bullet-headed man" with his misleadingly comic face. He is "a policeman in a thousand," "a policeman in soul," "a stickler for police etiquette," "dependable, exact, conventional, tenacious." Moving through the Minoan, he assumes "a purposeful nonchalance which stamped 'police' all over him"; and looking for evidence against Carados he is "like an old woman looking for a postal order she thought she had somewhere," searching "on and on and over and over, never tired, and always remembering just one more place to look." Like Oates on an earlier occasion, he is ill-at-ease with upper-crust suspects, finding "class" an irritant in an investigation, though he likes it "in its proper place...on the stage." By nature "the kindest of men," he retreats in "in bad order" when his well-intentioned attempt to show sympathy towards a suspect is overthrown by an emotional outburst. Campion's appreciation of the head woman's mutual agreement with her husband to meet him only occasionally finds him "out of his depth," and though he professes himself "not too old to learn," he has to confess that Mrs. Yeo would be outraged by the situation Campion's words are shaping: "If my missus heard you talking, she'd put you across her knee."

He is perhaps at his best at his "unofficial head-quarters," a back room at the Coach and Horses "up the wrong end of Early Street," where we find him sitting

...at the table, his collar loosened, his spectacles on his nose, an evening newspaper neatly folded into a wide wafer in his hands, and a tankard at his elbow.
Campion surveyed him with open satisfaction.
"Got your boots off too?" he enquired vulgarly.

Here he is relaxed and confident, chuckling and grinning in "ferocious good humour," gratified by Campion's compliments on the speed with which the investigation is being wound up, and enjoying in his turn a mild revenge: "faintly amused at Campion's disapproval: of and "shocked respect" for his casual analysis of the murderer's psychology, he expresses a matter-of-fact contempt for "trick-cyclists" and "modern guff": "You were laughing at me yesterday because I didn't cotton on to one or two high-class ideas...but I'm not unsophisticated when it comes to crime. We've known about that for a long time."

Yeo has been promoted Superintendent since last we met him, but Oates, of course, can go no higher (though he is oddly described by Campion as "the new chief of the C.I.D.," as if he had not already attained to this eminence four years earlier in *Traitor's Purse*). Although his "long face" seems rather less melancholy than formerly— "as if the world catastrophe had cheered the old boy up"—and he greets his friend with "a faint sad smile," it is not long before he is adopting an "inquisitional approach" to questioning him, and oddly unwilling to accept his story where it diverges from what he had already been told.

There are a number of instances where he relaxes: when he sounds "privately pleased with himself" at having tracked Campion across London in the dark; when he makes belated amends by linking his arm through Campion's and taking him off for a private chat between old friends; and the entrancing moment where he shakes himself gently "like an elderly dog." But despite these touches, the pipe and the raincoat, and the occasional warmth and charm, there is nothing very cozy about Oates during this investigation. He is moved to rare passion by the thought of treachery, and as long as he believes Johnny Carados to be one of the "Judases. The men who kiss and serve and sell; the lads who sit smug in one way of life and still serve the other," he is determined to hunt him implacably: "If Carados is the man I'm beginning to believe he must be, then from my point of view he's an evil thing and I'll treat him as I'd treat a typhus germ... I don't care what I do to catch him and crush him." At times, he is more like a dour old tiger than a comfortable old dog, his eyes "cold" and "dark, as they always were when the chase ran close": and when his prey continues to elude him he is "harsh" and "unrelenting," speaking "bitterly," "grimly," "savagely."

Oates is to some extent bemused by Carados, whom he admits to liking: "he's a good chap fundamentally; he's brave, he's original, and he's used to thinking nothing's too big for him." There is even at times a curious feeling almost of kinship between the two men, particularly when it becomes clear that both hunter and hunted have much the same experience during the pursuit of the one by the other, and both posit some form of madness to try to account for it. When Oates says "that the fellow doesn't know if he's guilty or if he isn't," he is echoing "some of the remarks which had...sounded so fantastic" during Campion's "last conversation" with Carados. But whereas Oates, as befits "the most nearly just intelligence" Campion has "ever met," is calm and rational, presenting so cogent an argument that, when Campion turns it "over in his mind," "everything but his reason revolted against it," Carados draws a nightmare picture: "The devil of it is that it keeps coming back to me. Whichever way one turns, whatever new line one takes, all paths lead back to me. To *me*, mind you. Whenever I get a thread and follow it up and see a vague figure disappearing at the end of it, and I press on until I see his face, whom do you think it turns out to be? Me, Campion. Myself. My God, it would almost be a relief to think I was mad."

The theme of madness is introduced in the novel by Carados himself when, having seen him into his taxi, he confesses to Campion "I believe I'm mad." But though he touches repeatedly on the possibility of madness, or at least irrational behavior, either in himself or in one of his circle, in conversation, at least, he appears obstinately sane. That he may actually be mad seems just possible at times, but only when he is being discussed by others. There are repeated references to his living in two entirely different worlds, and from them arises an implication that the stress of sustaining a "dual personality" may have undermined his reason. Eve sees his quixotic engagement as evidence that "the war strain has got him *right* down": "He was going to marry her because he's promised her young husband to look after her. That's insane, really insane...I'm terrified. He's unbalanced, what else can it mean?" Dolly says much the same thing, but more briefly and bluntly: "He's gone out of his mind, Mr. Campion, the war's gone to his head." Oates argues that, if they exist, Johnny's madness and guilt interlock to form a moral state rather than a mental one: because he has settled his conscience by rationalizing his actions, he may even be unaware of his own guilt.

The most potent image of madness in the novel is that of the "vague figure" that proves to have Carados' own face when he catches up with it—yet the frisson this image induces, in us, as in Campion, is undermined by the clear indication in what follows that, in his own mind, at least, Carados sees himself as *sane*: it would be a "relief" if he were mad. The possibility that he may really be deranged is thus made difficult for us to take seriously, and the novel's varied speculations on "the exact nature of Johnny Carados' madness" takes on increasingly the limitations of an academic exercise.

Unfortunately, it is not only Johnny's putative madness that is difficult to take seriously. Miss Allingham lavishes on him so many gifts that he becomes a fantasy figure of truly heroic proportions. He is quickly established as a major influence on the civilized life of his time, "a great patron," who has "had every opportunity to give his genius full rein," with an imposing roll of achievements to his credit. In addition, he has been "one of the leading amateur fliers of the age," able when war came to get "himself into the RAF at an age which at the time appeared fantastic," and sufficiently brave and skilled to undertake single-handed "a sticky job" from which, having done "a certain rather useful bit of damage," he returns on "nothing but a horrible noise and a strong smell of fire."

His gift for inspiring devotion and a remarkable capacity to "belong wherever he is" have made him "a hero, both here and there," in the civilized world of the arts, and the perilous war-world where "everyone might die tomorrow." To Gold, he is "sans reproche," and to Onyer a figure "over life-size...on a pedestal," to whom it is an emotional necessity to look up.

Physically, he is very clearly seen, but in terms too often reminiscent of *Woman's Own*." He is "wide and long-armed," with a "strong sensitive face" that is also "clear-cut" and "terrifyingly intelligent." (Why "terrifyingly"? If the implication is that his intelligence is so acute as to put him near the borderline between madness and sanity, the point is not clearly made: one fears that the author is merely being smart and slack at the same time.) The Carados chin is predictably "strong" (how could it be otherwise?), but his eyes are oddly uncertain, varying within a few pages from a "serene smiling grey" to "bright blue" —though a "grey-blue" compromise is reached thereafter. His "short fingers" are "delicate on the notes" when he plays "scraps of Scarlatti"; and there are "little muscles at the corners of his mouth" which twitch when he is amused (the author tells us that "much of the charm of the man lay there," but she is unjust to attribute to Campion a thought that is so palpably her own).

The grandeur and intensity with which Miss Allingham clearly aims to invest Carados are regrettably little in evidence, largely, one suspects, because his achievements and immense personal magnetism seem aspects of his pre-war self, seen in retrospect, and reported to us rather than shown. Inevitably, war has suspended the artistic activities, and the dramatic solo raid is not only delayed perforce to the end of the action, but has its impact reduced by the jokey wartime understatement (though, to be fair, it probably read much less stickily in 1945). On the one occasion when we encounter Carados in mid-entourage, the fact of murder has just been established, and none of them is at anything like his best: Johnny is edgy and sullen, and when he tells Ricky, with "tremendous authority" in his voice, to "shut up," the little designer continues to complain vociferously! Even the attempt to give him an idiosyncrasy of his own—"his passion for going out of his way to do little things to assist people he knew but slightly"—is interesting less as a personal insight than as a trait that plays into the murderer's hands, and later shows unexpectedly in Johnny's favor.

Finally, like Lee Aubrey, Carados is imprisoned by his role, a concept rather than a person, the product less of his author's creative energy than of her calculation. In the same way, she can do little to animate the ingenue and jeune premier roles of Susan and Don, Johnny's fiancee and the young American soldier whom she eventually marries. Both are intelligently and attractively presented, perfectly acceptable in their roles, but at the same time fatally limited by them. Even within the Carados circle, there are variations in the author's degree of commitment to a character. The Onyers and Gold virtually elude definition: Gwenda, "sandy and petitely graceful, like a whippet," her image as an intriguante dashed by Eve's view of her as "the silliest, woolliest little rabbit in the world"; Peter, with his "sleek, handsome head" and "graceful elegance" and, frankly, very little else; and the Captain, hardly more than a beard, a deep voice and, in our final glimpse of him, a pair of "fat, pointed feet."

But Ricky and Dolly and Eve are more persuasively drawn, and though we warm only to Eve, all three capture our interest. Ricky is an exception to the general rule that Miss Allingham's people take war like everything else in their sophisticated strides. When, in anger, he accuses Johnny of being "like the animals I have to spend my time with. I'm having hell, I tell you, absolute hell." it occurs to Campion that he "was probably speaking the truth. The life of a man like Ricky Silva as a conscript private in the British Army did not bear consideration." He is an interesting development from Rex in *The Fashion in Shrouds*, but though his effeminacy is blatant— the author associates him successively with flower arrangement, matching silks, Lady Laradine's dresses and the corpse's corsets—he is seen predominantly as a childish rather than a feminine figure. The author naturally attempts no assessment of the nature of his emotional dependence on Carados, but it is reasonable to see his fear of rejection in terms of a child's need for a father: he is asexual rather than homosexual, and the weeping and howling at the thought of the wedding arise not from Johnny's marrying, but from his marrying a stranger.

We meet him first "shut in by a sort of playpen of chairs," his "plump babyishness...encased in...battledress...absorbed in himself, and completely unconscious of the picture he presented." He has "full, childish lips" and is said to have "wept and howled...like a baby" when his position in the household seemed threatened. He is easily provoked to tears and appears "on the verge of weeping" during a spat with Gwenda: "His childishness was extraordinary, but there was no silencing him." When he makes an objection, he is "as sulky as a child"; and when he returns to the room after a mischievous exit, he assumes "the studied nonchalance of the naughty child." Anticipating the opening of a parcel, he is "so frank and innocent" in his curiosity that "Campion saw for the first time a reason why Carados had ever liked him sufficiently to allow him to live in the house"; "there was an honesty about his faults which was engaging." At the end, as Campion's "last possible source of information," he is predictably more concerned about the fate of his puppet theatre than whether his friend and patron is a traitor; and as he seeks assurance of its welfare, he stands "questioningly, his large youthful eyes raised trustingly." Sensing that, despite all the odds, Ricky does have the information he wants, Campion reacts to him as to a child, "keeping the conversation simple," hardly daring to breathe once he has begun to talk, and finally jolting him by ridicule into revealing what he knows.

Dolly Chivers is direct from a Betjeman poem, "a thundering English rose," whom one could well imagine in a Home Counties garden thumping the rhododendrons with her tennis-racquet. For a time, she has Ricky's approval because she is so "unfeminine," and it is noticeable that the author invariably qualifies her attractions with rather masculine adjectives: she has a "big, well-modelled head," a "heavy but by no means unhandsome face" and "fine, hard eyes." The expected words accumulate—"hearty," "brisk," "sensible," "cheerful," "forthright," "efficient and splendid," "clumped," and "thrust"—but she is saved from becoming a routine figure by an interesting dichotomy between her image and what she actually says. Though she is said to be "jolly... with a big, frank smile" and has a "confidential friendliness of manner," we have to take these attributes largely on trust. In word and deed, she appears "one of those people who have the misfortune to cross all their t's and dot all their i's," uttering "careless words"; "laughing irritably"; speaking "dryly," "dully," or "with vehemence"; voicing a potentially damaging remark about Eve, a harsh assessment of the dead woman, and an imputation of madness in her employer; and at one point giving Campion "a push which all but unbalanced him."

Admittedly, we see her only in situations calculated to test even the most equable temperament, but even on the one occasion when she is apparently relaxed, her "broad, open face...alight with amusement," she appears so perverse and stupid in her refusal to acknowledge the seriousness of Carados' reaction to the rose and the pearls, that Campion is reluctant to accept what she says: he feels that her statements carry "conviction in spite of their unexpectedness," but only because she is so "strong and intelligent looking."

Eve is a more attractive proposition altogether. Alone of Carados' circle, she feels greater concern for him than for herself, desperate to account for her lover's sudden engagement to a stranger just out of her 'teens, aware that he still loves her, afraid, even, for his sanity, and yet in no way attempting to assert her own emotional claim on him. She is understandably at sea with the "two worlds" theory as an explanation of Johnny's odd behavior, and is gratifyingly curt with Campion when he advances it. Miss Allingham's account of her as "shrewd, kind and, above all, adult" seems justified on the whole, though her unprotesting acceptance of Carados' emotional betrayal has the odd and surely unintended effect of making her seem masochistic.

Her quality as a "character" is immediately apparent, as befits a revue star of the first magnitude ("the most lovable comedienne in the world," no less). She is "exquisite of form and absurd of face," with "vivid honey-coloured eyes," dark hair with a "narrow yellow curl in the front" of it, a "wide, sophisticated mouth," and "long dancer's legs." The picture of a stunning jolie laide emerges, with a force of personality that takes "the colour out of" other women, their "pretension to beauty" diminished by her "unbeautiful, unforgettable face, which possessed so much more than beauty." Her smile is "famous," her voice a "familiar, squeaky whisper," her appearance "incredibly chic." Her "ridiculous lavender fez" is clearly akin to the objects Val wears on her head, and even in extremis her dress sense does not desert her: though "a ghost of herself" at the end, she is nonetheless "a chic and tragic ghost."

Outside the charmed circle, two contrasting old women take precedence, Johnny's mother, Lady Carados, a Gladys Cooper part, and Miss Dorothy Pork, the eccentric guardian of a curious treasure-house. Edna, Dowager Marchioness of Carados, to give her her full dignity, is a maddening old woman who is possibly less charming than the author intended. At first, with Lugg, one warms to her as a woman of spirit, or as he phrases it, "a real old sport" who, "even if she was a marchioness...was showing very game": (and it it, after all, to her that we owe the superb opening sequence of the novel: "The man and the woman carried the body cautiously up the stairs... The two who were alive in that grim little group which writhed and breathed so hard in the gloom were both elderly people. They were an unexpected couple..."). Lugg's contention that she has "not a nerve in 'er body" is supported by Campion's sudden perception that, though she is "frightened," she is "finding the experience invigorating"; and her effrontery during an encounter with Campion, engineered by Oates, at Scotland Yard, offers even more striking support, as well as knocking "the breath out of" him.

Lady Carados has been in her time a beauty, a "fabulous" postcard beauty, whose charms have matured from their Edwardian heyday, so that she now resembles Reynolds' portrait of Mrs. Siddons (but Reynolds' Siddons is noble and tragic; Gainsborough's is the feminine version). Still "young in everything but years"—in responsibility, as it emerges, most of all—she is "a woman who never from babyhood had expected any consideration whatever to stand in the way of her desires": "things to inconvenience her had not been allowed to occur." When at last something does occur to discompose her—not the war, which appears to stimulate her, but a corpse in her son's bed—her instinctive reaction is to get rid of it, presumably as a necessary preliminary to forgetting about it.

So used is she to having the course of events geared to her personal requirements that she now has "an original view of law and order, all probably based on the fact that she used to tip the Home Secretary half-a-crown when he was at Eton." For decades, clearly, men have eaten out of her hand: her husband "could refuse her nothing," and her son, speaking "very gently, almost casually and certainly reassuringly," perpetuates "the method by which Lady Carados had been able to survive so long." As a result, she has perfected "such poise and authority," such "unshakable ease of manner," as to explain "the behaviour of the police, for one thing, and Lugg's unaccountable obligingness, for another." The police are "stodgy" and best ignored— "they're blunted and warped, and no good anyway": Yeo is a "stupid little person," and the house arrest he imposes on her is "silly and officious" and not to be taken "literally."

The expression of arrogant contempt for Yeo is almost the last thing we hear from her, and by that time, certainly for Campion, and probably for most readers, such charms as she has are measurably on the wane. Increasingly, we range ourselves with Campion, who, despite his recognition of "where her tremendous charm for her menfolk lay," shows himself at least as having learnt from earlier encounters. Her performance at Scotland Yard having taken his breath away, it is a matter of pride, that on their next meeting, he should not even be "surprised" by her: "He felt he had had that." He is ready for her this time—"She smiled at him frankly as he thought she might"— and when the emotional level of her story rises in proportion as its probability dwindles, he reflects cynically that she would acquit herself "nobly in the witnessbox."

He comes, even, to see her as a menace, her "potential dangerousness" growing "at every moment...like a beautiful high-powered car driven by an engaging maniac." Oates' view, that she is "loose without a keeper for the first time in her life," has already been formulated more soberly in his own reflections: "He wondered just how spoiled she was, just how far her notions of her private rights to do things which in more ordinary people were not permissible ranged into that abnormal which is politely called eccentricity." Finally, "a new and startling idea" occurs to him: "Here was a person who had a curious outlook on life if ever there was one; here was a person with an imperious will, who believed in astonishing privileges for certain people; here was somebody whom Johnny would shield."

After Lady Carados, Miss Pork blows like a breath of fresh air through the closing stages of the action. It is even a relief that she has no pretension to beauty, and when she steps towards Campion and looks up at him it is with "a sudden gesture which in almost any other woman would have been wholly charming." Her house is unappealing, too, "an essay in Victorian Gothic at its worst," "angry-coloured...puce rather than red," skulking "at the end of a narrow drive with too many shrubs," its hall "discouraging" to "searchers after beauty," with a "dreadful door," set with "panels of iron-work and glass."

Despite her lack of the appeal of the conventional leading lady, she makes the delayed entry of the star actress, determined to finish her breakfast before receiving her callers:

> She came at last, bustling through the baroquerie, a surprise to everybody. Miss Pork had never been an English rose, nor any other flower; she was made of different stuff. She was very small, a fact which she countered by holding herself bolt upright, and she was scarlet. Mr. Campion thought he had never seen a redder human being; red face, red hands, she even had limp reddish hair, which escaped its moorings and hung fiercely round a protuberant red forehead. Her clothes were utilitarian and dropped backwards, and on her feet were large upturned, patriotically wooden shoes. She had a wide mouth and a voice with a quack in it, and, as she said herself, she was usually talking. Bright round eyes peered at them each in turn, and flickered as Oates rose to meet her.

Under pressure of extreme indignation ("This is the limit...Really the outside edge"), she turns "darker in colour, a surprising and even alarming sight," and her gratification, too, "her exertions and her triumph," bring her "to boiling point." Aggressive at first, she is disconcerted by Oates' disarming mildness under attack: "It was not that she melted so much as that she cooled a little. She smiled, too, widely, transforming herself into a slightly merry old dragon." Later, she is moved to offer the company "a glass of wine—beetroot. Homemade, but before the war. Very nice, rather like a very sweet port with a taste of cloves."

She is refreshingly direct and honest, cheerfully aware that people
often shout at her, and freely admitting to being "an old snob": "The
aristocracy is dying, I know, but they mustn't be hurried." Her
cooperation once enlisted, she heads precipitately for the cellar,
"steaming along like a little red train," and calling out a well—
intentioned warning to "Be careful of the third step from the bottom,
there's only half of it there." ("Since they were descending from the
top, of course this last injunction took everybody's attention.") All
unknowingly, her drawing-room harbors the Croker Venus, a
masterwork of some celebrity, flanked by one of her own "treasures,"
"a small print framed in loops of brass wire" of a "little Scottie with
his baby mistress." The print she finds attractive, albeit sentimental,
but her comments on the Venus are less what one might expect: "That
girl in the chemise... is a picture I'm minding. One or two people
have admired it, but I was in two minds about having it up... It's
not everybody's meat and some years ago I should have hesitated to
hang it in any downstairs room. But times have changed, haven't
they? And a good thing too. I like to see these Land Girls in their
knickers; so sensible and healthy." She later dismisses the Waterlow
Ivories as "some little figurines which I put in the spare bedroom...
ugly little things in some sort of ivory." Mr. Campion may be forgiven
for appearing "lost in wonder and delight."

Yet it is a mistake to underestimate Miss Pork, as she demonstrates
when the murderer makes a last-ditch attempt to pull the wool over
her eyes. For a moment, her "aggressiveness" is "startling," and her
"gooseberry eyes" are "embarrassingly shrewd": "Don't you treat me
like a silly old woman. That's one of the few things I'm not. I've
got my wits about me."

Her view of life is decisive and unequivocal—"Good white soap
and water never hurt anything"—and she expresses an invigorating
philosophy of life: "I never write if I can help it, and I don't read
either. I believe in action." She has her own distinctive codes of conduct:
"If one's known a parcel a year, one feels one can take liberties";
and approves of proper domestic impulses in the young: "I like a
boy to be interested in the home." At one point Inspector Holly is
"rendered speechless: by her assessment of the war" "You never can
tell with the war...I've experienced many wars, but this one is far

more inconvenient than any I can remember... There seems to be so much more going on in it than usual." At the inquest on the murderer, she expresses surprise that the deceased had no relations: "I thought everyone had relations of a sort. Of course if one's mad that probably makes it less likely"; and her account to Carados of why she moved his art objects up from the cellar is reminiscent, in another context, of Dickens' Harold Skimpole: "Pretty things need air, everything needs air, we do ourselves; look at the flowers." Emphatically, she is "one for the memoirs": "God made her...no one else would have the nerve."

None of the male portraits in the book matches up to Miss Pork, but Miss Allingham gives us entertaining accounts of all four of the older men involved in the affair: Susan's father, Admiral Dickon; Fred Parker, the ancient waiter at the Minoan; Campion's uncle, the Bishop of Devizes; and Theodore Bush, "the greatest authority of the unfortified wines of the world."

If the Admiral is a type rather than an individual, he is nonetheless drawn strongly and with humor. He is an "old lion-fish," an "exuberant giant," a "vast red Drake of a man, with a head like a St. Bernard and the same dog's air of rigidly controlled energy." As Eve Snow has the power to make other women seem drab, so the Admiral makes other men look small: his presence is such that even Carados seems reduced beside him. He has gained fame "by sinking the Prince Otto," fighting "an old-fashioned sea battle in precisely the way he said sea battles ought to be fought." Thus confirmed in the Victorian principles which he had reluctantly been preparing to abandon, his policy now in a crisis is "Straight from the shoulder, go-in-and-win-action." In contrast with Carados and his circle, he is "essentially a normal man with normal reactions," and in "that sophisticated company his naiveté and directness" strike "a slightly alarming note." His conversation is as explosive as his personality: Carados reports on a lunch with him spent "laying mines for the police," and he has earlier talked of putting "a little gunpowder" behind them to "wake 'em up and spur 'em on." He is confident of his powers to make the police "pipe a different tune," and he evidently puts "the cat among the pigeons" to some effect, since Yeo refers to him as "that perishing Admiral," and mentions almost with respect a cataract of "questions, chits, memos coming down every two minutes" from his superiors. Long after his single brief appearance he is kept alive by constant awed references from those who encounter him or his methods.

The "ancient" and "decrepit" Fred, who "sees himself as the Hand of Fate," has been "enticed" to more glittering pastures in Soho from "some country town hotel" (subsequently specified as the Totham Sun in Suffolk, "a very dull place" compared to the Minoan). He brings with him "the happy provincialism of his kind," an unabashed interest in all that goes on that prompts him to cut into conversations while waiting at table. Like the Admiral's, his remarks are explosive, and he invariably launches some form of conversational "depth-charge" to ginger up his patrons.

Campion begins by taking him at face value: "Wonderful to live to that age and still be indiscreet... His life must have been one long fall downstairs and still going strong"; but he comes to adjust his view after further exchanges, detecting a "dreadful thirst for entertainment" or a "glint of wicked amusement" flickering deep in the "sunken and watery eyes." Although Fred appears "outwardly... as casual, as ineffectual and as disinterested as an old brown leaf in the wind," and despite his protest to Campion that "things kind of slip out" and "my old tongue...runs away with me," his effects are deeply calculated: "Things happen when you're around, and if they don't you help them on." He makes sure that he is never "gravelled for lack of excitement." For all that he spends much of his professional life wavering, drifting, fluttering, shaking, stumbling, shuffling, shambling, and sidling, he maintains in fact only a "show of doddering inefficiency." Occasionally the mask slips, and the "sinful old face" cracks into "a purely yokel smile," or he utters an "evil chuckle," "soundless" and involving "the display of a dreadful assortment of tooth stumps."

The Bishop is Campion's uncle, his father's brother, and he is by way of being a revenant, having been reported dead by his nephew in an earlier Campion tale. He is now a silvery, sweet old man, "tiny...soft-voiced and gentle, with the bluest eyes seen out of Scandinavia," "patently innocent" and yet with such a natural dignity that, when he is discovered "sitting demurely...by himself" at the

Minoan, it is "not he, but the Minoan" which appears "a little out
of place." (His kindly-meant observation about the restaurant—"This
place looks very clean"—makes Campion feel that "any debt the
Minoan owed him was repaid.")

Although we see the Bishop in a wholly secular situation—at
one point in Oates' office, where he *does* look "out of place"—his
saintliness is implicit in all he says and does, whether laughing "his
gentle little laugh which had made so many people his slaves in his
long life," or speaking in his "beautiful, precise voice," "charming
and amazingly adroit" in an unorthodox social situation, and with
a fund of "masterly" "small talk" designed to put an anxious host
at his ease.

He has come prepared for a rite of homage to a bottle, producing
from "the folds of black silk" that envelop him a pen-knife and a
reading-glass. His winesmanship is impeccable, and when he uncorks
the wine, "his slender hands revealing practised skill," the cork emerges
"with the ghost of a pop...a beautiful sound, regretful, grateful, kind."
Faced with irrefutable proof that the wine is stolen, his face is "as
grieved as a mourning cherub's," and he is relieved and happy to
"put crime behind him" and plunge "into fairer country," with his
personal account of the rare vintage, "his bright blue eyes" "alive
with unconquerable youth" as he talks.

It falls to the Bishop to perform the ritual rather than the oenophil-
in-chief, Theodore Bush, since the latter is prevented from attending
the ceremony by an attempt to murder him. Bush claims to have devoted
his life to wine, and, whether serious or frivolous, most of the references
to him in the novel enforce this idea. He was "Secretary, Curator
and High Priest of the Museum of Wine"—(is there a hint of
opportunism in Campion's remark "He got himself put in charge"?)—
and as an authority runs "neck and neck" with Don's father, his
transatlantic counterpart, for "the ultimate arch-connoisseur stakes."
Even his house resembles a wine-bottle, in that it is drab and dusty
without, and rich and fine within.

He is a "rather grim old man," "portentous" but nonetheless
"impressive," with "the head of a Victorian statesman," "a structural
appearance round the skull and much superfluous drapery about the
chin." He makes a modestly flamboyant impression, wearing a "wide-

brimmed black hat" and an "enormous brown tweed overcoat" that hangs "jauntily" and brushes against the tables at the Minoan as he moves. Despite a suggestion of humor—"he had a way not so much of smiling as of hinting that he was about to smile which lent his face a pleasant uncertainty"—and an assurance of intelligence—his eyes are "bright and very intelligent"—he emerges as solemn, self-important, and ponderous. When, in cloak-and-dagger style, he hands Campion a note under cover of a hand-shake, he acts both mysteriously and uncharacteristically.

At the inquest, he addresses Miss Pork "with a pompousness which he appeared to have decided was her due"; and neither Carados nor Campion appears willing to take him at anything like his own valuation. Johnny regards him as "heaven's own peculiar prize bore," a "silly old ape" of limited humanity who believes in "all the wrong things" and bewails the fall of France principally because he can no longer obtain a particular brand of stomach powder. Both he and Campion, while clearly respectful of his expertise, highlight his self-importance: Johnny with his remark that Theo is unable to "give his opinion on a rare bottle if he isn't in virgin linen"; and Campion with an account of the traditions of the Museum of Wine that implies the absurdity of the man even as it establishes his authority as an expert: "Certain approved connoisseurs...were allowed to mature small quantities of their rarest vintages under Theo's pontifical eye. No one was permitted to take anything away...until Theo pronounced it at is zenith, and at the psychological moment out it had to go, and Theo would come and help you drink it, if pressed." The author herself joins in the fun at Theo's expense by naming his niece Hebe. Campion claims that she sprang "fully armed from a champagne bottle," and was destined at fourteen for "a serious drinking tour of the world," designed to create in her "the perfect palate."

Miss Allingham's gift for what used to be called thumbnail sketches is superbly in evidence. We meet Eve Snow's dresser, the "consequential" Mrs. Phipps once, and there are no more than four brief references to her; but we need only to be told of Eve, seated at her mirror, "while Mrs. Phipps, who reminded everyone of a hare in petticoats, moved around her in efficient bounds," for an indelible impression to be made.

Similarly, the Coroner at the inquest on the murderer appears once only, at the end of the action; but Miss Allingham takes the trouble to create for him a reputation in advance of his appearance— he is "an old publicity hound," who knows that "a coroner is king of his own pub parlour, and trades on it"—and then to endow him with a presence and manner worthy of the reputation:

> He was a small man, thin and shrivelled, who bore, and knew that he bore, a striking resemblance to the best-known portrait of Laurence Sterne. His lips were cruel and his eyesockets as dark as if they had been painted, but his whole face was rendered less impressive than it might have been by an incipient naughtiness, a lightness and vanity which partially explained why such an obvious personality should blossom so obscurely. Before he sat down he glanced around him with brisk professional interest, not at all unlike an actor manager appraising the house on his first entrance. Then he settled himself, took up his pen with a flourish and opened the proceedings in a quiet, intentionally dangerous little voice, rather unpleasant to hear.

Stavros and Pirri, the joint owners of the Minoan, are explosive and temperamental foreigners interesting primarily as mystery men: Stavros, because he proves to have been married to the dead woman, has quarrelled with her shortly before her death, and is clearly in a state of anxiety over the bottles of wine subsequently broached by the Bishop; Pirri, because he abducts Campion and persists in following him for no apparent reason; and both men, because they erupt into a violent quarrel, "bellowing at each other in several different languages," Stavros, at least, "with intent to kill; his arm...raised, his face white with fury, and his small eyes blazing." Their activities form a running subplot to the main action, dovetailing into it only with the explanation that Campion extorts from them at the end.

Mrs. Stavros, formerly Moppet Lewis, is the only corpse in the novel until her murderer stampedes in panic through Miss Pork's drawing-room window and crashes into the area below. She is dead on the first page but, much as with the malignant Andrew in *Police at the Funeral*, a lively picture of her personality emerges from what others say about her. Campion, who sees her only after death, speculates as to her having been "in life a birdy little creature, bright-eyed no doubt, and even pretty in a faded, possibly over-excitable fashion."

Eve, who speaks from experience, confirms the "birdy" impression, calling her "that little crow of a woman," once "a little gate-crasher" who, ironically, in death has "got in at last." One of Johnny's "fans," who "took the whole gang of us too seriously altogether, she got into the house once and I remember Gwenda trying to stop her trying on all our clothes. She thought we were all too "sweet and brittle' for words, and ...was always offering to get things for us wholesale." Dolly's view is, characteristically, more "forthright": she was "a bit of a trial, nosy and possessive"; and this opinion is echoed by Pirri, who considered her "a difficult woman, a worrying, nagging, importunate woman," who "bothered someone so much they killed her."

Johnny is less brusque and more generous: he admits to having "taken her out to lunch once or twice" (like an incipient Falstaff, he immediately upgrades this to "three or four times"!) and some memory of the brief fascination she had for him makes itself felt as he reminisces: she was a "jolly, vulgar little person with an interesting approach. You always felt she was just about to be terribly witty and yet she never was. She had an indescribable promise of romance, too, which turned out to be rather prim sentimentality; and yet you felt kindly towards her. The worst thing I remember about her was her energy, but I can't see anyone killing her for that. Besides, she was one of those people you like even when you can't stand them about any longer."

Stavros has already expressed much the same idea: having "loved her enough to marry her," he find that he "still loved her, but not so much. She was not a woman to live with every day." He alone is distressed by her death, and his questioning by the police prompts an outburst of grief: "The man stood before cracking visibly; his dignity and sophistication...gone,...tears in his eyes...his mouth...ragged and hideous like the mouth of a tragedy mask." Whatever her faults, Moppet was at least capable of inspiring that kind of emotion. Even the corpse has life in this vivacious novel.

Chapter 9
Treasure House

The distance of years between *Traitor's Purse* and *Coroner Pidgin* was the start of a slower rhythm of creation that Miss Allingham maintained for the rest of her life, and *More Work for the Undertaker* appeared after a further three years in 1948. The author apologizes in a dedication to "all old and valued clients...for unavoidable delay in delivery of goods," but, in fact, she never again achieved the regular pattern of, on average, a book a year that she sustained in the pre-war years. For the 14 years from 1928 to 1941, there are 14 books (15, if we include the American anthology, *Mr. Campion, Criminologist*), whereas the eight later novels are spread over a period of 24 years, from 1945 to 1968.

Whatever the reasons for "unavoidable delay in delivery" the "goods" were supremely worth waiting for: *More Work for the Undertaker* is one of the richest works in the canon, within its chosen convention. The qualification is important, since, in some ways, the novel might be seen as a retreat from reality, its characters engaging oddities, its villains clowns, its killer a toy, with trivial passions and designs insufficiently motivated. For all its murder and attempted murders, its surface tensions and sinister underground traffic, Apron Street is cloud-cuckoo land, its atmosphere is festive, and the overriding impression is of humor, warmth, and charm.

But within her self-imposed limitation, all Miss Allingham's gifts come into play, and she achieves an entertainment of consummate grace, at once cosy and menacing, stately and suspenseful, reassuring and unnerving, complex and crystal-clear. In terms of character and incident, dialogue and narrative, the book is an Allingham treasure-house, alive with wit and invention, dense in texture, and crammed with entrancing detail, its perceptions acute, its sympathies wide, its excitements subtle and sure. The author's prodigality might seem reckless were she less palpably in control of her enterprise: she judges impeccably the pace of her narrative, the shaping of her design, and the timing and placing of her effects.

The writing has both vigor and sophistication: it is stylish and relaxed, practical and precise, truthful and illuminating, and yet fanciful, unexpected, and exhilarating. Images and insights crowd the pages, from our initial view of Oates' raincoat bellowing "out behind him like a schoolmaster's gown," to Campion's final fear that the "curious smothered wailing" he can hear is Lugg's voice raised in song. Renee Roper pats Campion's shoulder "as if it were the situation she was jollying along." The actor, Clarrie Grace, has "horizontal wrinkles across his forehead," which, "under the uneven line of the receding tide of hair," give his face the look of "a mask of anxiety painted on a kite." Oates pauses before "the mock—moorish facade of a furtive tavern which huddled its pottery pillars between two large gown shops." An unspeakable odor has "crept up" from a basement, unwinding "a thin coil of appalling affront." "The D.D.I. was pulling off his coat as if it were attempting to resist him." "...every port has been watched like the last bun at a school—treat." A sheet in the darkness is a "macabre highlight slid into" a "dark picture." The proprietor of Madame Pernelle's Supper Bar is "as big as a barrel and as good as the beer." An old woman comes "wruffling up the pavement." A phone-box is "a little red temple" and the police—station clock is "freckle-faced."

There is some engaging invective, too: Lugg dismisses his undertaker brother-in-law as a "poor worm shoveller"; an anonymous letter writer becomes "foul-mouthed Freda"; and a callous landlady is successively described as an "old tank-trap," an "old shorthorn," and an "old bath-tap."

Miss Allingham's feeling for an environment is strongly in evidence. As always, her geography is scrupulous, and her map is a bonus, both informative and attractive. Apron Street has a remarkable tally of institutions and inhabitants: the Thespis Theatre, "highbrow" and, therefore, "harmless"; the grocer who "keeps the cheese too near the paraffin"; the china swan in the dairy window; the legless cobbler at work in the doctor's basement; the greengrocer's daughters, "with paint all over their faces and dirt all over their hands"; and the chemist's "emporium," with "great jars of coloured water in the window, dozens of little drawers of muck, smell of old lady's bedroom enough to knock you back," and "every...patent medicine the world has ever known." Across the way are the undertakers, Bowels and Son, offering "Reliable Interments. Taste, Efficiency, Economy, Respect," and the Apron Street branch of Clough's, "an Emett-train sort of bank," "a fantastic anomaly in a modern world," where "the cashiers hand you your notes with white-gloved hands," and the manager's office has "a rich Chinese red and gold paper, a Turkey carpet, a coal fire, and a corner cupboard which might have well have contained sherry and cigars."

At the top of the street is Portminster Lodge, home of Mr. Campion's old acquaintance Renee Roper, and of all surviving Palinodes, the family of autocratic intellectuals around whom the case revolves. All three show intellectual accomplishment: Lawrence, at work on The Origins of Arthur, while preparing "all the crossword puzzles for the 'Literary Weekly' in his spare time"; Evadne, prepared, "if one wasn't so occupied already," to contemplate Social Stratification as "a very jolly second subject"; and Jessica, solving Latin crosswords, and "slapping the words in" with daunting ease. Even their niece, Clytie, at eighteen, works on the "Literary Weekly" and intends to be a writer.

The author endows the Palinodes with a detailed literary and academic heredity. The fame of their parents was sufficiently widespread for even the schoolboy Oates to have heard of them: Professor Palinode, a critic and essayist in the Leslie Stephen mould, and his wife, Theophila, the "poetess of the 'sixties." Jessica quotes from one of her mother's verses, and Lawrence reads an appealing piece of family history from the third edition of "Elegant Extracts." Miss Allingham also gives us, for good measure, an extended passage from Jessica's improbable bible, "How to Live on One-and-six" by Herbert Boon.

Her villains are equally well set-up, from the hapless little chemist, Pa Wilde, whose stocks include "Old Ma Appleyard's Dynamite Cough Cure and Intestine Controller," to the mourning Bella Musgrave, whose "speciality" is "Death": "She...used to go round with the cheap bibles. She'd look up the deaths in the papers and then trot round to the 'ouses. 'Wot, not dead?'...Oo I'm ever so sorry. Such a loss to me too. The Departed bought one of these 'ere and put down a small deposit. Only fifteen bob to pay.' The sorrowers forked out to get rid of 'er, of course, and took in a bible worth nine-pence 'olesale." We are also offered an outrageous yet utterly plausible reason why the fatal poison should be at hand when the murderer wants it; and, for Bowels and Son, a bizarre little jingle designed to inspire confidence and boost trade: "If you're Rich, or count the Cost, We Understand there's Someone Lost."

The details of the main action are in every way as enticing as the incidental treats. Campion does not merely enter the case: indeed, he actively resists it, and three different forces combine to coax him into it. Renee Roper's household is of a variety and an oddity to foster suspicion and unease: all six of her boarders show a disposition to devious behavior, and Renee herself has something to hide. The youngest Miss Palinode cooks noxious foods at night and sits in the park each afternoon, dressed like a tramp, awaiting alms from the wife of a local businessman. Her brother and sister converse in a mixture of crossword clues, quotations from the poets and "the one unbreakable code known to man, the family allusion." Their niece habitually enters the house by way of the roof. The undertaker, Bowels, summons Campion to his aid, later to deny having done so. He uses the small hours for shifting coffins, one of which bears the name and dates of the eldest Palinode, dead and buried seven months earlier. An anonymous letter writer menaces the district with hysterical but accurate abuse; and in Charlsfield Prison, Looky Jeffreys, a delirious housebreaker, reiterates his determination not to be sent up Apron Street.

The victim of the Apron Street murder is Ruth Palinode, another of the Professor's children, newly exhumed on the prompting of the local poison pen. Various theories are advanced to account for her death: she was accidentally poisoned by a herbal concoction brewed in the cellar by her younger sister; her wits were going, and her siblings eliminated her to spare themselves social embarrassment; she was gambling away the small remnant of the family fortunes and had to be stopped; a parcel of dead shares had come to life, and a greedy heritor saw his chance; her money had finally run out and she had killed herself.

Campion almost misses all this, from an access of middle-aged solemnity that threatens to engulf him. The mock Paladin of *Sweet Danger* is here all set to govern a colony in earnest, to abandon Lugg, and to bring Amanda into line as governor's lady; and he resists all attempts to persuade him to resume "the old hobbies of his pre-war life." Renee Roper has appealed to him, and Oates has led him "with a certain assumption of casualness" to the park where Jessica awaits her alms: but "two crows don't make a summons...According to the adage one needs three for that," and so he returns to Bottle Street to telephone his acceptance of the post. "After nearly eight years he was again his own master and was finding his freedom a thought unnerving, like a man out of prison or a boy out of school. The great carpet of his half-finished private life hung on a shadowy loom before him, the threads tangled and dusty, the pattern but half remembered, and the task just a little, if guiltily, wearisome to contemplate." No longer a younger son, he has spent "five months of uncomfortable hesitation," and now "the most important decision of his middle life was practically made." Although he is awed by the face of the woman in the park, and very much wants to know more about the young couple who avoid an encounter with her, at all costs "the ancient spell must not be permitted to work."

But "the enchantment which had been striving to overcome him for the past few months had never been more strong. Yeo's remark that his intervention in the Palinode affair was 'intended'   nagged like a prophecy. All that week coincidences had occurred to keep the case before his mind. A fresh fish - -hook of interest had fastened into his imagination each time he had released himself. Opportunities to interfere had opened wicket gates in his path at every turn : and when he encounters a great lady in her crested limousine, there is a "bleakness in his eyes," and she recognizes his need for reassurance. However, despite her efforts, "the lead was still in his eyes" at the end of the interview, and he returns, "in the same state of depression," to "the sanctuary which had been his ever since he left Cambridge," where he is "shocked" by "its jungle growth of trophies and their associations," and turns away to the phone.

Here, with exemplary timing, the third crow awaits him: Bowels' letter, from Apron Street, pinned to the blotter, with awesome symbolism, by "a memento of his first adventure," the Black Dudley Dagger, no less. Even Campion is not proof against this, and at last he begins "after a while. . . to look quietly happy."

The case which he resists so resolutely proves a major personal triumph, and Oates' prediction that it will be "one of the classics of its kind" is at least borne out by Campion's performance. If he fails to establish either the identity or the motive of the man who coshes Clytie's lover, in all other respects, he sweeps the board. Once he has seen the coffin bearing Edward Palinode's name-plate (dubbed by its makers "the Queen Mary"), he never loses sight of its importance, establishing by leg-work that it is still above ground, despite Bowels' assertion to the contrary, and subsequently keeping tabs on its comings and goings till its final macabre appearance. He assembles the evidence to establish both the nature of Bowels' sideline and the way that it operates: from the ubiquitous coffin; from the positions of two chairs at Pa Wilde's; from the appearance of Bella Musgrave on the scene; from the delirium of Looky Jeffreys; from a rumor caught by Thos. Knapp and Lugg; and from the denials of various bereaved families. He pursues the money motive for Ruth's death beyond the point of its authoritative dismissal, prompting at the highest level—from the top brass at the Treasury—a reaction which defines the motive exactly. On internal evidence supplied by one of her missives he identifies the anonymous letter writer; and he perceives why Renee Roper provides a home for the Palinodes despite considerable pressure on her to eject them.

Acute and sensitive at all times, he wonders if Evadne Palinode is hiding something when she sits so still in her chair, and registers exactly what is on her occasional table each time that he sees it. He recognizes why Lawrence Palinode washed up when his sister died; understands why Renee's military friend, Captain Seton, spectacularly drowns his sorrows; and detects a "tea-party atmosphere" during a conversation with Bowels, arising from the undertaker's awareness of an eavesdropper. He assimilates into the final pattern even the bank clerk's confusion as to the time of Ruth's death; and from a chance remark about a wine-glass deduces the identity of the killer.

While his police collaborators are "stunned" and fearful of having pursued the wrong man, Campion persists that they are right, certain that the outcome of the final chase will be total vindication and triumph.

As always, his personal progress is meticulously observed. He is at this time "a tall man in the forties, over-thin, with hair once fair and now bleached almost white. His clothes were good enough to be unnoticeable and behind unusually large horn-rimmed spectacles his face, despite its maturity, still possessed much of that odd quality of anonymity which had been so much remarked upon in his youth. He had the valuable gift of appearing an elegant shadow and was...a man of whom at first sight no one could ever be afraid." The familiar characteristics recur like old friends: "Mr. Campion looked like a thin owl"; "the slightly high voice was misleadingly foolish"; "the lean man was expressionless as was usual when he was very excited"; "his tread was lighter, his back straighter and his pale eyes more vacant at every step."

Miss Allingham charts his way with her customary care, through his relief at finding a trace of "the professional crook element"; his separation of the "two different colored threads in the ...coil"; his speculation as to whether they are "tied at the end"; his awareness of the "definite point at which reconnaissance" becomes "attack" and "Phase Two" begins; and the mulling-over process during which his "thoughts...boil gently" as the "basic design" emerges. The news of Looky Jeffreys' dread of Apron Street even induces the "familiar trickle, partially and shamefully pleasurable, running slowly down his spine"; and he feels again "some of the old thrill" when, having backed "a hunch of the wildest kind," he sees "the card turning up." The final revelation has the preternatural clarity of a Joycean epiphany: "The words detached themselves from his immediate present and hung in front of him, very small and clear, as if they were printed in hard block type across a picture of the room. Immediately afterwards, with a series of jolts which were almost physical, a string of hitherto unrelated, and in some cases hardly noticed, items jerked into line. Each little knot pulled out like chain-stitch and suddenly the single end of the cord lay in his hand."

Campion's occasional histrionic impulse has a brief but happy showing: "He stood wavering, a lean column of open indecision, guaranteed to arouse the executive instinct in any practical woman... It was a princely dither, and she took pity on him": and his unempathetic wit surfaces repeatedly, whether he is teasing Clytie on her entry from the roof: "'Been on the tiles?' he enquired affably"; or ribbing Bowels, about to shift the ubiquitous black coffin from one side of Apron Street to the other: "Good evening, sir." His tone was brisk but subtly deferential and a thought knowing. "We did not disturb you, I hope?"

"Think nothing of it," murmured the torchbearer magnanimously.

"What are you doing? Stocktaking?"...

"Not exactly sir, not exactly, although there are likenesses. It's all perfectly in order. All above ..."

"Ground?" suggested the thin man helpfully.

"No, sir. Board, I was going to say."

He even out-Applebys Appleby at one point, capping a quotation from an obscure Elizabethan dramatist, whom he had been "moved to read...only the evening before in search of the name which had been tantalizing him." (Palinode, of course.) That he knows where to look is proof of such staggering erudition that we are obliged to overlook an earlier lapse, when he attributes to Caesar a remark made by Cassius in Shakespeare's play.

Amanda, absent owing to pressure of work, again provides an effective tailpiece, this time with a letter: from which we learn that "the new Cherubim jet is almost ready for her trials," and that Rupert— still not officially named and here referred to as Sexton Blake—is emerging as a true child of the atomic age, for all his tender years. We also learn, in a postscript, Amanda's guess as to who the murderer might be!

Oates and Yeo make characteristic contributions from the sidelines of the case, Oates at the beginning, Yeo at the end. To Oates falls the marvelous opening sequence, where he rambles in apparently aimless reminiscence through his old manor, while actually edging Campion ever nearer to Jessica Palinode. His progress is "Like the serene sailing of a big river fish from whose path experienced small fry consider it prudent to scatter," and he retails his recollections with a certain macabre relish. Despite the evidence of earlier books, he is said to have had only "eighteen months as Chief of Scotland Yard."

Yeo, now the "senior member of the Big Five" and a "heavy breather" in "his late middle-age," reveals an irrational prejudice against wireless cars for the force, and later takes the opportunity to grow "ponderous, giving his celebrated imitation of Counsel I Have Known, a sure sign that he was enjoying himself enormously." In the chase that crowns the case, his "legendary" knowledge of London takes them through "the dark built-up streets" in time to trap their quarry.

Charlie Luke is the official detective in charge of the case, the last recruit to Miss Allingham's permanent staff, and one of her grandest achievements. His investigations into the Palinode case are largely unsuccessful: the poison pen eludes him, though not unknown to him; he fails to react to the item from Charlsfield that gives Campion the "trickle"; he is unable to prevent Pa Wilde from committing suicide before his horrified eyes and he is "stunned" by "shock and disappointment" at the climax of the chase. His failures appal him: "His face grew dark with anger... 'I hate a surprise like that in my own manor' "; "I ought to resign on this...I had all the aids and missed it"; "I've done it this time. I ought to be shot."; and he is often low in spirits, "grief-stricken" at the loss of the coffin; laughing "bitterly" and making "a face like a smile" in response to the "suppressed triumph" in Bowels' voice; "rattled" when Pa Wilde dies before his "wretched" eyes; "restless and unhappy" after the interview with Clytie's boy; and, at the end, "more tired than a man could be," "his wide shoulders" sagging and "suddenly less square."

But despite all this, we are left in no doubt of his quite exceptional ability, of the "pile-driver personality" that makes him a D.D.I. at 35, "sensationally young for his rank." Three of his fellow-investigators acknowledge his formidable quality: Yeo, who bursts out "with uncharacteristic abandon" in praise of the son of his old colleague "from the Y Division in the great old days"—"he's poor old Bill over again plus his mother's brains, and I don't see why he shouldn't pull it off alone"; Lugg, who pays tribute to his amazing energy: "That chap'll go far...'e can't leave it alone...No five-day week for 'im.

"E'd 'ave apoplexy waitin' for Monday' "; and Campion himself, who has only to see him to understand "something of Yeo's enthusiasm," and is quickly assured by his own observation that "Charlie Luke was going to be one of the great detectives."

Our first encounter with him is an exhilarating experience: he not only tells us about Apron Street and its inhabitants, he recreates them for us: "Campion had never heard before of this particular Dr. Smith but suddenly he was in the room with them. He took shape like a portrait under a pencil, vigorous with the startling vividness of truth. . . . Charlie Luke spoke without syntax or noticeable coherence but he talked with his whole body. When he described Dr. Smith's back his own arched. When he mentioned the shop front the squared it with his hands. . . Campion was made to share the Doctor's scandalized anxiety. The man talked like an avalanche."

He looks like a gangster, "his hands in his pockets, his hat over his eyes, his muscles spoiling the shape of his civilian coat." He has "compact and sturdy bones" which tend to "disguise his height," a "dark head on which the curls were as tight as a lamb's," "a live dark face with a strong nose, narrow vivid eyes" and a "ready" smile which has "yet a certain ferocity." His voice, "as strong and pliant as his shoulders," is "liable to set the panel vibrating," "even when suppressed." There is "a graphic quality" about "his every movement," and his energy is "a visible thing."

If he is a "favourite" with the landlady of the Platelayers' Arms, he is no less adored by his creator. Miss Allingham dwells on him lovingly, highlighting his features, pointing up his talk, transcribing his gestures, and registering his glooms and elations like a sympathetic barometer: "Some of the enthusiasm had gone from him and his angled eyes watched Campion gloomily over the embankments of his cheekbones"; "Charlie Luke's murmur was like the roll of distant artillery"; "His muscles looked like stone under his coat and his diamond-shaped eyes were. . .bright"; "His great hand shot out, painting in the little greedy flames in pantomime."

Despite his being occasionally taken by surprise, he knows his manor and its people—the doctor's shrewish wife; the bank-clerk's "bull - frog" of a sister; fat Mme. Pernelle with the supper - bar in Suffolk Street. He knows which is the Captain's "secret pub"; and is aware of Pa Wilde's ephemeral taste for "a certain miserable ladylike funereal type" of woman. By resort to Cockney rhyming slang, he scores a neat small revenge over Lawrence, whose allusive talk has continually baffled and irritated him; and he reveals a written style as laconic and forceful as his conversational mode: the decision to exhume Edward is memorably expressed as "Proposed have up pronto." He tells the time by a silver turnip watch which he thumps "vigorously."

Even at a moment of maximum excitement, he has time to be kind to Clytie, and he is, by rather veiled implication, drawn to her sexually, even: why else should his face darken and his speech emerge "sulkily" at the mention of Mike Dunning, her lover? His final remark, dismissing Mike's love as "just teaching her the words," suggests that his expressed intention to take Clytie "to the pictures" may have been rather more than kind encouragement: in which case, Campion reflects, "Miss White was certainly going to have fun."

Campion's apprehension as to how Lugg and Luke will react to each other proves groundless: Luke responds to Lugg with "a collector's appreciation," "a certain raptness" apparent in his face as he listens to a characteristic narrative; and Charlie's youth enables Lugg to enjoy the role of battle – scarred veteran—he has a rich, self-satisfied moment when the inspector fails to react to the name "Bella Musgrave": "'O' course you're only young,' he murmured, smugness oozing from him."

The old villain maintains a vintage level of performance, his "lush personality" pervading the room "like a smell of cooking," and the "rich rumble" of his voice sounding in Campion's ears with "an expression and flexibility...which many actors might have sought to imitate in vain."On Campion's return to Bottle Street, he is preparing for an unsentimental withdrawal, but the "truculence" in his "beady eyes" fails to "hide the reproach or even the panic lurking there," and Campion is able to meet his gaze only when startled into doing so.

Reprieved by the "third crow," he promptly establishes both feet in the enemy camp, moving in on Bowels and Son, his brother-in-law and nephew; and when next we meet him he is a "pale bleary-eyed bundle of resentment" recovering from the knockout drops added by Jas. to his "guinness and two half bitters," and able to " 'ear a fly stamp." But before long the "little black eyes" are "sparkling," and he is "sufficiently nettled" by Campion's stealing his thunder in the matter of Ruth Palinode's gambling to "forget that they were not alone" and growl at "young Viscount Clever" (just as, later, he is mildly pleased to find that "Little Clever's still in a black-out... That's a nice change for yer").

There are two reminders of his intermittent parade of virtue: disapproval of Mr. Knapp, late of *Mystery Mile:* "I say, don't ferget yer place. We've come on since them times, I 'ope. What's to be forgave at twenty ain't the ticket at forty-five"; and his comment on "the Greek Street gunman": "Mr. Lugg looked down his nose. 'There's too much of that break a jooler's winder, fire at a copper, and 'it a bloomin' civilian,' he said virtuously...'We'll 'ave gangs next.' " He has a lovely definition of "official" behavior: "Don't listen and then ask": and, in his response to "the elder Miss P.," a resurgence of the kind of admiration he had for Johnny Carados' mother: "I took a fancy to 'er...We ain't on Christian-name terms yet and very likely never will be, the class system bein' so stoopid, but a lovely woman! 'You're dirt and can't 'ardly understand what I am a—saying' of, but I 'appens to like you.' That's the sort she is ... They call it charm." His comments on Miss Evadne's "blow-out" are also worth recording: "Somethink from another world, this is. Make up yer mind what you're goin'ter 'ave, cup o' yerba mat or a small nettle hot. There's a ration of somethink else as well, smells as if it come out o' the flowers in the 'all. There's not a lot of call for that."

He plays a loyal part in the investigation, identifying both Bella and Jelf, the driver of the truck that nearly kills Campion—"Reunion, that's what this case is, cock"—and reporting on its return the Queen Mary's most remarkable property. With the help of Thos. Knapp and the "contac's" of which he is so proud, he tracks down Jelf, and even names the man who turned Apron Street from "a bit of a joke" to a topic no longer "considered 'ealthy."

His collaborator, Mr. Knapp, is a changed man: he "nearly works" and is "almost respectable," now that   Muvver's gorn (those who treasure the "recollection of that ragbag of a giantess" will be happy to hear that her end was characteristic: "Went out like a light when 'er time came, bottle in 'er 'and.'') With a wife with social aspirations (or, as he phrases it, "a missus on the up and up"), he is "out of the know these days." But despite his disclaimers, his ignorance irks him, and he accepts with "a flicker of the old enthusiasm" Campion's invitation to "look about" him. Something of the old aptitude evidently remains, too, since he and Lugg achieve a fair measure of success.

Another figure from the past is Renee Roper, whose warmth, gaiety and mother-hen instinct were already well-established during Campion's previous encounter with her when she was landlady to Chloe Pye, Peter Brome, and the Brock Brothers, in *Dancers in Mourning*. Having remembered Campion from those earlier days, she now turns to him when she needs his kind of help. To the household at Portminster Lodge, he is a lawyer from Bury, her nephew on the "nobby side of the family," and her attempts to sustain the fiction are "staunch" and "valiant," like the small-talk under which she conceals her fears. Her distress at the "evil cloud" that has spread over her house has a "genuine intensity," and when her bright rattle stops and the mask slips, she looks "small and old" and "networks of red veins" push through "the powder on her cheekbones and over the bridge of her nose." She is "a ghost of a warmer world," retaining a certain "histrionic instinct," a sense of being "still more or less before the footlights," despite her resolutely domestic situation. A question sounds like a "cue for a song," and she calls her char in "a sort of musical scream." In her kitchen, to remind her of the old days, are "some hundreds of theatrical photographs...covering half the walls."

Invariably, she dresses to suit the moment, in her "receiving costume" when Campion arrives, "unexpectedly magnificent in solid black" when the occasion demands "a speck of mourning," and "looking like a travesty of something out of one of the lesser chapters of his youth" for a companionable drink with Campion at three in the morning. She is "utterly feminine" with a "small red bird's face," a "tip-tilted nose," hair of "a wonderful if unlikely brown," a "rattling tongue," a "compact" figure, and a "pretty" laugh that wells up "fresh and young from a heart nothing had aged." She is naturally flirtatious and responds in a flurry of delighted chuckles and mock reproaches to the slightest hint of flattery: when Campion says "Come on, darling, tell me the truth, what's cooking?", it is, typically, "the endearment" that she hears "most clearly" and to which she reacts.

She is intensely generous, like a benevolent old pantomime fairy, spreading sweetness and light, and determined that all shall be right in the end. Clarrie claims that "she can't look after the perishing world," but one feels that Renee would if she could. Her protective instinct is boundless, and only when this is challenged does she lose her temper, standing up physically to Luke to shield the Captain from him, and quarrelling spectacularly with Clarrie over her determination to take Mike into Portminster Lodge—and,even then, "in the height of her rage," her eyes are "troubled and kindly still."

Her sympathy for Clytie is entirely charming, both in its fellow feeling, recalled across fifty years—"'I can just remember being like that,' she said with a ruefulness which was delightful"—and in its shrewd but kind perception: "She's head over heels in love and she's like a bud unfolding... Thorny, you know, but with a little bit of pink just showing... Blushes whenever she hears a petrol engine, and thinks nobody knows." Her comments on the older Palinodes are equally perceptive but considerably more tart: what she says about Jessica, particularly, contains marvelous insights into both women: "The poor old girl is a bit of a crank, that's all. She believes in New Food and so on. I let her go her own way, although she does make me wild when she wants to eat grass and send her rations to the people who tried to kill her two or three years ago. 'You do what you like,' I say to her, 'but if you want to feed the hungry with your two ounces a week, there's your own brother downstairs with every bone sticking out through his homespun. Give it to him and save postage.' She says I'm 'doomed to insularity,' whatever that may mean." Her self-mockery is delightful, when Campion suggests that her affection for the Captain might be the confidence she intended to make to him: "My dear," she said with cheerful vulgarity, "we've lived in the same house for nearly thirty years. You don't want a detective to find out any secret there. You want a time-machine!"; and her idea of a reassuring remark is irresistible: "If you hear any thumping, it's just the undertaker."

Mrs. Love, Renee's char, "all of eighty and still brimful of what it takes," is a supporting player with star quality, whose three short scenes have astonishing impact. A ripe old Cockney, red-faced, rheumy-eyed, heavy-breathing, hoarse-voiced and deaf, she nonetheless shares with Charlie Luke "the energy of a light engine" and a determination to defeat the forces of evil. In the interests of keeping "above ground" and outwitting the Portminster Lodge poisoner, she locks the porridge in the "'aybox,'" and leaves her chops safely at home. To fox her friends, who look askance at "mixing with the police and that" and think she's at the pub, she reports for duty at night, ostensibly out of loyalty to Renee ("I couldn't let 'er down. I come with 'er from the other 'ouse"), but more probably because, despite her disclaimers, nothing would keep her away. Clarrie's contention that "she's loving this business" is borne out by the relish with which she pats "her lean bosom," repository of the haybox key, and her zestful account of how her loyalty overcomes her fear. Her subsequent reaction to press coverage of the Apron Street "'appenings" is more openly ecstatic: "Mrs. Love's excitement was dreadful to watch, although there was little in it which was ghoulish. She was proud and possessive, rather, like a child with a birthday. 'I've got the Evenin' 'ere,' she said,... 'They've gorn orf them others and we've come up in front.' "

Encountering Campion for the first time, she regards him "with interest" and detects a likeness to his supposed aunt. She plays up to Clarrie Grace with an innate sense of theatre, clearly enjoying the fiction that he will lead her to the altar should her established friend defect: "Having achieved one effect, she shot out for another. 'Still got me evening doodah on.' She waggled her ribbon at Clarrie, who touched an imaginary hat to it, making her laugh like an evil child. ''E's my second string,' she said to Campion. 'I say 'e's my second string.' "

She works "like a navvy...Can't stop in case she falls down dead," and is continually reassuring Renee that she is up-to-date on her chores: "I've done yer porridge" or "I done me floor." By an idiosyncrasy of speech, she repeats many of her statements, with an entrancing effect, that distinguishes her as an individual, and is both comic and convincing. Her curiosity is intense: she is "uncomfortably shrewd" about her employer, listens eagerly to the quarrel with Clarrie, and reports a scene between Lawrence and the Captain, the "inquisitive" eyes in the "ancient rosy face" watching Campion eagerly, avid for any gleam of surprise or disapproval."

Despite her extreme age, she is, like all the women who have the author's approval, "wholly feminine," wearing pink by night and blue and white by day, "exactly like a kitten which has been dressed up as a doll." When she whispers, the effect, most memorably, is "like a fall of sand."

In comparison with this uproarious ancient, even the Palinodes pale a little, and some of the other members of the household seem positively underpowered: her "second string," Clarrie Grace, for instance, or Renee's Captain Seton. Clarrie is at least theatrical, a seedy juvenile, long out of a "shop," but still flying the flag, poverty notwithstanding, "gallant if shabby in an impossibly long-waisted blue overcoat." He strikes "an attitude unconsciously theatrical," or finds "a heaven-sent audience," or offers a "hideous...professional" smile, or weighs Campion's remarks for their effective stage potential. He advances an impossibility melodramatic theory of the murder, and at a carefully judged moment in his quarrel with Renee "sat down at the table, folded his arms, and laid his head, hat and all, upon them."

Captain Seton, "a slender Edwardian drying into old age very gently," has only poverty in common with Clarrie, whose mocking name for him is "excuse my glove." Miss Allingham describes him with affection and delicacy, but in general he is more interesting for what he does than for what he is. He has a slender motive for killing Ruth, is known to have quarrelled with her, and finally drinks himself into a stupor after a mysterious assignation in the small hours.

Of the Apron Street contingent, by far the most formidable is the undertaker, Jas Bowels, a foeman worthy of the steel assembled against him. Lugg is uncompromising in his view of his brother-in-law: "When you're dealin' with Jas, you want a warrant and an eel-'ook": he is "Bowels by name and Bowels by nature," "a 'orrible man," who "will talk about your dead sister until you're all crying and then slip you the knockout drops."

Appropriately for an undertaker, he looks "as imposing as a fine marble tombstone," "large and solid with wide shoulders and the breast and belly of an ox." He has a voice "like a gong," "rippling white hair" and a face "as broad and pink as a gammon rasher," with "heavy chins" and innocent blue eyes that appear at their most "childlike" when he is at his most treacherous. His "ugly little mouth" has two large front teeth that make him resemble on occasions "an enormous parrot fish." In the professional garb that would have looked absurd on anyone else, he is a "splendid figure," nothing short of "superb."

Bowels is a very capable rogue, devious and wary, quick to think and act, and with a cool head in a crisis. In some ways, he is a descendant of Falstaff, one in the long line of engaging villains who relish their own wickedness and talk themselves out of trouble. Repeatedly, he shows himself as "equal to the occasion," revealing "his mettle" and "behaving admirably," "damned naturally" or with "remarkable control." In a tight corner, there is "no panic, no undue haste. Only the sweat betrayed him"; and after long hours of police interrogation, he is "pallid and sweating, but he kept his head." The author herself records and clearly admires in him "the saving grace of guts."

Because we never encounter Bowels when he is free of the need to watch out for himself, there is a continuous tension between his persona and his real self, between his "mock subservience" and his actual assurance. Campion responds to his performances with a connoisseur's appreciation— "Mr. Campion was diverted but not beguiled"—reflecting that "his villainy had a gentle polish and his hypocrisy was practiced and flatteringly concealed." Even when he feels that Bowels is not lying, he credits him with nothing more positive than "some sort of version of the truth." His "carefree ease of improvisation" compels admiration and it proves difficult to disconcert him: a probing question from Campion prompts an immediate reproach and a leisurely circumstantial reminiscence that gives him time to think of a story: it is a masterly performance to a hostile audience, and when the undertaker finishes "the lie with a flourish" and sits back "well pleased with himself," we feel that he has good reason to be so.

His professional patter is invariably diverting, whether he is commending the Queen Mary to Campion—"It's not too much to say that any gentleman who *is* a gentleman would be proud to be buried in it. It's like going below in your own carriage" — or mocking the grandeur of his ceremonial black—"I call these me Mourning Glory." From time to time, he strikes a philosophical vein, contrasting public splendor with domestic modesty—"We see enough of magnificence, me and the boy, so in private life we like to be homely" or musing on the craftmanship of Rowley, his "aggressively legitimate" son: "Rowley could have made very different furniture from what Nature's called him to. 'You might have made things the owners were in a position to be proud of, son,' I tell him, 'but none what becomes them more. Remember that!' "

Pa Wilde and Dr. Smith have the advantage of being described in Luke's power-hammer style (as Bella Musgrave is almost wholly defined by Lugg). The little chemist is vividly seen, surrounded by his astonishing stock, "looking like Auntie's ruin with his dyed hair...little black tie threaded through a woman's ring with half the stones out, striped trousers, black cutaway all grey with the filth of years." He was "always very quick on his feet, like a spadger and about as scruffy," "a silly vain old chap" with a "little dyed moustache" that was "the pride of his life." The Doctor gets one marvelous paragraph to himself, and when Luke has finished we need no more: "A tallish old boy...fifty-five, married to a shrew. Overworked. Over-conscientious. Comes out of his flat nagged to a rag in the mornings and goes down to his surgery... Seven-and-six for a visit, half-a-dollar for a squint at your tonsils or a thorough once-over if he isn't sure, and a bottle of muck which does you good. Stooping. Back like a camel. Loose trousers, poking at the seat as if God were holding him up by the centre buttons. Head stuck out like a tortoise, waving slightly. Worried eyes. Good chap. Kind. Not as bright as some (no time for it) but professional. Professional gent. Old school, not old school tie. Servant of his calling and don't forget it."

The manager of Clough's bank seems dwarfed by the establishment he serves, not inappropriately, since he is preeminently an upholder of tradition. He has the name of a great novelist, Henry James, and is "a dapper little man of forty or so," "neat to the point of fussiness," immaculately and discreetly dressed, and yet "modern and slightly uncomfortable" in his antique survival of an office. The Bank is his god—he gives it "capital letters, like the Deity"—and he is evidently embarrassed by the shortage of staff and the implication that Clough's is not what it was. He is adamant in his refusal to discuss the Palinodes' finances, and comes fully to life only when moved to recall the vanished "great time" of his childhood, when "the district used to revolve round" the Professor and his family.

His clerk, Congreve, looks like another survivor from that age, "so old that the skin of his head clung with almost embarrassing tightness to his naked skull." He is perverse and unlikeable, at various times "old and obstinate," "superior but forbearing," tempering "offence...with magnanimity," his voice "harsh yet hollow," "his blob of a lower lip quivering" as he mumbles to himself. This "unpleasantly unsteady lower lip" earns him the nickname Bloblip and serves as a disquieting reminder of his malign curiosity and sinister ubiquity.

The solicitor, Mr. Drudge, is unexpectedly youthful, the "frank apple blossom and innocence" of his complexion "enhanced to absurdity by a tremendous sink-brush moustache." Both this and his nickname, "Clot," are relics of his wartime RAF career, during which he also gained "a D.F.C. and bar" with a distinctive conversational idiom. He talks about "chinning with the old Skip," and at one point actually says "I care for that," thereby raising irresistibly the ghost of Flying Officer Kite, a 'forties radio character, whose braying weekly catchphrase, 'Oh, I say, I rather care for that!' gave innocent pleasure to the nation.

As a solicitor, "Clot," though short of thirty, is only token young, whereas Clytie and Mike, Miss Allingham's lovers, are palpably, even nakedly, so. Young love is not the author's forte—sentimentality too often saps her strength in this area—but largely by making things difficult for this particular pair, she arouses for them our sympathy and concern. True, Mike does defy credibility with that old romantic novelist's stand-by, a face simultaneously "ugly and pleasant," but Clytie is saved from cliche by the unrelieved oddity of her situation. (Even her birth was hazardous, as Luke's succinct account makes clear: her mother "married a doctor who took her to Hong Kong. On the voyage out the boat went down and they were both nearly drowned, and the baby was born while her Ma was still wet with sea-water.")

Improbably, with aunts around the sixty mark in 1947, and a grandmother who gained fame as a poet in the 1860s, she is 18½ for the dates to work comfortably, she needs either to be a *great*-niece of Lawrence and his sisters, or to be ten years older—and for seven months she has been leading a double life: an accredited, shackled Palinode existence, working as a clerk for the *Literary Weekly* and dressing as if she were of an age with Evadne and Jessica (specified garments include "a dreadful cardigan in khaki wool" and a "tuckered saffron blouse" suitable for "a woman four times her age and bulk"); and an anxious, exciting, lyrical life with Mike, on the back of his bike in the clothes of his choice, "like a cross between the chorus and washing-day." Her re-entries to Portminster Lodge are by way of the roof, which marks the point of transition: here, she sheds her finery and resumes her life of drab docility.

Although she is "not beautiful," her "round dark eyes" are arresting and her hair shines "with the blue-black sheen of poppy centres." Campion is at once "aware of her charm," with its latent sexuality, "a shaft of animal magnetism like a searchlight held inexpertly by a child" in tandem with the "real innocence" that Renee attributes to her.

For all that she is so young and vulnerable, she is recognizably a Palinode, with a "force" that Campion finds "disquieting," an "indefinable assertion of intelligence" in her face, and, on occasion, a "slightly alarming...composure." She has sufficient self-possession to withstand a crazy attack by her uncle, accusing her of obscene behavior, insulting her mother; and even, with "a faint irrepressible smile of sheer naughtiness." shows herself aware during his demented diatribe that her own knowledge of human sexuality is already greater than his. When she achieves her emancipation, we rejoice the more because of the utter enormity of her upbringing and the sheer weight of the family tradition that has threatened to crush her. Lawrence's horrible outburst is simply the last straw, as Charlie Luke, at least, happily recognizes.

The Palinodes dominate the novel, as they dominated Apron Street in Mr. James' golden age, providing the murder victim, the rather improbable top suspect, and a part, at least, of the killer's motive. Most of the other characters in some way dance to their tune: Renee gives them a home; James and Drudge administer their diminished affairs; Clarrie rails against them but takes up their trays; Charlie Luke is baffled by them. The Captain quarrels with Ruth and Lawrence; the grocer and the dairyman are doctored by Jessica; Bowels and Son are spurned in Edward's will; and the Thespis company perform for Evadne.

Even the dead members of the family are lightly characterized: Edward, a "pompous old idiot," "full of smarty ideas," vengeful against the undertaker who shattered his sleep, a reckless innocent abroad on the stock market, with "vision...and courage, but not judgment"; Ruth, "a great big woman, larger than the others" and not "quite so clever," with a mathematical rather than a literary bent, as foolish as her brother on a smaller scale, squandering her last few pounds on the horses, and capable of the "brutal joke" of leaving worthless shares to someone she disliked; and their mother, Theophila, an indifferent poet but considerable beauty, whose "dark vivid face burningly alive with the quest of the sweetly impracticable" has been inherited by her youngest daughter.

Jessica's appearance takes no account of this particular inheritance: matted elf-locks replace her mother's ringlets, and her face is "full of wasted beauty and wasted cleverness." Her clothes are squalid, ill-fitting makeshift, her hat is made of cardboard, and she puts grass in her shoes (or banana skins to cool her feet). She carries a bag "made of a piece of an old waterproof tacked together inexpertly by someone who understood nothing about sewing save the principle," and apparently containing "papers and kitchen waste in equal quantities, since both made attempts to escape from every dubious seam."

She is "a real witch," who makes Luke "think of fairy tales" and Campion feel "a superstitious apprehension" when first he looks closely into her face. His telescope reveals a face that "blazed with intelligence" and he receives an "outstanding impression...of a mind." Later, he is "shaken" by a demonstration on himself of her capacity to "will people to speak."

Renee calls her "the cleverest of the three," but her cleverness, like her beauty, is "wasted." She argues persuasively in defense of her eccentric mode of life—dressing like a tramp, cadging alms in the park, living entirely on herbal messes, concocted in the small hours because they smell so dreadful—and her self-sufficiency is undeniably complete; and yet Campion feels that she is "such a terrifyingly and indefinably wrong thing." He is moved by her and even "afraid of her," and he bursts out "uncontrollably" in a sudden need to understand her.

Miss Allingham does not side-step the question of why Jessica is as she is: she is not just a quaint old "character" with instant appeal, but a genuine eccentric, with a reasoned philosophy of life that sustains and even nourishes her. Her defense is simple: "I have no gifts...I am dumb...I cannot make, or write, or even tell"; and she quotes from her mother's work in support of the pursuits that occupy her and help her to survive in poverty in a world to which she can make no positive contribution.

Ironically, even the small contribution she does make is potentially dangerous: had she dosed the old dairyman with "the right kind of poppies at the right time of year," he would have died from "a basinful of raw opium"; and even the "Saxon leechdom" for the grocer's knee arouses the doctor's apprehensions.

Her sister Evadne—the elder by "some ten or fifteen years"—is a stately, florid woman with a "creased and mottled" face and a "gracious cultured voice," "educated and brisk," "packed with authority," and impossible to disobey. (Lugg calls it "a voice like a beak.") Campion's hand trembles as he pours out her Slepe-Rite, and a senior Treasury official wrestles ineptly with an intractable electrical plug at her behest. She is gratified by Campion's capping of her "little piece of Peele," but takes "any wind there might be right out of his sails" by taking him for an actor, whose stock-in-trade will naturally include facility in quoting from the more remote Elizabethan dramatists.

Her conversational mode is occasionally reminiscent of rather daunting works of scholarship—"Is it a question of parallel taboos exerting their restraints or is it actual?"—but at other times she is playful, quoting *The Tempest* at the Treasury expert to soothe his ruffled feathers, and taking him, too, for an actor in need of a "shop": "You must both come in tomorrow, of course. I don't know that there will be anyone particularly influential there this week. However, it should be amusing, I think." She makes an instant conquest of Lugg, and invites "half London" to a conversazione at which she dispenses apples from her dead sister's bag, to provoke, as in *Hamlet*, "some obviously guilty reaction": "The theatre, it would appear, was in her blood." Her manner of dealing with her dying sister also commands a certain astonished admiration: "She spoke to her sister, but when the poor woman didn't wake she looked about the room and picked up a book from one of the shelves, read a little bit, and then told me to send for the doctor as if I hadn't thought of it."

Evadne is pure fun, but Lawrence has a frightening aspect to him. He is "a far more nervous subject" than his sister, as we see mildly in his initial concern over the errant Clytie, overwhelmingly in his later insane attack on her. Lawrence undergoes a patent sexual crisis, and is pushed dangerously near the edge of sanity by the combined impact of the "madness cold and festering" of the poison pen letters, Clytie's bid for an independent emotional life, and his own consequent researches into adolescent sexuality. His challenge to Clytie is obsessive and shocking: "You look like my sister...creeping out, slyly to make love in the streets like a drab... The itch is in you, is it? Hot hands over the pavement in the reasty dark, and the shuffle of the curious rustling by. Do you know, you make me retch? God! you disgust me!"

He reveals the intense and fascinated prurience of the classic case of puritanical repression: "He was wrinkling his nose with disgust" and yet his eyes were eager; and there is a dreadful "Physican-heal-thyself" irony in his concern that the "hidden lunacy" responsible for the letters arises from someone in his own immediate circle. His grotesque frenzy is "terrible rather than ridiculous," his "dreadful self-inflicted agony" "a living thing in the room."

Charlie Luke's decisive intervention returns him to normality and to the lucid, analytical intelligence that is usually his. Once the crisis with Clytie is past, his explanations and reactions are entirely reasonable, and even after the attempt to kill him at Evadne's party his brain draws acute well - founded conclusions: "Lawrence lay looking up at them, a living gargoyle, his damp hair on end and his face glistening, but his eyes intelligent as ever." He and Luke find each other mutually exasperating, since neither talks the other's language-witness the confusion over "Mme. Pernelle," which is Lawrence's name for "foul-mouthed Freda," after the scold in *Tartuffe*, and also, by mischievous coincidence, the name of a local restaurateur. (Lawrence, inexcusably in the context of "a matter of ordinary education," applies the feminine gender to Moliere's celebrated hypocrite.)

Physically, he is the most gauche and charmless of the Palinodes, relentlessly clumsy, upsetting ink or books, or spilling "a bushel of assorted papers out over the parquet" to create "unholy muddle on the floor." His neck sticks out from his body "like a stalk," and his voice, "queer," "honking," "gooselike and unreliable," has a life of its own, "jarring like piano wires," its volume "flaring and dying like a faulty loudspeaker." Even his nearsightedness becomes absurd when he pursues Captain Seton in mistake for Clytie.

All three Palinodes exert a continuous fascination, burgeoning like exotic fruits, each strongly individual and yet demonstrably from the same fantastic mould. However outrageously they behave, their conduct is explicable in human terms: they are genuinely eccentric people, and not just caricatures who act oddly for effect. They are stimulating company at all times, and both singly and in harness their bizarre vitality enhances the appeal of a most accomplished and diverting novel.

Chapter 10
Havoc

The next novel, *The Tiger in the Smoke* (1952), dispenses with the whodunit element for the first time since the early adventure stories. In the fourth of nineteen chapters, Oates reports Jack Havoc's escape from prison, and from that point on we know what we are up against. Nonetheless, the author's delight and skill in mystification are evident throughout, from the bizarre opening sequence, where an attempt is made to establish that a dead army officer is still alive. Apparently recent snapshots of Martin Elginbrodde have been sent to his widow, Meg, and a racecourse photo in the current *Tatler* also appears to include him. An impersonator is soon exposed, but the full explanation of his deception is gratifyingly delayed: despite her change of direction, Miss Allingham preserves such familiar strengths as knowing when to divulge a secret.

Other mysteries occur as the narrative proceeds. Martin's coat is quickly identified on the newly-killed impostor, but it is not till much later that we learn how he got hold of it. Meg's new fiance fails to phone as promised and suspicion accumulates against him in his absence. We know at once it is Havoc who has killed three innocent people at the offices of Martin's solicitor, but we move on a hundred pages before we know why he is there at all. Only gradually do we learn the full story behind Havoc's obsession with the Treasure of Ste. Odile—from the recollections of a group of street musicians, from Meg's references to a wartime episode in her dead husband's life, and from Havoc's own account of this sinister event.

The novel's main themes emerge as these and other mysteries develop, and for all the intentness of her aim, her preoccupation with good and evil and the nature of justice, Miss Allingham never forgets what is due to us as mystery readers. Canon Avril, Meg's father, is the principal agent of good in the novel, but he is also, more practically, the means whereby Martin's jacket is traced from a hook in the rectory cloakroom to the body of the man impersonating his dead son-in-law. Geoffrey Levett, Megg's fiancee, reaches the point where his jealousy of Martin is extinguished while his very life is in danger from Havoc and the street band. The final scene, where Meg encounters Havoc on a cliff-top in France, operates finely on two levels, as a realistic encounter between an unsuspecting woman and a vicious killer rendered harmless by exhaustion and disillusion, and as a climactic triumph of good over evil.

If there is any tension in the novel between the old, zestful Allingham and her rather somber new self, it occurs in the treatment of familiar friends. The old guard is present in force—Campion, Amanda, Lugg, Oates, and Yeo—but their total contribution is curiously muted. Significantly, it is Charlie Luke who takes on Havoc and controls the forces that hunt him down: Campion's main concern is to avoid him and to keep Amanda and Rupert safely out of his way.

As Canon Avril's nephew and Meg's cousin, Campion has the best of reasons for becoming involved, but he is not on his own admission in anything like his element: "The days when little Albert charged singlehanded into battle have gone for good. Havoc is police work, good hefty police work, with medals and promotions at the end of it." Amanda, for once, is largely passive, reaching her point of greatest involvement as a near-addition to Havoc's tally of victims; and Oates is here largely to define the specific danger that Havoc represents, that of a "truly wicked man" who "kills if he wants to." The paragraph devoted to Val's "town car," the "fine old Daimler" familiar to us from pre-war days, but now re-upholstered "in olive—green and an intelligent maroon," strikes a fussy, incongruous note after the high tension of Amanda's brush with Havoc.

Least at his ease is Lugg, and it is noticeable that he never has to face the reality of Havoc as the others do. Though he accompanies Campion to the street band's cellar, he is given his head only in the rather strained comic interlude that precedes Geoffrey's discovery. Otherwise, he is reduced to the status of child—minder, and becomes the object of some implausible whimsy attributed to Rupert. It is even suggested that he can "speak proper" if he so wishes. Only once is he permitted a characteristic "mot," when he hoots in the fog at Marble Arch and remarks: "I thought she was takin' 'er time."

Despite his avowed unease, Campion has his successes, and we are grateful that Miss Allingham did not exclude him, as the film version of the novel subsequently did. He is still the "easiest of men to overlook or underestimate"; "still the slight, elegantly unobtrusive figure exactly six feet tall, misleadingly vacant of face and gentle of manner, which he had been in the nineteen-twenties"; still alert and intelligent, "his hands ready," or his curiosity aroused by a maneuver to divert his attention. His triumph is the inspired deduction whereby he traces Geoffrey and by doing so saves his life.

His emotional development continues to concern the author, and among other insights we are given a report on the state of his and Amanda's marriage: "Now that Rupert had grown out of babyhood her prime allegiance had returned to himself and they were partners again. She would look after him and he must look after the three of them. It was not the only sort of marriage but it was their sort."

These reflections are prompted by Amanda's decision to stay in London with him whatever the danger from Havoc, and his feelings for both her and Rupert are intensified in a context of terror. Meg's early conclusion that he is, among other things, "unemotional," is confounded by his later shows of feeling. When Amanda is alone with Havoc in Meg's new home, he is distraught: afterwards, "more badly rattled than she had ever seen him," he jerks her "roughly" towards him, holding her "so tightly round the shoulders that he hurt her." Later, even the act of looking down at Rupert finds him "shocked at the intensity of his emotion and more afraid of it than of anything he had ever known." The boy is "one half of his life, more than half," and to his father his innocence and vulnerability are frightening. He feels "uneasy," helpless as never before, and out of his depth: "It was not often that he wished for police with rifles, but he could have welcomed them now."

Miss Allingham comes in this novel as near as she has ever done to recording directly Campion's love for Amanda, but even here the threat to his wife and son is a necessary preliminary to the revelation of his feeling for them; and the intensity of his concern for Rupert takes even himself by surprise. The author avoids a head on confrontation with Campion's dreadful fear that Havoc may actually kill Amanda by showing it through Luke's jokey account of how he "took on just like any other common chap," and through his own outburst when he knows she is safe: he exclaims—"irritably," merely—"Really, ducky, how damned silly." Both devices effectively distance the emotion while making its extremity apparent.

Elsewhere, Campion's admission that he is of the generation that "feared romance like the devil" gives us, perhaps, a retrospective insight into his curiously detached courtship of Amanda. He regards his exclusion of romance as one of his "sins of omission," and now that romance "sneaks up on" him, "dangerous with all the charm of the untried," he begins to perceive what he has missed. In such a context, a reference to Amanda's looking much "as he had first seen her long ago in the shabby drawing-oom of the Mill at Pontisbright" implies that time has at least taught him what he should have experienced then.

With the new relationship of Meg and Geoffrey, Miss Allingham is much more direct. Whatever the trials that beset them, they are clearly destined to achieve "the kids and the house and the happiness" postulated by Geoffrey at the beginning. They are extreme examples of the standard view of masculine and feminine, Geoffrey all man and Meg all woman. We take Campion's virility on trust, but Geoffrey wears his like a panache. A single reassuring reference to Amanda's heart-shaped face is enough, but Meg is shown through a flurry of fragile, fine-spun detail.

Meg is the more limited by the kind of type-casting to which the author subjects her. Her femininity is of the intense, suffocating kind that characterized Val and Georgia in *The Fashion in Shrouds*, and the initial account of her has a preciosity reminiscent of that novel: "her clothes seemed a part of her. Her plum-coloured redingote with its absurd collar arched like a sail emphasized her slenderness. . . Exquisite bone hid under delicate faintly painted flesh, each tone subtly emphasising and leading up to the wide eyes, lighter than Scandinavian blue and deeper than Saxon grey." Her "husky voice," "her new perfume," "her long slender legs," her "very high heels, her "gentle obstinacy," her "sweeping and gracious" gestures, her "small gloved hand," her "big handbag," her "valiant parting smile," "the silk over her knee and the diamond on her hand" — these and other characteristics endear her to everyone else in the novel but tend to alienate the reader.

Perhaps predictably, Meg is a couturier, a disciple of Val, actually working at Papendeik for her cousin, as "one of her most successful discoveries." Her sitting-room recalls the world of Val and Georgia and Caesar's Court: "Van Rinn had done the decor for her in the latest lush or Beaton manner, and between the damasked grey walls and the deep gold carpet there ranged every permissible tint and texture from bronze velvet to scarlet linen pinpointed and enlivened with daring touches of Bristol blue." Her new home has an "Edwardian" bedroom with "flower-show wallpaper and a . . . Honiton bedspread," and a bathroom "like a comfortable lily-pool." On the "elegant side-table" that she uses for her work is a litter of "sketches of dresses, swathes of material, samples of braids and beads, and the blue spidery designs from which jewelers work." She even inspires a return to the soppy epithets that Val used to evoke: both Geoffrey and Amanda call her "pretty," using the word as a vocative.

Geoffrey has rather more to offer. He may be "a good steady sensible manly sort," who looks "solid and splendid, like the man who supports the human pyramid at the circus," but he does at least have elements of surprise in him. However "uncommunicative" and "sober" he may appear, however "stolid. . .unadventurous, even," he has in fact been "one of the biggest gamblers on this side of the Atlantic," who has "quadrupled his fortune." He reveals, too, an unexpected "sensitivity" that makes Campion think "how surprising the man was. Just when one thought one knew him, one stumbled on new depths."

In addition, his behavior appears gratifyingly suspicious. Campion catches sight of him lurking where he has no business to be; he is clearly the man with the "Phoenix Rugger Club tie" whom the landlady of "The Four Feathers" describes to Luke as having drunk with the false Martin shortly before his death; an envelope on the dead man's body has Geoffrey's name and address on it; and he fails to phone as promised and cuts important appointments with distinguished people. Later, it is as a victim that he holds our interest. Miss Allingham places him in a bizarre and increasingly dangerous situation, and at the moment of maximum danger switches our attention away from him so that we must wait to know his fate.

Both Meg and Geoffrey have their emotional trials as a result of the imposture. Geoffrey undergoes "the most grueling emotional experience of his life." He finds himself both "terrified" and "tortured. . .by anxiety," in a "nightmare" that becomes "very nearly unbearable." At one point, he discovers "with horror" that he is "in tears."

Meg keeps "remembering and dreading," uncertain where her love and loyalty lie, and showing both relief and disappointment when Luke tells her that the man in the photos is probably not Martin: "Hope died. . .but also hope appeared. She was saddened and yet made happy. There was shame. . .and bewilderment." When the imposture is exposed, she is "incoherent with embarrassment. . .she had been so sure."

Both make discoveries about themselves in the course of their ordeal. Geoffrey had not "realised before that he was capable of such jealousy"; and Meg's eyes are "sombre with new information about herself." The false Martin drives them apart, but their enforced separation has the ultimate effect of making their love more certain. Meg comes to know that it is Geoffrey she loves: ". . .the photographs brought not so much Martin as my husband back and I don't know what I did feel. Sometimes I seemed to be being unfaithful to them both and then tonight the whole thing crystallised and no—one but Geoff existed any more for me. I can think of Martin objectively now as an ordinary person. I never could before." Finally, she is able to recall Martin "with great tenderness but no sorrow. . .he had been absorbed into the fabric of her life which was the richer for him."

Geoffrey overhears Havoc talking about Martin and what he hears kills his jealousy of Meg's first husband: "All the jealousy Geoffrey had ever felt of Martin flared up to its highest peak in a searing sweep and died outright like an exhausted flame. He felt freed of it suddenly as Meg became, mysteriously, entirely his own."

In fact, Geoffrey's jealousy does revive for a shameful instant at the end of the novel, when Meg asks to be left alone with her bequest from Martin, the Treasure of Ste. Odile. Stripped of its trappings, the essential action of the novel is a treasure hunt, and everything that happens — the impersonation of Martin, the abduction of

Geoffrey, the killing of all Havoc's victims— springs from the greed for the unknown hoard. This is the cause of Havoc's obsession, and his desire for the treasure is such that nothing must stand in his way.

For the members of the street band infesting the area, the treasure is "the one thing they believed in all the world," and they live only to secure it. As they tell Geoffrey the story as they know it, their faces are "solemn, engrossed and avid. Treasure. The ancient word had worked its spell once again. It was holding them together as nothing else could ever have done, and was supporting them even while it sucked them dry." They fear that Havoc "has collected the treasure" and is "a-living on it in glory." A miniature and the memory of a musical box bolster their expectations and intensify their subjection to the "immemorial romance of treasure trove, gold in bars and jewels in bucketfuls, spilling out over a cave. . .in glorious technicolor." Later, even technicolor is "inadequate" for the full fantasy that emerges as Havoc tells the rest of the story, the "secret of a ship's treasure handed down in a wealthy family to an orphan boy at twenty-one": "It lit up the cellar with a radiance. . .more enchanting than moonlight itself."

The leader of the band, the albino, Tiddy Doll, is "of them all . . .the most completely enthralled." That Geoffrey learns "the tremendous news" of the treasure's existence is "agonising to him." He alone is obsessed enough at the end to climb the cliff after Havoc in search of his dream. He has been "tormented because of his deficiency" and dreams "wildly of becoming a tyrant in a city paved with gold": the treasure becomes his hope of escape from the freakish lack by which his life is impoverished.

He is "so white that he was shocking, his close-cropped hair so much the colour of his skin that the line of demarcation was scarcely visible." A "big, shambling figure, stooped and loose-jointed, middle-aged but still very powerful," he is by turns commanding and pathetic, astute and ridiculous. In negotiations with Havoc, he is capable of a "master-stroke," and yet Havoc's brutal account of his career strips him of all dignity, and his idea of fine food is pickled onions. He has courage and cunning and a streak of sadism that cannot resist "the opportunity to hurt: even when it may rebound to his disadvantage. But he is, nonetheless, "the basic material of which great fools are made, a country dolt," superstitious and credulous under the bluster and the undeniable force that he commands.

His position in the band is that of the one-eyed man in the country of the blind: he is "declared leader and main personality," and Geoffrey immediately realizes that he has "but one man to deal with." At moments of crisis he invariably keeps his head, "quite equal to the occasion," his tone "perfectly easy and ingratiating" or his voice ringing out "clear and belligerent." When the band runs out of control, he roars at them, "forcing his authority upon them as he had done a thousand times before," his voice "like a sergeant-major's and the brutal strength of his personality tremendous." Even when embarked on "a sort of mendicant sing-song of apology," he makes an effect "urgent and powerful and quite horrible": and an aura both grotesque and sinister remains with him to the end, as he clings to the cliff "looking like a white slug with a black head," his "pallid torso" a "wonderful target" for the rifles that finally destroy him.

The band is a "feckless rabble" of "shuffling ghosts" for whom Luke expresses a fine contempt. Each man has "something odd" about him: a dwarf with a "bulbous head," playing a mouth-organ in "an ecstasy of excitement and pleasure"; "a hunchback. . .with a jaw like a trowel and lank black hair which flapped as he moved"; "a wall-eyed thin-necked figure who. . .clutched a pair of cymbals"; a "one-armed man, his sleeve swinging mightily"; and "a flying figure, festooned with picturesque rags and moving with amazing speed and dexterity. . .between a pair of crutches": these, and other "oddities collected. . .for their freak value," constitute the band. Apart from Doll, only three are named: two fisherman brothers from Suffolk, who speak in "the gentle sing-song of the coast," Roly, talkative and truculent, and Tom, like "a chunk of Suffolk soil, long—suffering and eternal," "strangely dazed" after a wartime explosion that has bereft him of his wits; and Bill, the "iron" or homosexual, "the effeminate to whom fear was an excitant," with a "weak face. . .actually painted with shadows" and "a strange febrile gaiety of his own."

The music of the band rackets through the opening sequence of the novel, a recurrent motif, filtering through to Campion and Luke, "the ghost of a tune, not recognisable yet evocative and faintly alarming, like a half – remembered threat," or, later, "thumping" in "the thick air," "an almighty affront of a noise, importunate and vigorous." Their song is linked to the theme of violence in the air, an unseen presence that is "always there in London under the good temper": from the brutal words that Luke supplies to the tune there flashes out for Campion "for an instant the reality of the thing which had been chasing them all the afternoon. . . "Violence," he said aloud." The recognition sends "a thin trickle down his spine," but for once it seems a shiver of fear rather than the shiver of excitement familiar to us from previous encounters: "The band and its bellow had become hateful to him, and the fog bone-chilling and menacing." The "bray" of the band seems to "devitalise" Duds Morrison, the pseudo-Martin, and the very title of their song, a sentimental ballad called "Waiting," reverberates with ferocious irony, as the air waits for violence, London for Havoc, and they themselves for hidden heaps of gold.

The atmosphere of the book is cold, dark, and damp. London is fogbound and to the habitual heaviness of "the smoke" is added the density of fog, "like a saffron blanket soaked in ice-water." It oozes "ungenially, to smear sooty fingers" and spread "greasy drapery" over everything, "rolling up from the river dense as a feather-bed" and slopping over the city "like a bucketful of cold soup." It hangs in "blinding and abominable folds," turning people into "scurrying shadows," causing brakes to "scream" and tires to "hiss. . .on the wet road"; and giving Jack Havoc freedom to move, to kill and to flee. An irritant to everyone else, the fog is kind to him, helping him to get clear of the "wave of outrage" that spreads in his wake, or to melt like a "shadow" from a house besieged by policemen.

When Campion's spine is chilled by the perception of violence, it is an abstraction still, but almost at once Luke anticipates "a whiff of it the moment" they begin to talk to Duds Morrison: "That shady little mouse. . . was frightened of somebody, wasn't he?" The news of Duds' death turns threat to reality: the cycle of violence has begun and as Luke walks to where Duds died, he has "a presentiment. . .that he was about to encounter something rare and dangerous. The whiff of tiger crept to him through the fog."

For "the ordinary Londoner" Havoc is "an escaped convict berserk in a city, a wanton knife striking casually and recklessly in the mist": but for Canon Avril and his household Havoc's violence is specific.

As they come to realize his objective, the danger he represents approaches "too close to be discounted" and the very atmosphere of the rectory is violated. Even the fog has had a genial aspect in St. Petersgate Square, where it is seen as "cosy, hardly cold, gentle, almost protective"; but the threat of Havoc is real and terrible: "the whole house had developed a startled and piteous appearance. . .it was as if one suddenly saw water seeping through a painted ceiling. Irreparable damage was being done to a lovely thing and there was no telling when it would stop."

We are reminded of Miss Allingham's distress at the spoliation of beauty in *Coroner's Pidgin*. She was clearly deeply moved at the thought of the destruction of any "lovely thing," whether an exquisite decor shattered by German bombs or the living tradition of a civilized home threatened by a vicious killer. When Amanda watches Havoc smashing a spice cabinet of mahogany and ivory in Meg's new home, she feels "sudden rage at the wanton destruction of the pretty thing" and almost utters a protest.

Havoc's blind insensitivity to beautiful objects seems central to his nature, and the author takes pains to establish his incapacity to know beauty when he sees it. As a boy, he had rifled a toy theatre "to get the glitter out of it, and got nothing. . .but old bits of paper"; as a man, he wants to smash the Ste. Odile treasure, which is of a beauty to move Meg to tears, in case "there was something worth having buried inside." In his childhood, he had got "an awful row"; now he is finally destroyed by the devastating realization that "It was not even a new mistake. He had made it before."

Meg's request to be left alone with the treasure is not just a plot device to clear the way for her meeting with Havoc. It rings emotionally true as a final act of sharing with her dead husband, and it prompts a last flicker of jealousy from Geoffrey. The encounter confounds expectation: Meg is serene and strong, Havoc "nearly done," exhausted beyond further endurance, a spent force with no more physical strength than Meg herself. The girl is "not afraid of him, but for him," and "the authority in her voice" is "frightening because she sounded so so strong." He perceives through the haze of his exhaustion that "the power in her was greater then his power because he was so tired" and with the added force that Miss Allingham gives it her "sudden laughter" at his final pathetic show of violence becomes "the most terrible sound that he had ever heard."

Even the knife is denied him. Meg seems to be inviting her own destruction when, with hair-raising irony, she is irritated by the feebleness of her nail—file into exclaiming: "What we really need is a good-strong-knife." But, like some fabled weapon in an allegory of good and evil, it disintegrates at the first thrust and Havoc is finally deprived of his most potent strength.

Earlier the knife has flashed through the narrative, glinting with menace, the teeth of the tiger, even, at times, an extension of Havoc himself. Roly recalls the wartime raid to kill a foreign VIP and his mistress: "The Gaffer done the job all right, both of 'em we reckoned, though he never said anything about the woman. He liked the knife, Jack did." Later, when the "enormity of his crime" is filtering through to the band, they see "that a knife had appeared in his hand. It had come there as if by magic, or as if it had grown there, springing from his bony fingertips." With the knife in his hand, Havoc's power is absolute: he is "on top of himself. . .almost joyous. . .all trace of weariness banished and gone." The company sniffs the "odour" of "genuine violence, real menace, which tingles in the nostrils with a pepper which histrionics can never match." They recognize that not only would he be willing to use the knife, he would be happy to use it.

He has always been vicious, even as a child: acts of destruction and "intentional sacrilege" are reported from his boyhood. Luke gives a summary of the savage exploit that sent him to Borstal at sixteen and an account of the hold—up for which he was imprisoned, so "vivid and . . .unspeakably brutal" as to chill and appal the "gentle civilised company" at the Rectory. Oates regards him as "a phenomenon," one of only three "truly wicked" men in his experience: he would "like to see him dead," and has only to hear of the manner of the killings to know that "This is where Havoc has been." Miss Allingham intensifies the horror of the murders he commits by making one victim a bedridden old woman and another an only son, a promising young policeman, whose death moves Luke profoundly: all are totally innocent people, one who thought he was helping Havoc and three who merely got in the way.

Evil is a palpable force in the novel and the word "evil" recurs like a leitmotif. The smell of the fog is "evil"; so, too, is the "attempt to reverse the process of mourning. . .to kill the spirit" to which Meg is being subjected by Duds Morrison. Mrs. Cash, the money-lender, a "green baytree in St. Petersgate Square," is evil, and the Canon has long ago subjected her to his "ultimate personal rebuke of another human being, to cut him off, to shut him out of his heart, to eschew him, in fact, as evil." His account of her progress through the neighborhood distills an atmosphere of evil that is genuinely chilling: "As she passes down these great airy streets ". . .window curtains tremble, blinds creep down, keys turn softly in locks. She passes by like a shudder. The air is always a little cooler where she is." When the threat of Havoc comes very close to St. Petersgate Square, Campion senses "the ancient smell of evil, acrid and potent as the stench of a fever. . .creeping through the gentle house. . .defiling as it passed."

The Canon pays Evil the tribute of a capital letter when he reminds himself that Havoc is "of Evil" and always has been, even "as a babe." When, in the words of the Lord's Prayer, he prays to be delivered from Evil, it is specifically, "that night," from the Evil that Havoc represents that he seeks to be saved. The great abstraction of the prayer is limited and made human in Havoc.

Not only is he evil made flesh, but he is violence personified, too. Geoffrey, overhearing his account of the raid and the "dreadful necessary thing" that was its object, realizes with horror that "Havoc had not found it terrible." He has been the "perfect but unfeeling weapon, as it were a living knife." Killing elates him: when he swings himself into the cellar to confront the band, "His spirit danced behind his shallow eyes mocking everything"; and Tom recognizes "the state" he is in: "You're like you were that night. . .after you'd done them that time." Amanda, too, senses "the extraordinary atmosphere of the man" as he rushes past her in the darkness.

Physically, he is "remarkable," "just under the six feet, with long bones and sloping shoulders, most of his phenomenal strength in his neck and in the thigh muscles which moved visibly under his . . .clothes." His physique is "flaunting and magnificent" with "the grace that belongs to strength alone" and movements that are "graceful and exciting." He has "a great deal" of beauty, his face "conventionally handsome," "full of drawing," fine-skinned and "excellent" in feature. But it is a "tragic face," with a quality of "ruin. . .integral to the very structure. The man looked like a design for tragedy. Grief and torture and the furies were all there naked, and the eye was repelled even while it was violently attracted. He looked exactly what he was, unsafe."

He is seen repeatedly as a beast of prey, as the tiger of the title, of course, but also in a host of other references: to the "huge animal" he resembles as he bolts past Amanda; to the smile on his "wide thin-lipped cat's mouth"; to the "whiff of tiger" that comes to Luke through the fog. Campion sees him as "a scarce and dangerous beast, the rogue which every herd throws up from time to time." The police campaign becomes a big game hunt, following the "spoor" of the quarry and the stopping his bolt-holes, as "the net grows smaller and smaller." Oates insists that although he has for the moment slipped the net "the animal is trapped," and Campion's feeling that Havoc is "something to be trapped and killed" makes him welcome the chance of escape to Ste. Odile: he is "no great man for blood sports."

Havoc is very much Luke's meat, however; and he becomes "of all his many quarries. . .the chief enemy of his life." Curiously, they are alike in that both possess a vitality and "force" beyond the ordinary. Amanda detects the similarity: "He was urgent, somehow, rather like you, Chief Inspector"; and the author later emphasizes their kinship: "Personal magnetism remained glowing in him, as it did in Luke." The possibilities of a shared quality between hunter and hunted are not thematically explored, however. Luke and Havoc are seen as individuals, and not as opposing halves of a symbolic whole.

As before, Luke is thumpingly larger than life, such a "very male person" that he shocks Meg "at first glance." Fierce, vivid images bring him before us: we see "the kite-shaped mass of his shoulders," hear words come "pumping out of him, bright and alive like blood from an artery," sense "the power of the man. . .as if a truck engine had suddenly started up." In Meg's sitting-room he is "like a black curly retriever arriving unexpectedly in fairyland"; and a sudden access of hope makes his "dark face. . .glow again as the fires of his energy reddened once more."

Repeatedly, he suits the action to the word, "sketching in a pair of horns with his toe on the pavement" to accompany a speculation as to someone's "playing the goat"; thrusting "a long curved hand under Campion's nose" with "an expression of rapacity which was startling," to intensify his condemnation of Tiddy Doll's band; and speaking in "a new light voice, with a careful clipped accent" while "twisting his body slightly" to recall "the absent Duds. . .to the mind's eye." The account of the hold-up that so alarms the Rectory household is "an astonishing performance," during which Luke talks "like a pump, in gusts, using little or no syntax and forcing home his meaning by what would appear to be physical strength alone."

Failure again induces in him the bitter self-reproach of a man "furious with himself." His allowing Duds Morrison to go to his death is "a professional slip of the worst kind," one that "he hated himself for making"; and after Havoc eludes his net he is full of harsh irony directed at himself: "We shall get him in the next hour or two. We can't help doing that. If we continue to be lame, blind, half-witted and clotheared for the rest of our naturals, we shall pick him up. Alive, too, if we don't crush him to death getting out of each other's way."

Even at the eleventh hour, just before the luck turns, and his spirits begin to rise "so violently that they took his breath away," he is still reflecting grimly on the "thirty-five hours of rushed and unrelenting work" resulting in "nothing, not one pointer, not one useful clue."

Yet, despite all this, he makes an impressive showing here, and we are again assured of his destiny as "one of the great policemen"; "He possessed the one paramount quality which appears in all the giants of his profession quite apart from any other merit which they may display. He had that utter persistence which only derives from an almost unnatural interest. The man was a living question-mark, and he hunted his quarry with the passionate patience of a devotee hunting salvation." Convinced that the Canon can help him with vital information, he sets "himself out to understand every minute detail of the man." Given a lead, however slight, he is prepared to talk "for a long time, expending the precious minutes deliberately, putting everything he had into the job, feeling his way, watching like a cat, letting his intuition stretch out beyond where the mind could take him."

For all that he is such a formidable tough, Luke is not without his sentimental side, capable of consoling Meg with "a tenderness unexpected in him" (though his earlier concern for Clytie might perhaps have prepared us for it). He is "dismayed" by Canon Avril's apparent grief for his long—dead wife and blushes at having provoked it. His reaction to the death of one of his "white hopes" is an extraordinary moment of "self-betrayal": "He did not speak as he heard of his death but a grunt escaped him, a sound of rage, and he stood momentarily arrested, one long hand outstretched, warding off realization. No great actor ever expressed the instant of tragedy more vividly or with greater economy. To see him was like glimpsing a flame, an epitome of grief's impact." Later, the recollection brings him "within an ace of tears."

Luke's anger at what Havoc has done is intense and savage and it threatens to master him, as Canon Avril recognizes. He sees Havoc as "killing mad. . .knifing right and left as though human life had no value and any poor beast who gets in his way has no right to exist." His certainty is absolute, his statements exact and devastating: "He's got no right to live. There's no place for him under the sun. Of course they'll hang him."

The Canon's reaction to Luke's outburst demonstrates the distance between them: though he is sympathetic, he cannot share his emotion. He regards Luke as "untried, as yet," a "dear fellow. . .sound and shrewd and very likeable" — not surprisingly the Canon is often seen as "disconcerting," with an "approach to life" that is "clear-sighted yet slightly off-centre": even his "quality of blazing common-sense" is qualified by the phrase "in his own queer way."

He is in many ways a character in the conventional Allingham mould, a fitting brother for the Bishop of Devizes and the central figure in a distinctive household. The author observes his physical aspect closely, recording his "great frame, untidy white hair and. . .ease of manner," his "fine face" and "slender, clumsy scholar's hands whose fine almond nails took care of themselves." She gives him an innocence that allows obscenities to pass over his head, and an "imagination. . .as wild as a small boy's," a power of "conjecture" so vivid that he is sometime "shaken" by his own "imaginings." She clothes him individually, in a Phil May coat that is frequently pawned in the interests of charity, or a robe made "from the formula laid down in the archives of a thirteenth century monastery"; and she surrounds him with fine furniture and loving friends.

He lives on the ground floor of St. Petersgate Rectory, a 'Regency block' in a small cul-de-sac somewhere near the Barrow Road and Apron Street (the author refers outrageously to Luke's acquaintance with 'some very shady undertakers' in the district). Over him live his daughter Meg and, at attic level, Sam Drummock, an 'elderly and distinguished sporting journalist', and his wife; under him, the Talismans, his housekeeper and her husband, and their eight-year-old grand-daughter, Emily. A near neighbor, Miss Warburton, handles his finances.

Both Sam and Miss Warburton have a contribution to make, Sam functionally, as a custodian, Miss Warburton more decoratively, as a personality. Sam is chiefly notable for his irritating habit of referring to Meg as his 'old Queen' and to Emily as his 'little Queen', but Miss Warburton is decidedly good value. She enters on a 'burst of. . .cheerful noise', a plain "middle-aged gentle-woman', on whose thin, bony form 'every garment' looks 'as if it was still on its hanger'. She has moulded 'her social personality at a period when gay and feckless madcaps of the Paddy-the-next-best-thing variety were much in vogue'. The effect now, some 'thirty years later', is 'mildly embarrassing, as if a maiden aunt from the Edwardian stage had elected for a day to be untidy, offhand and bright'.

She enters a room 'tiptoeing exaggeratedly' or withdraws from it with 'the carefree crow of her chosen role. . .dropping a hairpin and a handkerchief behind her'. In her dressing-gown, she is 'so determined not to be embarrassed' that she achieves 'a skittishness not at all suitable in the circumstances'. On the threshold of the Canon's bedroom, she lingers 'against the doorpost, dying to gossip but quite incapable of taking a step inside'. He has only to remove his jacket for her to hurry off 'at once, as he had known she would'. Yet, despite her affectations and her innocence, she is astute enough on occasion, using her 'eyes and common-sense' to draw shrewd and accurate conclusions.

To the Canon Miss Warburton is 'a gift from God in his life', and we cannot doubt that he genuinely regards her in this light. Beyond all the skillful detail of Miss Allingham's conventional characterization of the Canon is an immensely subtle and searching study of a man whose very habit of mind is determined by his devotion to God. Campion remarks that it would be 'presumptuous' of him to worry about the Canon's safety because 'Someone else looks after Uncle Hubert', and Luke sees the old man's survival after Havoc's attack on him as proof of 'God looking after His own'. Both are surely right.

Luke has earlier shown some insight into the kind of man the Canon is: "By ordinary standards" he and his ilk are "not safe out. They ought to be starving in the gutter, imposed on by every crook in creation. But are they? Are they hell! There they go, picking their way like a drunk on a parapet, apparently obeying instructions which no one else can hear. They go barging into filth and it runs off them as if they were lead glazed. They see all the dirt and none of it shocks 'em. They hand over all they've got and yet they never want." Luke's account states the apparent contradictions in the Canon's character clearly, but it does not profess to understand or explain them. The author, however, goes on both to understand and explain him, offering him to us as a genuinely spiritual man whose negation of self is the dominant element in his personality.

He is incapable of acting out of self-interest and material considerations are irrelevant to him except insofar as they affect his ability to offer charity. He feels "sincerely safer and more at ease when he had given away all he had, like a man passing a ball in a game." Despite his having withdrawn himself from Mrs. Cash, he continues to include her in his blessings within the church, "for not to have done so would have been presumptuous, since in that house he was a servant." If he feels a human weakness threatening him, he resists it rigorously: "He pulled himself together. There he was, as usual, sneaking off into the luxury of idle intellectualism, lazing, arranging to be elsewhere when the new task. . .was about to be put before him." He regards anger as "the alcohol of the body" which "deaden the perceptions," and he solemnly warns Luke against it, having had cause himself to regret an earlier occasion when he had given way to it. Incapable himself of lying, he is contemptuous of his housekeeper's pathetic attempts to protect herself by this means: "Lying wastes more time than anything else in the modern world." The self is human, fallible, easily persuaded from the true path, and a source of wonderment; "What an astonishing number of pitfalls there are. . .We seem to be like contortionists at fairs. . .able to fall down in absolutely every way conceivable. It's very wonderful."

He is the kindest and most charitable of men, and yet at times he appears almost inhuman, displaying "utter ruthlessness" as an "extractor of the truth," seeming "to spot deceit as if it reeked like a goat." Harsh and implacable in the pursuit of the truth, he appears even to withhold forgiveness from his errant housekeeper, whom he values enormously: but, faced with God's work, his "human" instincts utterly excluded, he is totally uncompromising—and it is God's prerogative to forgive. In practical terms, he is "hardly safe out," viewed by Sergeant Picot as "a harmless idiot," and "loved and protected" by "simple people. . .as if he were daft." Yet he goes straight to Duds on hearing of his death, wiping the blood from the dead face with "no trace of distaste or hesitation," pulling "the lids down over the dull eyes": "It was clear that along with sin blood had no terrors for him." He expresses no shadow of resentment or bitterness towards the dead man, who has caused his daughter untold mental distress: the "poor boy" did what he did in ignorance, and all the Canon can do for him is to wipe his face and close his eyes, expressing "in unselfconscious regret" all "the wastage of Duds' manhood."

God's work must come before the personal convenience of any individual: if Mrs. Cash is needed to establish truth, then she must be fetched whether she is in bed or no, and even confronted with Martin's blood-soaked jacket, to the surprise of Sergeant Picot, "who had not expected a parson to get so tough." The sergeant is repeatedly surprised, shocked or "scandalised" by the Canon, and Luke, too, is later bemused and confounded, "doubly put out" "annoyed," "taken aback," and finally "startled out of his wits" by him. Miss Allingham's masterly account of his interview with Luke is a complex exercise in non—communication: the Canon holds the key to Havoc's origin and thus to his disappearance, but such is the nature of the man that he cannot communicate to Luke what he needs to know, and

Luke is powerless either to coax or wrest it from him.

The Canon owns a certain professional expertise and eloquence: commenting on the plot against Meg, he "stepped back onto his own territory and became a different being. . .his helplessness vanishing and his voice becoming wise." But he cannot offer moral or spiritual panaceas. Though he advises Mrs. Talisman that she has almost certainly suffered enough for the lapse that has subjected her to Mrs. Cash, he is unable to "promise" that this is so. He can give Miss Warbuton religious consolation—"The one hundred and thirty-ninth psalm is the one if you're frightened"—but he cannot tell her what should be done about Havoc: "If only we could tell anybody else anything. If only one could know by being told." Though he himself seems to be craving a moral absolute here, he makes it clear to Miss Warburton that only God can direct us to positive knowledge. Talking to Luke about the problem Havoc represents, his face wears "the authoritative but withdrawn expression which only appears in a man when he is actively engaged upon his skilled work"; but though he has thought "all day" about Havoc, he cannot match Luke's certainty as to what should be done with him.

Like Luke, he has no doubt whatever that Havoc is evil, but his reactions to Luke's absolute conviction that he must be caught and killed range through "astonishment" and "acute apprehension" to "sympathy but no sharing of the sensation." Since it is impossible to know whether or not a man should hang, and since a judge must not only face the question but answer it, Avril regards judgment as "a terrible job." Judgment demands a conscious decision by the fallible human self, and as Avril recalls his dead wife's guilt he reflects that "mercifully it was not for him to judge": his human instinct is to condemn her, but only God can do that, just as, earlier, only He could forgive Mrs. Talisman.

Avril reaches the apex of his self-negation when he goes to meet Havoc in the church, having at no point made a conscious decision to do so. He acts without knowing why, in a state of "mindless" submission, recognizing "with a strange sense of absolute peace" that he has "no existence, no will, no responsibility save in obedience." He loses his self-hood, his conscious power to decide: instead he feels that "a new task" is "about to be put before him," and only when he raises his head "to see where the stream was carrying him" does he realize "what he was about to do."

His mind functions on two levels, through the conscious "forward" mind of the "wise prelate" and the subconscious "undermind" of the "essential Avril." The author sets up a dialogue between the two and the "wise prelate" comes to seem like the devil in a morality play, tempting the good man from the path of right: he is "practical" with "reason" and "common sense," but also "cunning," whereas the "naked Avril" is "shrinking and mindless, and without existence save in obedience."

During his conversation with Luke he has, effectively, not recognized what he knows. Only later does a light in the church bring "complete certainty": the relevant facts that his "undermind had known all along" cohere and "become assembled in his mind," clearly and conclusively. He answers without hesitation Luke's question as to why he has visited Mrs. Cash that afternoon. Not until later is he "filled. . .with doubt" as to which of three possibilities had truly prompted him. Whatever the answer, he is certain that there "had been no plan in his mind," no conscious "ulterior motive" behind his move. After a while, he find himself "perceiving the reason for his visit" and accepting "his stupidity as a mystery which would be explained. In his strange peacefulness, his own unprecedented shortcomings appeared to be only a part of something much greater and more important."

At the moment when he recognizes "the demand" and knows "that he would submit to it," he is most in danger from the "wise prelate," from his protective wisdom, from the sentimental, compromising human self that threatens to undermine God's work: "All his human weakness, his casuistry, and his common sense rose up to betray him and turn him from his work." When two domestic accidents on a trivial, and even a comic, level conspire to help him to "obedience." he goes to face the tiger, walking "like a child among the pitfalls."

Havoc's scene with the Canon, like his closing duet with Meg, operates on two levels: as an actual dialogue between an old priest and a young killer, and as a symbolic encounter between good and evil. The climax of the novel is here, rather than on the French cliff-top at the end: by the close of the scene, Havoc is "weeping in "his weary rage" and his "doubting" hand has "lost some of its cunning."

For the author it is a particular triumph to have achieved this end and to have rendered it plausible. Havoc is desperate and ruthless and a realistic first estimate would give little for Avril's chance of survival. But the scene does work, with a dual effect of symbolism and realism: evil begins to lose its ascendancy over good, as the old man's actual strength counters and consistently undermines the young one's show of strength.

Though Avril's body shakes, his mind is "peaceful, relieved and extraordinarily content," and he is sufficiently in command of himself to master the anger that threatens "his temper and his perceptions." Despite its "enormity," he is unshaken by the imputation that he is Havoc's father; and he denies the charge in tones which are "matter of fact, regretful even." He is "genuinely amused" at the idea of trying to save Havoc's soul, and even pursues "an intellectual digression, knowing quite well how absurd it was." When it seems at the last that he must die, since no compromise is possible for him, he bends "forward to put his head in his hands," his "resignation. . .complete."

Havoc, however, is from the first in a state of desperate tension, his whisper "the most violent sound. . .ever heard" within the church, his realization that Avril is alone, incredulous and immensely relieved. Avril smells the fear in him, the "stink of terror" that emanates from him, and he senses the "astonishment and mistrust and rising anger" that greet an expression of compassion for him. Havoc is "disappointed" that the "reason for the Canon's charity towards him. . .was not the shameful one he had chosen," and his suspicion of the Canon's coming creates a desperate need of something to account for it: "Then for God's sake," said the agonised voice. . ."why the hell did you come?" He meets Avril's caution and humility with "curiosity, fear, impatience," his voice "bitter" or "harsh and naive," his will oddly uncertain and "hesitating." Finally, unmanned by the doubts Avril has sown, he sheds tears of "agony" in his weary rage."

As the scene develops, a curious kinship emerges between the two men, between Avril's recognition that "every small thing has conspired" to bring them together, and Havoc's "terrifying philosophy" of life, the Science of Luck. When the Canon struggles to define the process that has drawn him irresistibly to the church, his explanation seems "inadequate and unsatisfactory," but to his "amazement," it appears to be "understood" by Havoc: "That's it," said Havoc. . ."The same thing happened to me. . . That's the Science of Luck. It works every time." Later, Havoc's faith ceases "to be a cult which he followed painfully, a mere series of opportunities which he could seize or miss," and becomes "a force which had swept him on without even his connivance"; and we are reminded of the Canon's raising his head "to see where the stream was carrying him."

But whereas Avril's surrender to superior forces entirely negates the self, Havoc's "superstition" is a brutal, greedy, and self-glorifying creed. He has earlier outlined to the band the nature of his belief: "There aren't any coincidences, only opportunities"; and "there's only two rules in it: watch all the time and never do the soft thing." From the time of his military selection for the raid on Ste Odile, he has seen himself as "special": now he tells Avril that he is "one of the lucky ones" who have "got the gift."

Faced with this kind of talk, Tiddy Doll has already feared for Havoc's sanity— "Doll. . .knew men were often a little queer when they came out after a long prison term, but he was frightened all the same"—and now the Canon in his turn is "frightened out of his wits," Ironically, at the very moment when he is making a dent of reason in Havoc's obsession, he undermines his hard-won ground by giving him the information he needs, thereby appearing to support his evil creed: "Havoc laughed aloud. "Got it!" he said. "The Science of Luck, it's done it again. See how it's worked?. . . You've told me the only thing I want to know, and I came here to hear it."

But for all his scorn and momentary laughter, Havoc *is* affected by the Canon's attempts to instill reason and a degree of humility into him, and when the escape that he offers the old man is wearily but unhesitatingly rejected, he finds for the first time that it is less than easy to kill.

The creation of Canon Avril is a profound and distinguished achievement that crowns a quite exceptional novel. Havoc and Tiddy Doll are powerful feats of the imagination, boldly and memorably drawn, but it is the Canon who gives the novel a depth, a density, a distinction that lift it far beyond the ordinary. Havoc and Doll are destroyed, but the Canon survives: rightly, good triumphs.

Chapter 11
A Late Idyll

If *The Tiger in the Smoke* is Miss Allingham's most masculine novel, *The Beckoning Lady* (U.S. title: *The Estate of the Beckoning Lady*), which followed in 1955, is perhaps her most feminine. There could hardly be a greater contrast between successive novels by the same author. The very titles point the difference: the Tiger harsh and menacing, the Lady suave and bewitching.

The killer is a far cry from Jack Havoc: unlikeable certainly, but well-meaning in an odd way, intending perhaps to be "merciful," and quite failing to appreciate "the full enormity of the act" of murder. In place of the icy fog-bound city is a Suffolk village in high summer. Campion, no longer out of his depth, is relaxed and observant and very much on his own ground: Luke is now the alien, dazed, quiescent, and forlorn. Detectives and victims apart, there are only three men of any importance, as opposed to five women and seeming hordes of adolescents and children—actually seven all told—including female twins known exclusively as Blue Drawers and Yellow Drawers. There are also a troupe of clowns and "a large and sagacious dog," miscalled "Choc" by Amanda's Aunt Hatt, who bought him from a crofter.

At the outset, a graveyard dialogue between Campion and a hyper-efficient "ministering female" called Miss Pinkerton offers a curiously bald exposition. Miss Pinkerton is said to be getting her facts straight, but a hostile reader might accuse Miss Allingham of putting hers across in a less than subtle way. The preliminary list of Dramatis Personae has already alerted us to the fact that Campion is only "thought to be on holiday in Pontisbright": actually he has been "brought down to Pontisbright on the pretense of holiday-making" by what Lugg calls "private business" (as Campion reminds Luke, he has "an extensive private practice").The inwardness of this is never explained, and the matter is satisfactorily resolved without any great effort on Campion's part. The answer falls into his lap, and though Miss Allingham treats it as a four-star revelation—"A white light of comprehension, as vivid as a star-shell, hit the thin man squarely between the eyes" — the entire affair seems strangely public at the end, when two crime reporters are shown to be fully aware of what has been going on.

Campion's personal commitment has, for once, the odd and unexpected effect of almost excluding him from the official murder investigation. Because of it, he is deliberately "over-cautious" and "chary of becoming unnecessarily involved in any other enquiry." Only when officially co-opted by Luke is he rescued from the "nerve-wracking" situation of being "placed. . .neatly outside the inquiry," with "no idea how. . .to get back on the band-wagon."

His particular anxiety for the right to be a party to what develops arises from his affection for Uncle William, who makes his final, posthumous appearance here. Sadly, from having been in his time both suspect and observer in murder investigations, he is now himself the victim. The novel opens with Uncle William's obituary from *The Times*, and the narrative is peppered with affectionate reminiscences of the old man that remind us how charming and fallible and lovable he was. One of Campion's reasons for so disliking Miss Pinkerton is the "monstrous epitaph" she pronounces on his old friend: "Eighty-two and he drank, didn't he?. . . What a very happy release for everybody."

Throughout the investigation, Campion keeps Uncle William in mind, although it is another death that principally occupies the police. Once he has established that "someone meant him to go when he did," his indignation on behalf of the old man is vigilant and unceasing; and he declares a warm personal interest: "He was one of the best old boys in the world. He was dying, and he wanted to live until Bonfire Night. And he wasn't allowed to make it." Campion is not by nature a vengeful man, but he makes it his business to establish how Uncle William died and who killed him; and when, at the end, Luke suggests a certain extenuation of the murderer, Campion reminds him that only someone "extraordinarily beastly. . .would have tidied Uncle William out of existence."

Beyond the fact that Miss Huntingforest's dog finds the body, in company with Rupert, Campion has no personal link with the other murder victim, a retired rent-collector, known generally as "Little Doom," from a combination of his initials and surname. But the fact of murder offends him deeply, as always, and it is noticeable that, unlike nearly everyone else, he never regards Little Doom as an inconvenience or "obtrusive item." Even Amanda has to be reminded of the "inescapable" fact that "the silly fellow happens to be dead."

Campion's investigation proceeds as calmly and unobtrusively as any in his career. His second crucial insight, arising from a domestic fracas between Amanda and Rupert, is mild indeed; and a late conversation with Lugg, phoning in to report progress, is little more than a faint echo of earlier, livelier exchanges (the best of it is the simile for Lugg's breathing—like "the strange soughing of a distant sea"). The claim made by the final chapter— "Mr. Campion exerts himself"—though undeniable, has a certain ironic edge to it.

Oddly, in the context of one of his lightest undertakings, and before either murder is even suspected, Campion is prompted to talk to Luke about his role and technique, his relevance, and the way his mind works. He wonders if Luke might find him "a bit redundant" and not capable of "anything that the police couldn't handle better"; and despite Luke's disclaimer, he tries to justify his own approach, and to demonstrate his own particular gift. Aware that the younger man is ill-at-ease with a floral message delivered by Rupert, he attempts for his benefit to fit it into a rational context. Having already guessed who sent the message, he takes Luke through the reasoning involved in reaching his conclusion; and when Luke grumbles about its being "Damned subtle stuff," Campion's reply makes it clear that this is exactly his point: "Of course it is. That's my line."

For most of the action Luke is insecure and out of his element, unnerved by much more than what he calls "the greengrocery" and Campion's interpretation of it. He is "Charlie Luke the Londoner," driven at times to "a pitiable state of nervous irritation" in a "merciless fairyland": alarmed by the discovery that he has been eating peacock pie; "dumbfounded" by an old countryman's demonstration of extraordinary powers; and "bothered and fascinated" by "Mr. Campion's strange world of nods and hints and mysterious understandings, among people who trusted each other because they were or were not related, or had been to school or served in a ship or regiment together."

As if to intensify his isolation and unease, the CID Commander reminds him that he is an outsider: "they want somebody who has absolutely no personal interest in the place, someone with no local friends, a whipping—boy, in fact, who can shoulder any odium which may be accruing." It is small wonder that he feels a particular need for Campion as guide and interpreter.

In addition to all this, Luke has fallen so abjectly in love as to be a changed man, in whom the contrast with his former self is embarrassingly explicit. "In the normal way, the DDCI was a considerably personality" who "looked like a gangster and was a tough." Now he is broody and morose, "a grim yet hangdog figure," softened and enfeebled by love, scaled down and deprived of dignity. Campion, who has seen Luke "with young women before, teasing them, patronizing them, showing off like a whole pigeon-loft," witnesses now an "entirely new departure," as his friend sits with "a dark brooding face," so protractedly and "unnerringly silent" that everyone is surprised when he suddenly sits up and takes notice. Later, "the force of unfamiliar furies most cruelly released within him" reduces Luke to making a daisy-chain and sets him awash with sentiment at the sight of a bird's nest.

Having fallen in love, Luke has at least done it, as befits the "sort of chap. . .liable to have mighty soul-shattering passions," "in the most thoroughgoing way possible." In disappointment, his voice is "naked," his eyes "tragic" as "an icy drop congealed and fell within him"; in anxiety, he feels "a physical pain in his chest"; when "exalted," his step becomes buoyant, his eyes and teeth gleam, and he preens himself "like a great black tomcat." Once only, he is "murderously angry," "consumed and almost choked" by "blind unreasoning rage." His despair is quite dreadful, concentrated into "one terrible revelation, swift and awful. . .a peep into emptiness," the "vista" of familiar "city enchantments" seeming "spoiled, dulled, devitalized for ever." Finally, in possession of the field, he looks as if "you could warm your hands at him."

The girl he loves is yet another complication: Prunella Scroop—Dory, known as Prune, daughter of the last Baron Glebe, and in Campion's words "about as useless as a gasogene" or "any elaborate thing evolved for a specific purpose which no longer exists." Her line is dead, and so is her purpose in life. As a "present-day product," she is "uneconomic," with the pathetic, forlorn quality of one who is "born too late." The party for which she "had arrived, meticulously turned out. . .had been over for some time," and now "there's no sort of job in which she would be at all suitable."

With Luke, the situation is exactly the reverse. From humble origins, he has risen to eminence in his sphere. After a gory triumph in "the Caroline Street raid," he is "at a turning point in a career which had promised to be remarkable," "almost certain to . . .become head of the Flying Squad" and in line for "the coveted Police Medal." A scathing comment makes the contrast brutally explicit: "She's no earthly good to that chap. He's alive."

To Campion, whose affection and respect for Luke are immense, the matter is cause for alarm: "In his view, Luke was a fine and useful man, far too valuable to have his progress hindered and his emotional balance endangered by any hopelessly unhappy experience of this sort." The thought of Prune makes him "uncharacteristically savage"; and his anxious concern for his living friend matches his alert consideration for his dead friend.

The essentially romantic nature of the novel demands that Luke's emotional crisis be happily resolved, but the willing suspension of disbelief is tested rather by Prune's fairytale transformation from goose into swan, from "as odd a looking girl as one could wish to see" to an "eyeful" impossible to forget. Old Mrs. Luke, who can "smell breath over the telephone," clearly has other magic powers, too. Effectively, she waves her wand, and Cinderalla goes to the ball, dazzles all beholders and seems set to live happily ever after (she doesn't, as it happens, but doubtless the author reconsidered the situation later).

As a consequence of this, Campion is involved in an extravagant volte-face inappropriate to the sanest of men: "A vista of years had opened before him in which Luke's genius backed by Prune's influence carried the remarkable pair to heights as yet unguessed." This amounts to a betrayal of his earlier concern, and it is evidence of a dangerous inconsistency of tone. In the same way, the Luke who walks out on his sergeant after a crucial phone call from Prune, is not the man who fought in Caroline Street, the future holder of the Police Medal. The effect of the scene, in one way, is charming, but in quite another way Luke's dereliction of duty is not charming at all, but disconcerting and even shocking; and it has the secondary effect of reducing the investigation to the level of a game.

But to a large extent, Miss Allingham has already achieved precisely this effect. It is as if, having decided to retreat from the realities of the Tiger to a state of rural innocence, she has gone about it, like Luke falling in love,"in the most thoroughgoing way possible." Because she has a veteran's craft and concern, the mystery is continually absorbing, but for much of the time it seems almost incidental, and we are reminded of Dorothy L. Sayers' summary of *Busman's Honeymoon* as "a love story with detective interruptions."

This is by far the most disgressionary of the author's mature novels. Luke's amorous upheavals constitute the most patent and substantial digression, since they never interlock with any part of the mystery, but there are many more—juvenile antics and incipient adolescent amours, a whole spate of silly stories about ludicrous incidents, a monstrous instrument called the glubalubalum, and a painter called Jake who never even appears.

We are back with a vengeance in cloud-cuckooland, where Rupert is allowed to find a body and murder is really rather a nuisance. From the beginning, the incongruity of murder is asserted: "It was no time for dying. The summer had arrived in glory. . .yet death was about, twice." Amanda finds it hard to "believe in murders here at all. . . Everyone is happy. . . It's all wrong here."

One murder would be sufficient to disrupt most communities, but here two are nudged aside and edged into the background; a little guiltily, perhaps, but no less firmly for all that. A party is planned at the Beckoning Lady, home of Minnie Cassands, a celebrated painter, and occasionally of her wayward husband, Tonker, and this "seems to be the only thing that matters." Preparations proceed with unabated, all-embracing zest: at one point three people investigate murder, while eight get on with promoting the party. Concern that it shall take place is obsessive in two of the principals, and even those who give the murders a little token worry from time to time confidently expect it to happen. Even when death impinges for the third time, at the height of the feast—and with brilliant effect—the gaiety merely falters and the revels continue.

The investigation undeniably proceeds, but in an atmosphere of domestic upheaval that repeatedly undermines its authority. At one point Luke and the local superintendent find themselves shelling peas while questioning a principal suspect; and later, in a kitchen full of cakes and children, though "determined in their official capacity," they are "as human beings acutely conscious that they were in the way." The very house betrays them: the cloakroom yields a human skull which proves "after some excitement to be a part of an articulated skeleton such as can be found in most art schools."

The local police are virtual buffoons whom the author constantly holds up to ridicule. The chief casualty of her method is the superintendent, Fred South, from 'Safer than Love' in *No Love Lost*, described as "no-one's fool" and a "tricky old monkey," and depicted as a sinister snickering figure whose unending "cloud of little giggles" veils a real menace and even a sadistic streak. Campion calls him "Nemesis" and finds his "alarming quality of jocund innuendo" "terrifying"; and he is later described as "one of the I'm-your-pal contingent," a disreputable old-style bully of the kind that gets "the clean boys a bad name."

But it is impossible to take any of this seriously, since South is continually undermined by the course of events and Miss Allingham's determination to avoid unpleasantness; also, she has come to dislike him so much that she is now bent on making a fool of him. His pouncing questions and confrontations repeatedly fail of their intended effect, and he seems to "have a story-book detective's fixation about idiotic exhibits." Twice he has to concede professional misjudgment: after alienating a valuable witness, and after withholding crucial evidence regarding Little Doom's skull. His final anxiety to tidy everything away neatly with the minimum of fuss makes it easy for Campion to manipulate him. Even his hair-oil becomes a source of embarrassment. Worst of all is the conduct of his own constable, who finds the weapon used to kill Little Doom, throws it on a dump, spends all night retrieving it, only to plant it so ineptly that the whole deception is immediately exposed. South's gleeful assertion that the discovery of the weapon brings the murder "very close" to Minnie's "pretty house" is immediately contradicted and quickly demolished.

From the reader's point of view, the scene that follows the constable's humiliation, though hugely enjoyable, is in practical terms superfluous, since we already know what it reveals. At the very beginning of the novel, we are given a detailed account of the eight days that pass between Little Doom's death and the discovery of his body, and we know the full history of the weapon from the time it became one to the time of its reappearance.

Much play is made, even by Campion, with the empty cigarette packet found under the body's right hand, but for the reader it carries no real force, since we know exactly how it got there. The bead from Tonker's party waistcoat, so dear to Supt. South, is rendered doubly ineffective, since not only do we know from the first how it came by the body, but as soon as Minnie is confronted with it we find that Tonker has not so much as seen the garment, which has been hanging in a cloakroom for weeks.

Other nominal indications of possible guilt accumulate— a venomous portrait by Minnie of Little Doom; her admission that she once threatened to kill him; the false denial of her only paid servant, the Cockney Miss Diane, that she was once married; and the "crash like the end of the world" when Diane is startled by a question into dropping a zinc bath; but they don't amount to a row of pins. The author is merely playing at distributing suspicion.

Such villains as there are offer no more than token opposition. Their concern is the larger villainy that Campion is privately commissioned to identify, but they seem half-hearted, an irritant rather than a threat, and far from frightening Minnie, whom they wish to dispossess, they simply badger her with letters and institute a rudimentary espionage. The "notorious" foreign enterprise that they plan to emulate in rural Suffolk sounds more like a game than a reality; and their scheme is finally defeated by the troupe of clowns.

Repeatedly, effects and devices used in the narrative achieve a tilt towards fantasy, an enhancement of the sense of unreality. Campion not only receives his message in the language of flowers, but assembles the necessary flora for a full reply. Tonker's flippancy leads him to vanish when the police arrive, and to send a parting message to Minnie in the guise of crossword clues. He refers in a telegram to the corpse of Little Doom as an "obtrusive item." Emma, Minnie's friend-of-all-work, claims to be "hysterical with joy" at Little Doom;s death: it will be a tragedy only if it "rots up the party." One corpse is robbed and another dumped in the river, but neither of the people responsible is punished, though in each case his act is wholly known. Miss Pinkerton's arrival at the party is scrupulously prepared, with an astute use of dramatic irony, but the macabre threat she poses is spectacularly averted at the last possible moment.

Many old friends surface briefly in the course of the narrative, as if to intensify the holiday atmosphere. None plays a principal part and some don't even appear, like Sir Leo Pursuivant and his wife, the former Poppy Bellew. We learn enough about both, however, to know that they are unchanged since the time when Pig Peters threatened Kepesake, Leo as resolutely blinkered as ever, Poppy as kindly and game. We do meet Leo's daughter Janet, at whom Campion smiles fondly "because he was so grateful that she had not married him"; and her husband, Gilbert Whippet, now chairman of the Mole, and warmly remembered as one of the most inventive anonymous letter writers in circulation. Amanda's sister Mary is sighted in the distance with her husband Guffy Randall, who dates from Black Dudley days.

The principal revenant, of course, is Pontisbright, in the heart of the *Sweet Danger* country, Amanda's home ground and, as ever, of an enchantment to make "the ancient concept of paradise appear both likely and sensible." With its "pocket-sized heath" it remains "as blandly vegetable as ever and a good deal more innocent than Mr. Campion had known it in its time" (as when Savanake was abroad, not to mention the unnerving Dr. Galley). The narrative is studded with features of the landscape, especially at moments when they appear more than ordinarily bewitching: the Beckoning Lady by moonlight, for instance, or the "country round the Mill. . .at five o'clock on a June morning."

All the visitors respond to the enveloping spell of Pontisbright, even Amanda for whom it is home ground. She appears liberated by the return to her native place: murders or no murders, she is having "a glorious, glorious time" and she seems to Campion "as gay as he had ever known her." Campion himself is invariably moved by the Mill House, its "low half-timbered facade windowed like a galleon and graceful as if it were at sea," and never failing to induce in him a "shock of surprised delight."

Lugg, too, succumbs without protest to the "hatmosphere" of his "favourite place": "there's nothink so loverly as a loverly drop o' Nachure... Whatever you say, you won't beat this." He, like Amanda, is liberated by Pontisbright, and he even embarks on a massive flirtation with Miss Diane, who is "built on aggressive lines like a battleship" and is thus a match for him physically. She proves a match for him verbally, as well, in a notable passage of arms during which, as in a courtship ritual, they declare a mutual interest. Mercifully, the entire episode is seen in comic terms, Miss Diane being won back to her regular lover by a bicycle bell.

Only Charlie Luke is ill-at-ease, aware of and responsive to the beauty all around him, but "like a Cockney on a outing," bewildered in a "lush fairyland" that has "something terrifying" about it: "It's so beautiful that you don't notice for a bit that it's sent you barmy." "The fairies, haunts and spells of Pontisbright" get "under his skin" and he enlists Campion's aid specifically because "he speaks the language."

Luke's own inadequacy in this respect is clearly illustrated by a conversation with Harry Buller, the amazing old countryman who so astounded him during the byplay with the murder weapon. Old Harry warns him that a third body is to be expected since "three in a row" is always the rule; but what Luke fails to understand is that the old man has already seen the third corpse and now regards himself as having "as good as reported" it "if the man had any understanding at all."

An earlier encounter between Amanda and Harry enforces the point. Campion observes that they "did not appear to be saying very much, but the way they stood suggested the wordless communication peculiar to the countryside." Amanda's subsequent smug claim that "to get on here you have to know the place" is borne out by the confirmation she is able to give of Harry's part in earlier events. Even speech seems unnecessary for "one who knows the terrain."

Old Harry is a crucial figure in the mystique of Pontisbright. In many ways the village is typical of the kind established in English pastoral comedy in the Angela Thirkell vein. The complex interdependence of a small community provides the individual with every support while divesting him of any vestige of privacy. Tradition and ritual are sacred: Admiral Bear holds his annual peacock dinner at the Gauntlett every 20th of June, peacock pie is served on Midsummer Eve, and the landlord's daughter offers tail feathers to ward off indigestion. Eccentricity is almost de rigeur, and an element of madness, even, is only to be expected in "a countryside which can boast the highest percentage of rare lunatics in the world." Prune's mother is "a Gallantry, and therefore mad, of course, as they all are." The village boasts a comic vicar who is terrified lest Minnie "go religious," and, in Leo and Miss Pinkerton, a Chief Constable in the classic mould and a bossy, bothersome spinster.

Harry, too, fits into this pattern, as the time-honored quaint old rustic who gets the better of people considerably more worldly than he is himself, and he has his share of what might be called the conventional eccentricities: he "keeps his gold in a tin biscuit box bound up with barbed wire," and he sings a song with a hundred and thirty-two verses. But beyond all this, Harry has a special, preternatural quality that sets him apart. He takes us into deeper waters of a kind that had fascinated the author at least since 1921, when she based her first novel, *Blackkerchief Dick*, on what had emerged from a seance.

When the Commander at Scotland Yard talks glibly of Pontisbright as "very primitive and near the soil," he speaks more truly than he knows. Harry actually looks something like a tree rooted in the earth: he is "a curious gnarled figure whose earth-coloured garments had such a quality of stiffness that the whole man seemed to be made of old wood." "He's the proverbial cartload of monkeys" who "hears nothing, sees nothing, says nothing," laughing "with ancient glee," and chockful of craft and guile and knowledge, both of what goes on in Pontisbright and of age-old traditions and beliefs.

Amanda's report that he is "practically a dog," who "goes by instinct" and "smells things out," is borne out by his extraordinary performance with the murder weapon. He knows how to catch birds, and makes a "wicked wheat wine" that Tonker defines as the "hydrogen bomb among beverages." He alone knows how the Pontisbright sewer is laid. His posies for the party, "very formal and conical in shape and doubtless of some ancient significance" include "one all-gold for Amanda, for she was of the nobility" and "a glowing crimson pyramid smothered in buds and cradled in maidenhair, which was special for a lover": Campion later identifies its design as dating from the fifteenth century.

Discussing Old Harry with Luke, Campion restrains "an impulse to glance sharply behind him." For him, at least, the old man is of a type one meets "from time to time," in a line of descent from the original Green Man: "Long ago it was thought expedient to give chaps like that a nice sort of nickname, just to be on the safe side." Campion's suggestion, "good-fellow," implies Shakespeare's Puck as Harry's ancestor.

Harry watches over the quick and the dead, over Little Doom in his ditch and over the sleeping Luke, whom he shields with a rhubarb leaf, thereby saving "his reason from being spirited away by the dangerous rays of the moon"; "Let the full moon soak into yer this time o'year and you won't never be the same again."

This is the benevolent aspect of Harry: his malevolent side shows briefly when Supt. South jeers at his powers: for a moment "an expression of such scarifying malignity" darts from his eyes that the entire company is subdued and disconcerted.

Something of rural magic pertains to the Beckoning Lady, too. Like the Mill House it shares richly in the natural beauty of the village, "the deep meadows and the fenlands, where the cricket-bat willows look like egret feathers. . . tucked about it like a pile of green cushions." The house dates from the fifteenth century and is thus as old as the design of Harry's posy for Prune. It's a "queer place: according to Amanda, with a legend of feminine ownership and destructive masculine covetousness: "as far back as anyone can trace it has been owned by a woman, and . . .it is said that as soon as a man sees it he tries to get hold of it to do it in." The house is aptly named according to Lugg: "It's got the ole come-'ither. Look at 'er. 'Come 'ere and be 'appy, dear,' that's what she's sayin'."

Lugg does not altogether trust the Lady's promise but there's no doubt that the house is intended to symbolize vitality and fullness, traditional values with a touch of eccentric poetry, and it properly survives the efforts of a greedy man, true to the legend, to dispossess Minnie and destroy it. It is deliberately contrasted with the neighboring Potter's Farm, which has already fallen a victim to Sidney Simon Smith, the ambitious predator who wants to oust Minnie. A touch of the old regret for beauty destroyed is apparent in the account of the flattened, ironed-out estate: in a place "where larks once had nested," "not a hedge, not a tree, not a ditch, remained." The grounds now look like "the beginning of a race-course: and the house itself is "a blank-eyed shell" of which "all that remained was something which looked like an architect's elevation or the facade in a child's box of tricks." It has "no depth and very little character" and it suggests to Campion "one of those terrible Irish fairies who have no backs. When you look over your shoulder at them you see they're as hollow as jelly—moulds." As if to enhance this idea of an ominous malevolence, even Miss Pinkerton, Smith's handmaid, is seen as an evil sprite: Tonker's claim that she "haunts" the Beckoning Lady "like the Fairy No-good" contrasts eerily with Campion's suggested name for Harry.

Minnie herself clearly dislikes Miss Pinkerton, though, typically, she tries to be fair to her. But her account of their relationship eschews gratitude and affection in a way that speaks volumes:

"She was coming to help." Minnie's high cheekbones were spotted with colour. "I seem to need a lot of it in one way and another. . .Pinky types. . .she offered to help me with any secretarial work I needed. She's been most attentive." She shrugged her shoulders, dismissing the subject.

But more significant than her dislike of Miss Pinkerton is her embarrassment when she talks of her; and the red in Minnie's cheeks takes its place in a larger pattern of uncertainty and oddity that begins to gather about her even before we meet her. The village posits blackmail to account for her becoming "more and more peculiar," and Amanda repeatedly expresses anxiety as to her mental state. Minnie herself is cheerful but noticeably evasive and enigmatic at times, and now and again it is clear that questions are unwelcome.

The house itself seems, in Amanda's words, "like an Alice in Wonderland factory—all crazy union rules"; and a series of odd details accumulates to give exactly that picture: Minnie's only transport is a donkey—and—cart because "a car is out of the question"; two bedrooms have been redecorated but no one sleeps in them; electricity is laid on for Minnie's studio, but also for the the two untenanted bedrooms and an unused dining—room. Campion witnesses a "mildly lunatic" sequence that confirms Emma's view of life at the Beckoning Lady as "so far round the bend that we meet ourselves coming back": at precisely four o'clock she shouts to Diane, who in turn alerts Spurgeon the gardener, whereupon he downs tools immediately and sprints to fetch coke for the kitchen.

These and other details together constitute a secondary domestic mystery within the complex total framework of the dual murder inquiry and the threat to the Beckoning Lady from the odious Smith. In the interests of the larger scheme, the lesser question has to be resolved: and about halfway through the book, Tonker confides to Campion that Minnie's whole life is geared to paying her income tax.

For seven years, she has tried to keep pace with spiralling tax demands, and as a result her existence has become "a lunatic farce." As Tonker elaborates, we are enlightened:

"There are only two good bedrooms in this house and she's not allowed to sleep in either of them. She employs a gardener but he's not allowed to grow vegetable's because she only paints flowers. She hates chenpers but she's not allowed to drink anything else, and then only when some dreary customer is present."

Minnie has now reached the point where she cannot get clear of debt however hard she works, and her only hope of salvation is to divorce her husband.

The author is understandably exasperated with tax laws so ludicrous that they turn a substantial gift into a liability and suggest divorce as the only way out of debt. Her indignation colors the narrative so fiercely that one wonders how much of it is derived from her own experience: but she avoids any imputation of riding an irrelevant hobby-horse by making Little Doom Minnie's tax adviser. It is he who has imposed its berserk obsessive routine on the household, dictating which rooms were used for what purpose, timing Emma making beds and Spurgeon hoeing flower-beds, and finally insisting on divorce for Minnie and Tonker. As a domestic tyrant, he was implacable and ubiquitous: as a murder victim, he was clearly asking for it.

Both Campion and Luke take seriously the possibility that Tonker, at least, may have killed him. The marriage of Tonker and Minnie, however is much more than a motive for murder: it unites the mystery with the tax theme, and it serves as an elaborate centerpiece for the eccentric sentimental comedy that sets the tone for much of the book. Given their largely separate existences, one can accept it as a plausible union, but here is no disguising its primary role as a source of amusement, charm, challenge, even outrage: we are rather too obviously intended to exclaim with delight at the fun the Cassands have, and to contrast the color and animation of their joint life with the settled drabness of our own.

They appear to have hundreds of friends and a wide celebrity as a "character" double act. Both are "famous" for specific attributes: Minnie for "the eagle's beak nose of the Straws," and Tonker for his "bronchial laugh" and the "lighting temper which has earned him his nickname." Their parties have been celebrated for decades: Campion recalls a pre-marital affair made to seem respectable by "stuffed relations" with balloons for heads all over the house. We see them in harness in Amanda's report of an encounter in the village, when "they looked like a seaside postcard," "wedged in the tub cart. . .with the donkey looking very knockkneed. . .and. . .roaring with laughter at a game they'd invented." Later, when they are looking at a picture, Campion reflects "that he had always seen them like this, their heads together, up to something."

Amanda sees the marriage as "one long friendly fight. A permanent exhibition bout"; and Rupert's idea of correct marital behavior is clearly based on exact observation of Tonker and Minnie: having selected his wife, he will "shout at her and put her across a bed and smack her until she cries, and then I shall kiss her until she laughs, and we shall go downstairs and pour out drinks for a lot of visitors."

Of the two, Minnie is by far the more attractive: she has character where Tonker has bravado. She claims descent from Pocahontas, through her father, Daniel St. George Straw, "the second most famous

American painter of the Victorian-Edwardian golden age," celebrated for his "lions and lambs and saints and rather nice interiors." Herself an A.R.A. with work in public collections, she is known professionally by her true maiden name, Miranda Straw.

She has a "strange, fierce face" with "piercing grey eyes" and the famous Straw nose. Her "slow deep voice" with its "very English...intonation" is in startling contrast with her antiquated American appearance: in the "Mother Hubbard" and "stout apron" she habitually wears, she looks as if a covered wagon cannot be far away.

To Minnie, Tonker is a perpetual irritant, but also the source of endless joy and entertainment. That she loves him deeply is apparent from her face when she talks of him; and she draws strength from him and basks in his "delight" in her work. But she has, too, the spirit to retaliate when Tonker attacks and to maintain, in severely trying circumstances, a distinguished independent existence.

She accepts the regimen imposed by Little Doom, not from meekness, but from an absolute honesty that makes any privation or restriction bearable in the cause of meeting her obligations. For this reason—and because it solves a minor mystery—Minnie's final good fortune is both aesthetically pleasing and emotionally heartening to the reader.

Minnie is essentially serene, stirred to anger only when Tonker provokes her. In comparison, he seems too often a charmless, intolerant boor or, at best, an insensitive buffoon with a great deal of schoolboy in him. Appropriately, Campion has known him since their joint nonage at Totham School, during the headmastership of Tonker's father Sandy, who also got cross from time to time (and perhaps when Fred from *Coroner's Pidgin* was a young waiter at the nearby "Sun"). A caricature depicts Tonker most aptly as Tiger Tim, "truculent, sandy and thinking of something dangerous to do." He is combative and vengeful, "compact and powerful," with a "freckled face" and eyes as "blue as a sugar bag."

His redeeming feature is his pride in Minnie's work. but some of his other positive qualities are less engaging than they are clearly intended to be. His energy, imagination and humor are all directed towards gratifying or glorifying himself in the most spectacular way possible. His work as half the "tiny, high-powered firm" of Perception and Co. sounds impressive until such typical "perceptions" emerge as colored margarine and latex "beauty" masks that mould themselves to the ugliest features. Minnie paints pictures of Boston: Tonker invents a hideous instrument called the glubalubalum, of which, incidentally, far too much fuss is made.

The selfishness of Smith is seen as odious and contemptible— he sees "life entirely and solely from the angle of his own desires"— but Tonker's selfishness is seen as a lovable foible about which it is plainly not done to protest: eight people labor for the party while Tonker lounges in bed, but Minnie merely snorts in humorous exasperation and calls him an "old cad." Even Amanda approves of the "valuable sense of proportion" that allows him to dodge responsibility and put his personal convenience first.

The secret, of course, is that Tonker has, or is said to have, charm. His victims are not sensitive and kind like Minnie, but humorless bores like the vicar and a hapless county councillor, both of whom he admits to having made publicly ridiculous. But Tonker's charm is not so potent that we can forget so much that is unendearing in what he says and does, whether it be trivial like tripping someone up at the party, or more serious like blacking Minnie's eye during one of his "Grade A rages." Tonker is severely cut to size when viewed with a detached and critical eye, and, inevitably, since he is in many ways its guiding and presiding spirit, the novel is somewhat diminished, too.

Chapter 12
Love and Justice

With her next novel, *Hide My Eyes*, (U.S. title: *Tether's End*) published in 1958, Miss Allingham resumes the intensive scrutiny of evil that so preoccupied her in *The Tiger in the Smoke*. The leisurely, sunlit, self-indulgent amplitude of *The Beckoning Lady* is displaced by a swift, stark immediacy, as the events of an exceptional day interlock in a complex, chilling pattern. Again, it's a city book, London through-and-through, firmly based in Luke's western manor, but overspilling south and east into other divisions, chock-a-block with traffic and theatres, shops and restaurants, pubs and people—barmen, waiters, barbers, porters, and policemen. As so often before, Miss Allingham roots her extraordinary events among ordinary people in a real city, and her affection for people and places is continually apparent: routines are established, interiors evoked, locations scrupulously defined. The commissionaire at the Porchester steps "down into the staff-room. . .for his mid-evening pint and sausage"; the elderly owner of the Grotto in Adelaide Street, Soho sits"as she had always sat" at her "high. . .grilled" cash-desk, "keeping an eye on everything"; the first act of "Bowl Me Over" at the Royal Albert Music Hall runs for forty-five minutes and is followed by "the long interval"; the Rose and Crown "stands directly behind" the Royal Albert; and Rolf's sinister, reeking dump is "right round by the Regent's Canal" with a "foot-gate" into Tooley Street. Over in Garden Green, Polly Tassie's Collection of Curios includes a "pair of clogs ornamented on the soles with the Lord's Prayer in coloured nailheads," a "coat for a French poodle in black sequins and monkey fur," a "six-foot replica in plaster of the bridal cake of nineteenth-century royalty," and a "collection of moustache-cups decorated with crowned heads and the flags of all nations."

All these details and a hundred more achieve a cumulative conviction from the zest, wit, and precision with which the author records them, and they frame a central action as sheerly exciting as any Miss Allingham devised. The killer's deviousness and Charlie Luke's determination together with the constant vigilance and concern of two other characters, create a total pressure that is hardly relieved. At the beginning of the day, Luke has only the haziest network of suspicion to guide him: at the end of it, he has established a comprehensive picture and made his arrest.

He is in "tremendous form," his "handshake. . .a minor ordeal," his habit of "pantomimic sideshow" to reinforce talk well to the fore. Pontisbright might never have existed. The new case is one of his "sixth-sense specials," and he does not let absence of evidence diminish his faith in it. What evidence he has resembles the kind of scraps found elsewhere in the Department of Dead Ends: but whereas Inspector Rason waits for his oddments to become relevant, Luke is convinced, in the teeth of Yeo's disapproval, that his are already so.

From a geographical link between items from four unsolved crimes—a glove, a ring, a letter-case, and a waiter's statement—Luke evolves his theory that one man was responsible for them all. He talks, even, as if he knows the man and expresses a personal need to hunt him down: "I've got him under my skin good and proper, haven't I? I worry about him. . . He's my enemy. . . My enemy. Professional *and* natural, and . . .either I'm going to get him or he's going to get me."

But from strength Luke moves to weakness, proceeding in such a way that the title of the novel becomes relevant to him: his own uncertainty is clearly intended as an echo of the major conflict in another protagonist. Having set his sights on Garden Green, the western suburb that links his four mysteries, he argues persuasively that his man, while living somewhere else, has some kind of "sanctuary" there "which gives him an entirely false sense of security. . .a pub where they know him well but in some different character to his real one, or . . .a girl friend who doesn't ask questions." Yet when he and Campion follow a trail to the "cock-eyed museum" at Garden Green, he is so taken with its elderly proprietor, Polly Tassie, that he is too easily convinced that no link is possible between her and his man. Polly is one of the author's "old ducks," "a human old party," "born on a Friday, loving and giving," "the salt of the earth" for whom "no-one is too much trouble," "a character, vital as the spring." Luke loves her on the spot, and when Campion suggests that she is perfect for the role Luke himself has outlined—that of the unsuspecting innocent who provides a refuge—he rejects the idea totally, so that we are bound to see him at this point as a victim of his emotions. He even uses the phrase that gives the book it title: "I may be hiding my eyes but I just cannot see. . .(Polly) involved in anything of this sort." When Miss Allingham goes on to describe as "unaware of trespassing" the colleague of Luke's who comments sympathetically on his decision not to trouble Polly again, and so implies that the old woman is something of a private preserve of Luke's, she neatly reinforces her point. Because he doesn't want Polly to be connected with the man he has envisaged, he fails to investigate her properly and so misses his chance.

Where Luke fails, however, Campion again succeeds, on a more modest scale than in *More Work for the Undertaker*, but no less decisively. He is fully alive to the possibilities presented by Polly's odd menage and perseveres when Luke has abandoned the field, "dithering slightly in the way which those who had cause to know him best might have found a little sinister," his "pale face. . .as vacuous as in his youth and his eyes. . .lazy behind their spectacles." By the time he has finished "wrestling with the conversational subject as if it was a wet sheet which had fallen on him," Polly has shown "astonishment and then incredulity, followed by a flicker of instantly suppressed alarm" and she is perceptibly "on guard" when she says goodbye. Later, when Luke seeks reassurance that Polly "was on the level" and "knew nothing," Campion feels unable to "commit himself."

Throughout, he is typically oblique and self-effacing, unassertive even when picking up threads that elude Luke, and offering a crucial discovery as something that has merely "occurred to" him. An exchange between Luke and Yeo confirms the characteristic impression he makes: "He's sloped off now, I don't know where. He muttered something and next time I looked there he wasn't."

"That's Albert." Yeo was amused. "He'll be back. He doesn't miss much. You'll find he's had an idea and trotted off to test it" In fact, he has seen beyond his initial perception to a further possible link between Garden Green and their quarry and when his message reaches Luke simultaneously with a similar nudge from another source, the gratifying effect of the double climax is to confound Luke and leave him "staring."

Twice within seconds Luke is asked by colleagues new to the enquiry whether Polly's address means anything to him; and so the point of his negligence is made again, subtly in terms of the titular theme and devastatingly in terms of the action. All through the novel, this kind of refinement is maintained. The author's mastery of the small climax at the end of each chapter is here seen at its best: when a phone rings in Luke's office it does so with the promise of enormous excitement, and we are later brought twice in entirely separate chapters to the same point of high suspense. The narrative method is enticingly oblique. Nowhere does Miss Allingham tell us directly how a sedate old couple came to be on the bus driven by the killer in the opening sequence: instead we are given the pleasure of assembling the explanation—from an innocent question by Polly's niece, Annabelle, from Polly's own revealing comments on the answer she receives, and from a reminiscent anecdote in a barber's shop (whereas Luke has only the hazy and misleading recollection of a waiter to guide him, until the old people make a dramatic reappearance). We learn that the man visiting Polly is the killer from the opening scene because his "unusual neck-muscles" are remarked on both occasions; and we know how he intends to kill Polly from his not looking up and his "casual tone" when she reminds him of a potential danger from her gas-fire

The novel is also distinguished by a pervasive irony that adds immeasurably to its subtlety and complexity. Annabelle's "joyous" joke linking Polly with the murderer is in fact a total deduction of a dreadful truth; and a moral judgment that she applies to someone in a film is so cruelly apt to Polly's own situation that she is "appalled" by it. The friendly remarks of a waitress impinge on the killer's mind as an incitement to kill; and his improbable account of "a great wall of oil drums" with a "mystery packet behind it" proves to have an unexpected macabre truth. A few words on a hotel receptionist's notepad create a chilling and "somewhat ominous" effect far removed from their intended import; and the title of the song the murderer plays while taunting a former lover alludes both to their past intimacy and to the damaging details that she subsequently recalls when the police question her: "How are you getting on with your forgetting?"

The action generates a continuous, concentrated excitement, from the meticulous, menacing prologue to the action proper, through the sinister assembly of the pattern of the past, to the enormity and urgency of the present with the murder and the threat of its sequel. Even *The Tiger in the Smoke* cannot quite equal the swift, keyed-up intensity of this novel, though the two are demonstrably akin, and there are echoes of the earlier book in the later one.

A detractor might even charge the author with having written the same book twice, and an element of deja-vu must be acknowledged. Again there is no whodunit element and the central figure, soon identified, is an evil man whose motivation is a prime concern. Luke again feels personal enmity towards his quarry and images of a big game hunt recur. The killer advances a philosophy of life—"the Chad-Horder discovery"—comparable to Havoc's Science of Luck, and the action rises to a climactic confrontation between good and evil, after which the killer dwindles to nothing.

But the author anticipates the charge of repeating herself, and is at pains to rebut it even before the action is properly under way. Before he has any tangible evidence of his existence even, Luke maintains that the man he is after "isn't a fraction like" Jack Havoc, and the action of the novel goes on to substantiate this claim. Where Havoc was reckless, "out of touch with the Peace-time world," and guided by instinct and obsession, "this man is different. He's almost refreshing. He's got a brain and he's got nerve and he's not neurotic. He's perfectly sane, he's merciless as a snake and he's very careful—doesn't like witnesses or corpses left around."

Luke in fact describes him very accurately and the man himself frequently echoes this uncannily close assessment. His name is Gerry Hawker, alias Jeremy Chad-Horder, and his confidence in himself is absolute. He sees himself as "indestructible," boasting of being "careful and. . .thorough always, every moment of the time," and claiming to have "no sentiment to make me shrink from any move when the need arises." Under pressure for perhaps the first time in his life, he appears "completely confident," convinced that he is "in no danger at all": "I'm careful. I'm like a good racing driver. I never take a risk. I've got no ties and no rules. I'm so safe it's boring."

His contention that he has covered his tracks so well that even if the police were to investigate him thoroughly, "they couldn't prove a thing," would sound like bravado except that Luke has already talked of "a snowdrift of suspicion" likely to melt"at the Old Bailey," and later deplores with Campion that "nothing quite jells. . . Every lead. . . is as thin as a bit of cotton. There are hundreds of strings but nothing that promises to plait up into a rope."

From the first, Gerry is an arresting figure, wound up to kill, meticulous and lethal, "a shocking and dreadful thing, as horrible as any deadly creature moving subtly in the dark places of an unsuspecting world." Initially, we do not see the whole of his face: only "the plane of his thin cheek and strong jaw and neck muscles" catch the light. When his eyes and forehead emerge from "their mask of shadow," he is seen to be "good-looking in a conventional way, his features regular and his round eyes set wide apart." "Only the heavy muscles at the corners of his jaw and the unusual thickness of his neck" detract from "the accepted fashionable picture."

On the two occasions that we watch him at work, he shows himself as calculating and impassive, with patience, foresight, and superb self-control. He sets about the murder of a moneylender to whom he is in debt with military precision, timing "to perfection" the arrival of his bus; positioning it unhurriedly and "with remarkable care" over the back steps of his victim's house; calling the man from a phone-box, but forestalling the suspicion this could evoke by pressing Button A "immediately"; and calmly hiring a taxi to remove the unexpected obstacle of Polly, who is on the spot and in the way (by a carefully documented coincidence).

The murder on this occasion is left to our imagination, but we actually witness the later killing of Polly's friend and solicitor, Matt Phillipson and the elaborate preparations for an alibi that accompany it. As he waits to shoot his victim, he seems to lack "any emotion": "Never once did he falter or make an unnecessary step, but carried out the entire operation with the smooth efficiency of a dance routine on the stage." His cool certainty and self-possession eliminate all possibility of the least hint of suspicion: "From first to last, he behaved as what he so nearly was, a well-trained animal without imagination or moral sense, and it was probably because of that that he aroused no instinctive alarm in the crowds through which he passed. There was no danger signal from him, no smell of fear" (in direct contrast to Jack Havoc, from whom an "extraordinary atmosphere" emanates).

When his entire complex alibi for the murder of Matt is overturned by a chance meeting, he is "by no means panic-stricken": rather, he feels "impersonal, almost as if his whole interest in the matter was academic." He denies a repeated charge that he was at Silverstone on a particular day without a hint of anger or self-betrayal; and though the charge is patently true, Gerry's "idle half-laughing expression" does not change and he persists in reiterated denial as if "his mind was only just on the subject."

Only on two occasions does his emotional guard slip: when he recalls his grandfather as "a brilliant man," making the claim "with a conviction not only out of character but clearly misplaced"; and when he is moved to tears by his final dialogue with Polly. Otherwise, it is as if he has schooled all emotion out of himself, and he denies specifically that he is subject to sentiment. When Luke expresses the fear "that he's that rare bloke who is not dependent on anyone or fond of anyone," he is echoing Gerry's own words, those of "the Chad-Horder discovery," the inhuman philosophy that informs his life: "I've never let anything tear the skin. . . I've never been faintly fond of anything or of anybody in my life. . . Any kind of affection is a solvent. It melts and adulterates the subject and by indulging it he loses his identity and hence his efficiency." (Interestingly, Amanda reaches the same conclusion in *The Beckoning Lady*, where the humiliating transformation in Luke forcibly demonstrates its truth).

From his implicit contempt for other people arises, inevitably, a disregard in Gerry for the sanctity of human life. Luke describes the notorious Haigh as the exceptional criminal who "went the one stage further" than the majority:"Most crooks will take anything and everything from their victims, except the one final item. Haigh was the chap who thought that one final refinement was silly." That Gerry, too, goes "one stage further" than most is for Luke "the really unusual thing about him": "He makes a living by taking all he needs from other people" and "kills quite coldly when it's the safest thing to do." Gerry dismisses the very idea of murder as "silly": "That's a damned silly term. Murder is a word, a shibboleth." The concept of murder is "hocus-pocus," merely: to be awed by the idea of taking a life is "to make something metaphysical of it, setting it up as the unforgivable crime." He maintains that "People get killed every day and sometimes it's called murder and sometimes it isn't. Sometimes it's war and sometimes it's accident, sometimes it's. . . well, it's just the logical conclusion of a sequence of events." Though the hesitation in this statement speaks volumes, the shift from war and accident to his own will in a situation he has engineered is hair-raising. He has actually convinced himself that if it is "logical" to kill, as the way to get money or to escape a difficulty, then it is justifiable. Death is something that happens to men, and "If you're prepared to strip everything else from a man, why not finish the job logically and take his life?" Gerry is quoted as saying that Haigh would be "alive today and still picking up a good living" in a "logical" way, had he not "lost his nerve and confessed." Clearly Luke's conviction that the basic concern of the man he is after is to make a living is correct: he is "simply out for money. . . and not necessarily big money."

Despite the excitement he generates, there is no danger that Gerry will seem a glamorous figure, and,. if there were, this in itself would be sufficient to destroy the illusion. To the thrill of the chase and the wish to complete the pattern of events is added a basic desire to see Gerry brought low. For us, as for Luke, he is "the enemy," and as Luke suggests where he might be vulnerable, we respond with instinctive sympathy to the "purr" in his voice (just as, with Campion, we experience "a small and secret thrill creeping down" the spine).

Luke's perception of Gerry's weakness is uncannily true: in particular, he pinpoints the element of fantasy in his way of life, what the author subsequently calls the "odd hypothetical quality in his appreciation of events." If a man feels that other people can be robbed and killed at will, he can have no perception of them as individuals: they exist for him only when he has a specific need to gratify. The coroly of this must be that they *don't* exist when he doesn't need them, so that he is at such times in his own estimation virtually invisible. Luke divines this "state of mind" in Gerry and the reader sees an example of it in action. To establish an alibi, Gerry draws attention to himself at a hotel he has "cased" the previous day: he wants the waiter to remember him only for the purposes of the alibi and clearly cannot conceive of him outside the role for which he has cast him. But the man in fact recalls him from his earlier visit and makes the appropriate deduction.

By such a device the author shows that Gerry cannot avoid involvement with others and that he interacts with them to a degree that he never suspects. Like everyone else, he is at the mercy of his own humanity—of his physical presence, his actions and reactions, his effect on other people, his fallibility, and his luck. People see and hear him, watch and wonder about him; he is deceived, or out of luck, or reminded of things he would rather forget. The events of the day compel him to acknowledge his common humanity with the rest of mankind.

The waiter's perception of his motives is central to the author's aim to show the undoing of Gerry by other people, the men and women he so despises and manipulates. Just as Luke has outlined his career and thrown light on his secrets, so the waiter conjectures what has actually happened to prevent Gerry's return to the hotel: "Maybe t'ings don' go too well. Maybe some feller bolts a door 'e don't usually bolt, or some cashier girl stays on too late at the office waiting for a friend. Maybe 'e jus' runs into someone 'oo knows 'im and 'oo could say 'e's seen 'im outside this 'otel when 'e ought to have been inside it telephoning."

In the same way, Gerry's barber, Mr. Vick, unconsciously reveals a good general knowledge of his criminal habits derived from observation over a long period. He knows that "every now and again 'e gets up to something—puts a big deal through"; that he calls in for a haircut "as part of a little programme 'e's set 'imself" that "'e's always in a tizzy about the right time"; and that "'e nearly always picks up the man who 'asn't got a watch." Clearly is has never occurred to Gerry that Mr. Vick's avid curiosity and garrulity constitute any sort of threat to him, but though the man is an overt figure of fun, with his "drawing-room" screams and "coy" effeminacy, he talks sufficiently to the point to make one of his customers conclude that Gerry is "a crook," and to confirm the suspicions of another who already has him under observation.

Richard Waterfield, the observer in question, is one of Gerry's worst misfortunes, since he already has reasons of his own for wanting to keep him in view, and by selecting him as witness to his current alibi, Gerry unwittingly plays into his hands. Again, he thinks of another man only in terms of what he intends him to do, and by doing so undermines his own security. Richard's observation of Gerry is constant and acute and he registers everything accessible to sheer vigilance—the pleased reaction to the absence of a watch from Richard's wrist; the lie about his own approach to the barber's shop that first alerts Richard to his being "engaged in" a "definite. . .plan", the fact that Gerry puts jacket and raincoat on together "so that the outside of the jacket did not appear"; the label on the shaft of the starting-handle of Gerry's car ("Hawker. Rolf's Dump, S.E."); the tensions that arise during his conversation with Edna, his former lover; and the odd circumstance of their sitting exactly "in the centre of the longest wall" of the deserted lounge at the Tenniel Hotel, directly opposite the corridor off which the telephone booths open. Even Gerry's reason for choosing Richard to guarantee his alibi is a stroke of pure mischance, since he has pawned his watch only minutes before entering Mr. Vick's shop.

Fate is at last playing Gerry at his own game of providing for all eventualities, massing its forces against him and pushing him to extremes. This is the end of his run of success, his last day in his established image of himself. From minor irritants like questions and reminders that stir unwanted memories—from Annabelle, from Mr. Vick, from Edna—the action moves through a succession of disasters: the shattering of his alibi by a chance encounter; a subsequent meeting with a man who remembers him as a child and thus knows his original identity; the appalling discovery that the murder he has laboured all day to achieve was futile; and the necessary consequence that he now must kill the only person for whom he has a shred of disinterested feeling.

Increasingly through the day, his early ease and confidence give way before disquiet and dread. Gently at first, he begins to experience human weakness, to know what it is to doubt, to be surprised, to feel anxiety. For the first time he feels and shows something other than the expression of "laughing shamefaced apology which Richard had begun to consider characteristic of him" or the "urgency" of the approach to the kill, the "strain and determination like a climber's nearing a peak," the "simmering" quality that Mr. Vick detects in him, the "dancing and quivering" of the nerves "under the stretched skin." He knows, for once, "a moment of indecision" and encounters "something he had not envisaged." His face shows an "expression of innocent surprise," "a sudden glimpse of helplessness" or a "strange dark blush." He begins to acquire a belated self-knowledge with the "surprised" realization that "his faith in himself" demands a new alibi to replace the ruined one. He finds the unexpected necessity to kill Annabelle "distasteful" and is "reluctant to implement" her death "until the last moment."

More terribly, he undergoes a series of mental and physical shocks that shake him beyond measure and finally destroy him. His reading of the letter that negates the purpose of the murder of Matt provokes in his body the kind of extreme reaction he has not known since childhood: "a flood of tingling blood rose up from his stomach to suffuse his face. . . The nerves in his face contracted to a net of pain and the blood in his heart felt icy." Simultaneously, his mind is paralyzed by the realization that his two alibis cancel each other out: the difference between his habitual refuge in a fantasy world of his own creating and his new "stark vision" is "as great as between sleeping and waking."

He faces with "open horror" the necessity to kill Polly and an "extraordinary conflict" arises in him, "part apprehension, part eagerness, part passionate despair," as he reaches the point of contriving her death. Like Havoc with the Canon, he is "agonized, weeping even, suffocated by the relentless compulsion" to preserve himself in his own image whatever the cost.

The need to maintain his own achieved identity emerges in the closing stages of the action as his greatest weakness. On the level of survival, he is actually at risk from the catastrophic moment when he leaves Matt's wallet on a cafe table; but the realization that he has so betrayed himself does not strike till he is already a prey to other doubts and fears. When he does realize what he has done, he is "stunned by the discovery" and begins physically to dwindle: "all his movements" become "a little smaller as if he was shrinking into himself as the old seem to do." Richard's subsequent attack brings him physically to the ground, unable to resist, and the recognition that follows it strips "the last flimsy shreds of illusion" from his eyes.

Now all that is left is a temporary refuge from "the naked horror" of his situation in Richard's belief that he is "some sort of small-time crook." The "extraordinary effect" of Richard's so regarding him is to offer him, however briefly and ignobly, a momentary escape into yet another identity, "a brief mercy, like a little screen to hide" behind. From the brisk way he addresses him, it is clear that Richard has no conception that Gerry is a man destroyed: "The notion that something a little less than a man might be trembling there, struggling feebly to wrap itself in the shreds of a false identity. . . casually created for it by Richard himself was something quite outside his imagination. It was an aspect of hell which, mercifully, was not in his comprehension."

Gerry, at the end, is "less than a man," no longer "he" but "it," no longer merely in "a nightmare" but facing "an aspect of hell." He crawls like Havoc in his ditch, into a "little dark hole," a "very cool, very dark" corner. As Havoc had found himself with "no decision to make" and "knew himself to be fallible," so Gerry is finally reduced to nothing: "He was nothing and there was nothing for him."

Before the end, Polly tries desperately to save some part of Gerry's spirit. Even as he sets about preparing her death, she cannot believe that the "lively boy" she has known and loves has moved wholly beyond her reach. If Gerry has a redeeming feature it is that something in him has made Polly care for him. Though described on her first appearance as "a mum if ever there was one," she is in fact a childless widow, and Gerry is her surrogate son. Polly's love for Gerry is the second great motive force in the novel.

Polly's feeling for Gerry suffuses the novel, and it is clear from repeated references that she would love him no more intensely were he indeed her own son. What begins as "pure affection" in a cosy, domestic context ends as "Disinterested Love. . .a force, like nuclear energy," a fact of life able to survive anything, even the attempt to kill her. When Polly admits to loving Gerry "like a son," she adds "and nothing can be done about that"; and her friend Mrs. Dominique confirms the implication that maternal love knows no limitation: "When one if fond of a son, real, adopted or step, one has no rules. . . One forgives. That is all there is to it, and the whole nature of the attachment. That's life." But Mrs. Dominique also maintains that "one still ought to *know*": while accepting that Polly will forgive Gerry, even if he has committed murder, she sees a necessity to discover what there is to forgive.

Polly finds that she cannot come to terms with this and refuses to authorize Mrs. Dominique to consult a friend in the police. She, too, has an image of Gerry, as the "kind good boy" she has known and loved since the war, and when this image is threatened she hides her eyes from what she knows to be the truth. Only when it seems that Gerry intends to kill her does she admit the full extent of her concern—though it has been apparent from the first, even during their opening demonstration of affection, when her "elderly voice" has "sounded the least bit flustered."

None of her encounters during the day is free of the tension between what her intelligence demands that she believe and what her heart would be very much happier to believe. The gentle scene with Matt Phillipson is pervaded by her unease: they may talk of Gerry as a "rascal" and a "wretched chap," who simply needs to "be pulled up good and sharp," but a darker picture emerges from what they say than either is prepared to acknowledge. (In the same way Polly's naive plan to bring Gerry and one of her nieces together in the hope that they may love and marry is seen as ludicrous in the light of his encounter with Edna, whose evident passion for him evokes no more in him than a mildly sadistic contempt: so much for Polly's idea of "the right girl to love him and boss him"). Even the innocent remarks of Annabelle, whom she has only just met, cause her to react so violently as to startle "even herself," or to speak so "huskily" that she needs to cough "to explain it." Her very denials make the conflict explicit. It is precisely by appearing to dismiss the idea that she acknowledges that it was Gerry who paid for the taxi on the night the moneylender was murdered: "I know some damn silly boys but no murderers, thank God. Besides. . . I had a postcard from Gerry, sent from Yorkshire that very evening. I noticed it particularly at the time." (Later, she admits that she has known all the time: "That night when it rained, you sent the taxi. . . I knew that in my heart. And when I got the postcard telling me quite unnecessarily that you were somewhere else that night, I was even more certain. But I wouldn't, I couldn't believe it.") In extremis, even as she learns that Matt is dead and knows that Gerry has killed him, she repeats the word "No"; and when confronting him at the end, she appeals to him "in the teeth of her own intelligence to make the mitigating claim," to explain away what he has done, somehow to justify it in human terms.

Even though Polly is forced to relinquish her image of Gerry as a "damn silly boy" who only needs a nice girl to set him on the right lines, she insists in the face of death itself on his need for love. When, during her luncheon with Matt, she states her belief that she is important to Gerry—"I don't want him to lose *me*"—she is talking on an intimate, personal level; but by the end of her climactic encounter with Gerry, she is concerned to save his humanity, his soul even.

At times when she looks into his face it's as if "there's no-one there," and it is this that frightens her more than anything. She asks God to let her see in his eyes that he is "still a man. . .and not a snake," and is relieved, "despite her sense of paralysed dismay," to see "sweat standing out on his forehead": "at least he was alive to it all, still there." Even when she realizes that he has drugged her, she still struggles to make him understand and acknowledge his need: "I am the last thing you love. . . If—you—kill me, Gerry, you will lose contact with—your kind. There'll be nothing—to keep you alive. You'll wither like a leaf off a tree."

Though Gerry averts his eyes from Polly's sleeping form, "turning his head whenever he passed her," he does so "like a sulking child," not like a man alive to the enormity of what he is doing. There is never any overt indication in him that Polly's words penetrate, and though he weeps as she sinks into unconsciousness, his tears are involuntary. As he continues with his plan to kill Polly and Annabelle, he denies his humanity, bent on a course that will quickly reduce him to "something. . .less than a man." As if he is trapped in his inhuman role and unable to function outside it, his behavior is "largely automatic"—"Just as a hunted animal will continue to run for some time after a bullet has killed it, so he pressed on with the plan he had made." Even as late as the encounter with Richard and Annabelle, when he knows that he has left Matt's wallet on the cafe table and realizes from a "pair of eyes looking in" that the police are outside the house, he is still intending to "silence" the girl, and is astonished that she is "not where he had expected her to be, upstairs asleep in her room."

Only when he leaves Matt's wallet behind does some kind of moral force appear to influence Gerry, and then only in the most oblique and impalpable way, so that the reader becomes wholly aware of it only in retrospect. When he discovers the loss, Gerry is chiefly appalled by the realization that some part of him knows already: "He had known all the time. He knew he had walked directly out of the cafe, leaving the leather folder behind him on the table, and he had done it almost but not quite deliberately. Only the finest veil of unawareness had hung between him and that suicidal act."

Whatever the force that governs Gerry in the cafe, its definition is clearly crucial, since the wallet constitutes the evidence that will hang him. For the police sergeant the oversight is a straightforward indication that Gerry "couldn't stand himself any longer," but the implication of a conscious self-betrayal is at odds with what we are told. Luke, more searchingly, posits the kind of drastic trauma that does in fact overtake Gerry as he formulates the need to kill Polly, of all people: "In my experience that kind of blackout always indicates an explosion. Either some unexpected idea or demand set off an emotional spark which he didn't know he had in him, or some force from outside suddenly succeeded in penetrating his hide and startled him out of his senses for a minute." Since both Luke's hypotheses accord with Gerry's "open horror" as he absorbs the "full implications" of his exchange with the waitress, either will serve as an insight into self-betrayal. Whatever the reason, Polly's love is at the root of it, and the force behind it is emotional, not moral. However elusive and complex Polly's triumph, however undermined by irony, it is finally absolute.

Chapter 13
Identity Crisis

After *Hide My Eyes*, there was an unprecedented gap of five years before the appearance of *The China Governess* in 1963. It would be instructive to know if this infinitely subtle novel was the full five years in the making and, if so, to what extent the author found her material intractable. It's one of the oddest books in the canon, described on the dust-wrapper as "a Mystery of Today" and with an intelligent awareness of contemporary tensions, but firmly set in a characteristic Allingham world, cosy, eccentric, sentimental, and above all, permanent: the sons of important families are still sent to Totham, and even an East End factory worker proves to be employed by Alandel.

It is preeminently a novel of contrasts: between Ebbfield past and present, the Turk Street Mile and the Phoenix estate; between the Well House at Scribbenfields in London and the Keep at Angevin in Suffolk; between two ways of life, one coldly aesthetic, one passionately altruistic; between a deluded older generation and a bewildered younger one; and between romance and reality, semblance and truth.

The novel is rooted in this old, pervasive literary theme: appearance and reality, the difference between what seems to be and what actually is. Most of the principals in the action are either deceiving or deceived, on a scale that shapes their lives: by the end of the novel, several mysteries have been resolved, but it seems even more important to the author that essential truths have been told, so that life may begin again on a more trustworthy basis. As he looks round the Well House, the home of the Kinnit family, Campion, finally, is "comforted": "It was a picture of beginnings, he thought. Half a dozen startings: new chapters, new ties, new associations. They were all springing out of the story he had been following, like a spray of plumes in a renaissance pattern springs up from a complete and apparently final feather."

At the center of the new beginnings is the coming together of Timothy Kinnit and his father. Tim's identity crisis is the main concern of the novel and the most extended development of the theme of appearance and reality. As heir to the Kinnit fortunes, he has always believed himself the bastard son either of Eustace Kinnit or his dead brother, "the original Timothy." When his fiancee's father suddenly objects to their marriage and he discovers that his parentage is in fact totally obscure, he is "shattered" and becomes obsessed by the need to establish his origins: "I've been thinking I'm a Kinnit ever since I've thought at all and now suddenly I find I'm not. Naturally I want to know who I am." To Julia, his fiancee, he is the Timothy she loves "and nothing and nobody else," but for Timothy himself this is an evasive irrelevance.

Divorced from his familiar identity, he is totally at a loss, "like an untethered balloon" floating "unattached and meaningless." His experience has been like "a sort of. . .birth": "I feel that until today I've been in a . . .an eggshell. But all through today I've been breaking out of it. Everything I've ever taken for granted has come apart in my hand." To Julia, he has "become completely insane on the subject," " *mad* to know" his origins; but Timothy himself argues cogently in defense of his need to establish a heredity to replace that he has lost: "I'm a component part. I'm the continuation of an existing story, as is everybody else. I thought I knew my story but I don't. I have been misinformed in a very thorough way. I've got to go on and find out who I am, or I'm unrecognizable even to myself." When, at the end, Timothy's true father remarks that Barry, his surrogate son, "takes his papers very seriously," Timothy's reply is "momentous and completely enlightening": "He takes his identity seriously. . . Naturally. It appears to be all he has." It is ironic that Timothy's discovery of his own identity deprives Barry of his.

Timothy's quest governs the action and impinges on almost everyone involved in it. By employing detectives to investigate his paternity, Eustace and his sister Alison precipitate a terrible violence that even enters their homes. Julia is bewildered to find her lover's energy "diverted from her to meet this new demand." Timothy's real father undergoes extreme distress of mind; and his established son breaks out into extravagant acts of destruction in an effort to preserve his own achieved identity.

The novel's exploration of heredity becomes an extension of the conflict between the seeming and the actual. Two views emerge, the false, advanced in the main through spoken arguments, and the true, surfacing irresistibly from resemblances between Timothy and his parents. Joe Stalkey, the Kinnits' detective, sees the transfer from "a vicious slum" to "something plushy" as harmful. He takes Timothy's pugnacious reaction to provocation as proof of his slum origins and an indication that he wrecked the flat in which Stalkey's brother was staying. Timothy's father accounts absurdly for the deficiencies in his false son by the experiences of his earliest infancy: "What sort of chance has a child whose mother . . . came from the most dreadful of slums?. . . Wouldn't that account for him, whatever he's become?" Charlie Luke wonders whether Tim's plebeian origins might not be a factor in his reaction to the loss of his identity. He argues that Timothy is not "specially bred. . ., conditioned over the generations to withstand a bit of cossetting, like a prize dog, but an ordinary tough boy," who must therefore be more vulnerable to such a shock. The idea of his "reverting to type" is even applied in malice when Basil Toberman, the Kinnits' business associate, uses it to color the suggestion that he has contributed to a servant's death.

Nanny Broome, the Kinnits' nurse, predictably discounts heredity. For her it is a "scientific fact" that "If you have a child until he's six it doesn't matter who has him afterwards": because she has trained him, she can vouch for Timothy, whatever his origins. (With unconscious irony, she talks of the infant Timothy as having resembled "a changeling in the fairy tales.") She maintains that "As long as a boy has a home behind him no one's going to ask what church his mother and father got married at." Her comfortable view that "he's got a perfectly nice family of people he's very fond of and knows all about and takes after by this time!" copes with the crucial issue by simply ignoring it (like Julia's resolve to love him whoever he proves to be).

Timothy himself is intellectually doubtful about theories of heredity—"I've never believed in heredity consciously before and I don't know that I do now"—but he finds in himself an instinctual need to "know what is behind" him and to "belong to someone's line." In conversation with Julia, he reminds her of the possibility of hereditary mental weaknesses and "other diseases one doesn't want in a parent," and he finally acknowledges to Campion that he believes in his heart that her father is right to keep them apart until the matter is resolved.

The novel asserts repeatedly that heredity will out. The family resemblance between the Kinnits and their niece Geraldine Telpher is so pronounced that observers are "made a little uncomfortable" by it. Basil Toberman drinks heavily "just like his father," and Mrs. Telpher's commiseration over the embarrassment he causes enforces the point: "Poor man, if it's inherited we should be sorry for him, I suppose." Campion is dismayed to find that Luke's daughter has the Scroop-Dory face, but reassured when he also sees Luke's "cockney intelligence blazing out of it." Barry and his real mother share similar strengths and weaknesses that confirm their kinship.

Once the initial contact is made, Timothy's own descent proclaims itself irresistibly. When Eustace reproaches him for being not like himself, Timothy replies that he is "not like anybody": but his resemblance to his father has already been observed by Tom Tray, the cobbler to whom he goes for information, and later by his stepmother. Campion is startled by a "raw force" in Timothy that seems "out of character in one whom he had assumed to be a typical young Oxford success-type"; and Julia and Timothy himself remark on a "curious gesture" that he shares with his father.

The effect of each man on the other is further confirmation. After talking to his father, Timothy feels "as if a skin had peeled from his eyes," and he is aware that "in the vast, blind, computing machine where the mind and the emotions meet and churn, something very odd indeed seemed to have taken place." Later, he is "astonished at his own vehemence" when defending him against denigration. With his own experience to guide him, the older man is more directly affected. He confesses to being "knocked. . .endways" by Timothy, less by seeing himself in the boy than by his amazing resemblance to his late wife:

"People keep mentioning that he resembles *me*. My God. He not only looks like her but he *is* her. He's treated his own poor little girl now just as she treated me. He's keeping her out of it, suffering all alone." Earlier, he has reacted with sudden hostility to a particular conversational trick of Timothy's, but only in a later scene with Julia is it made clear that this, too, is something Timothy shares with his mother. Barry's heredity resides solely in his papers: Timothy's emerges from his looks, his voice, his gestures and his temperament.

To the Kinnits, Timothy's identity crisis seems more an inconvenience that a cause for emotional concern. At "a moment of enormous danger," when Timothy is at his most vulnerable, Eustace reacts by changing the subject: "his protection was almost complete." Alison receives the news that Timothy is no longer helping the police with their enquiries with an "emphasis" that is "nearly generous": but she is clearly tempted to get on with ordering the luncheon, "only thinking better just in time." The subtlety of the author's treatment of the Kinnits is a constant challenge to the reader. They appear gentle and civilized, Alison "twittering" and "feminine," as delicate as "thistledown," Eustace "kindly" and urbane, with "shy charm" and a "disarming diffidence"; so that the reader warms to them instinctively as to cosy old dears in a traditional Allingham mould. But when their utterances are examined the picture that emerges is far from sympathetic, so that, again the question of appearance and reality is raised.

Alison is "pink and girlish" and wears a "little-girl dressing-gown, splattered with pink roses." She hangs her head "like a delicate child" when she fears to have given offense. Like her brother, she is "utterly embarrassed" by a direct confrontation of Timothy's predicament, and she provokes Julia's anger by her total failure to understand his reaction to police suspicion: "It's so unlike him to be awkward." But for all her fragility, there is "something a little frightening in the grey-eyed intelligence with which she confronted the world," and her eyes, though "innocent" are also "hard." When she is so minded, she is capable of subjecting Julia to a "ruthless dismissal."

Eustace, too, has an immature quality, "as if the world had never touched him at all." He has a "schoolboyish and charming laugh" and at times "an innocence of expression which was almost infantile." Because his mind is "always unhappy and fumbling when emotions of any kind were involved," he persists in seeking a "rational explanation for Timothy's behaviour" and seizes on a "purely factual point gratefully." Yet, again, there is another aspect to Eustace, apparent in his ineffectual attempt to "pull strings" to free Timothy from being harried by the police, and in his confident determination to govern his unruly partner: "Basil must stop drinking and be quiet. I'll see to it myself." More "godlike" still is his decree that "to save us all embarrassment" there shall be no post-mortem when a visiting servant dies suddenly.

Their niece, Ms. Telpher, seems by nature enigmatic, a grave, remote, silent woman of "considerable elegance" with "all the Kinnit tolerance in her quiet voice." The suggestion of arrogance in her actions and attitudes reinforces the point made by her physical resemblance to her uncle and aunt: temperamentally, too, she is "exactly like any other Kinnit." She is ordinarily "unforthcoming," "aloof" and "preoccupied," appearing "relaxed and withdrawn" even in company "as if she were out of the circle altogether": even her voice seems "intentionally inexpressive." Only twice is she "startled out of her natural calm" to the point where her eyes dilate and her face looks "grey and rigid."

All three Kinnits have the family "trick of making people feel slightly inferior without intending to or noticing that is had been done": they react to Basil's claim to connoisseurship with "exactly the same twinkling smile of good-natured derision." Even in the wider field of patronage, their celebrated benevolence is suspect, and their charity is bitterly attacked by Basil, who claims to be one of its victims. He regards the Kinnits as "natural sharks masquerading as patronising amateurs" and sneers at their kind of "philanthropy" which "always has an end product." The "Kinnit method" is to "take in lame ducks, don't ask too much about them but make devoted slaves out of them ever after."

Even Timothy, who loves Eustace and Alison, agrees that the "Kinnit family *is* what Basil said it was. They do tend to capitalize their charitable acts since they do them for the wrong purpose. They don't keep helping folk for the warm silly reason that they like the people concerned, but for the cold practical one that they hope to see themselves as nice people doing kind things." Nanny Broome takes this a stage further and observes, more shrewdly than she knows, that they "put up with the most extraordinary people" as if "they were trying to work off some sort of sin they'd committed."

Basil sees Thyrza Caleb, the original of the China Governess, as a prototype Kinnit victim. While employed as governess to two of Eustace's great-aunts, she was tried for the murder of their music-master: after her acquittal, she drowned herself, having no longer any prospect of a future. Interestingly, she enforces the central theme of illusion and truth in both her manifestations, as a woman whose established history is false, and as a prettification of something ugly, an ornament to commemorate a murder. Her exploitation both as a woman and image intensifies our dislike of the Kinnit family: she loses her life from her association with them, and as a rare collector's piece considerably enhances their fortunes.

She has her revenge, both dramatically, when the truth of what happened to her is brought explosively to light, and more subtly, as a skeleton in the cupboard, a constant reminder to the Kinnits of the "basic living sin which the original crime exposed." She is "not so much a ghost as their minds playing the goat," creating such a climate of anxiety that Eustace reacts with panic to the sudden death of her modern counterpart, Miss Saxon, who is staying at the Well House with Mrs. Telpher. Because of the link with Thyrza, Eustace cannot get her under ground quickly enough, disposing of her with such furtive guilty haste that suspicion is inevitable. Miss Saxon, like Thyrza, is not what she appears to be: (even her dyed hair is an enhancement of the main theme). Her revenge is still to come when the novel ends. As Campion observes: "The world is certainly going to hear about the Kinnit family and their governesses. . . No-one on earth can prevent that now." By a final irony, it becomes an advantage to Timothy that, as Julia points out, he is "not a Kinnit."

The Kinnits are especially vulnerable to ugly publicity of the kind that is imminent because their lives are ordinarily so secure and so secret, so "very civilised" and "very covered up." They live in a "Tudor merchant's mansion" that is "completely out of place in a modern world"; and they scratch the surface of life with "literary, charitable or political interests" or "endless writing" on "various aspects of the china collector's art."

Alison and her friend Flavia Aicheson are conservationists concerned for "the Preservation of the London Skyline," and their conflict with an East End councillor offers a further metaphor for the central theme. Councillor Cornish is the motive force behind the Phoenix estate in Ebbfield, "an enormous block of council dwellings" resembling "an Atlantic liner swimming diagonally across the site." He is "a living flame of a man, as passionate and fanatical as Luke himself," with a restless social conscience deriving from his experience of pre-war London slums. Throughout, Cornish stands for reality, the kind of harsh, uncompromising discipline that imposes standards so severe that the chance to escape a daunting responsibility seems a delusion to be resisted. Yet he, too, is not wholly what he seems: his very stoicism and strength make him vulnerable and credulous, so that what he has accepted as truth for twenty years proves to be appearance only.

Though he is not what one would call a comfortable man, he has a grandeur and intensity altogether lacking in the Kinnits. They inhabit an earlier Allingham world; he is very much of the present. His commitment to his "great project" is total: "It's not a municipal venture, it's a social rebirth, a statement of sincere belief that decent conditions make a decent community." Predictably, Alison and "Aich" are the enemy, more concerned for appearance than reality: "They don't like the look of the new flats. The silhouette is an affront to their blasted eyes, they say." Cornish allows that they "may feel that they're serving the Arts," but claims that his "life's work" is to "serve Humanity."

The author's detachment is admirable and it allows us to sympathize with either view or both. Neither side understands the other: to Aich, Cornish is "the poor wretched man with the dreadful temper," while to Cornish she and Alison are "half-baked intellectuals who never know when to stop." A comment by his wife shows that Cornish has drastically over-reacted to a single brief experience of a London slum, and yet the very force of his recollection threatens to make Aich and Alison seem trivial, their conservationist activities on a par with their attendance at an outre recital to make up the numbers.

Ultimately, the Kinnits are seem to negate life, to reject it, and even, in extremis, to destroy it. They lack the capacity to live other than intellectually, aware in themselves that they suffer the emotional limitations imposed by *their* heredity. In Timothy's words, they "know all about this and don't like themselves very much because of it. . . They know they're missing something by being so cold but they don't know what it is." Timothy comes finally to realize the absurdity of his desperate hope that he may after all prove to be Eustace's son. He sees not only that "Eustace couldn't be anybody's father," but that this is "what every adult must have felt about him." Significantly, it will fall to Timothy, who is "not a Kinnit," to perpetuate the family name.

Timothy's admission that he has clung to his false hope reminds us how tempting illusions often are, how necessary, even; but the idea of romance as a valid factor in life is repeatedly scorned. Eustace's unemotional dismissal of Timothy's appeal is like "a pail of cold water" washing away his "romantic swaddling—clothes" and leaving him "quivering and ashamed of himself for ever clinging to them." Flavia Aicheson dives even deeper into fantasy by suggesting to Timothy that his paternity "could be very romantic and exciting" because "one never knows": but even Alison ridicules this idea. For Cornish, reality beats romance at its own game, and he explodes at Eustace's suggestion that "facts. . .are dull and even a trifle drab compared with a tale of fancy, all moonshine and romance." He sees the truth as taking "the shine out of any old invention," and insists that to find romance one "must go to reality." Later, he shows himself sufficiently irritated by what the "old sissy" has said to repeat his conviction to Luke: "No nurse made up a tale like the real one."

Interestingly, there is no confrontation between Cornish and his true polar opposite in the novel, Nanny Broome, Timothy's childhood nurse. His apt description of her as "an old butterfly clinging to its wings in a bombardment" makes the essential point that reality is something she keeps at bay. She dislikes "people who are always seeing snakes" and believes that if you "don't pull pussy's tail" she won't "scratch you." When some failure of sympathy in Julia reduces "cosy chatter to the status of an old wives' tale," a "scared look" passes over her face "as she glimpsed reality's fleeting skirt." Whatever the pressures, her way of life deliberately excludes anything approaching an unpleasant truth. Timothy remarks that she "screams the place down" if she thinks "something is merely naughty. . .but once she perceives what she feels is Evil, she hides." She is "deeply frightened" when her coat is slashed, not so much because of "the physical attack" as because of an "unclean shadow falling across her bright nursery world." When reminded of the damage to her coat, she is startled into admitting that she "wasn't going to think about that until the morning."

She is a deliberate anachronism, whose conversation has "to be heard to be believed" in "the world of today." She actually tries to create romance in real life and seems to derive many of her ideas from a hazy mediaeval ideal of courtly conduct. Timothy has clearly been raised on this sort of principle, with the aim of making him a "chivalrous gentleman with a proper attitude toward women": "I used to tell him about the knights riding in the courtyard, jousting and saving ladies and killing dragons and so on." As her little Prince Tim of the Rose-Red Castle," he has always been promised a princess, and when Julia arrives Nanny Broome welcomes her in exactly this spirit, "trembling with excitement" at the realization of the dream of over twenty years. She has prepared the Bride's Room for her, a cold, white Victorian showpiece, "monstrous" in its arid formality. Her fervent hope for a betrothal between Timothy and Julia exactly shows her longing for something holy and mystic to seal their love: again, without "any clear idea what she was talking about," she harks back to Arthurian legend for her inspiration: "Long, long ago the man knelt praying before a sword all night." She is invincibly and unashamedly "romantically-minded": even the prosaic "private" rooms of higher court judges take on the added fairy-tale fascination of "secret" chambers in her recollection.

She talks continually in a mindless nursery gush, reducing everything to kindergarten level: children are "kiddiwinkies" and Miss Saxon a "poor old girlie": Julia is instructed to stir her stumps, or invited to pretend that she's Cinderella. She herself is seen in juvenile terms: her character has a "child-like streak," her voice is "ever-young," and she moves with "the agility of a girl." Her "resilience" is "indefatigable," and after the momentary doubt that Julia inspires she is soon "talking away again as happy as a child uncovering a surprise"; understandably, her face is "never in repose in the ordinary way." She cries "like a baby, noisily, wetly, and with complete abandonment," and like a child keeps "one eye on the audience" when she knows she is being outrageous.

But beyond her role as arch-apostle of romance-arch, alas, in both senses—Nanny Broome is too often merely an irritant, a silly and embarrassing woman considerably less endearing than Miss Allingham presumably intended. Much of the "dismay" she initially inspires in Julia is increasingly felt by the reader. Timothy is conditioned to liking her but we have the advantage of detachment. She is another of the author's intensely feminine women and since she is also "possessive" and "tremendously authoritative," she is in danger of taking control. Campion call her "the ubiquitous Mrs. Broome" and Luke agrees that she "keeps on cropping up," bossy, inquisitive, interfering, with the eye of a hawk and the disruptive force of a steamroller. She horribly embarrasses Basil Toberman by reminding him publicly that he was always "an ugly little thing" afflicted by "that tiresome weakness," and, incredibly, reduces a blushing Luke "to half-pint size" with her parting shot. She has only to cry to inspire "terror" in men and render them "helpless," and her entry with Julia into Campion's flat has "the full force" of an "invasion," so that Lugg and Campion are "dispossessed in a matter of seconds." Though she is described as essentially "warm" and "unselfish," she makes quite a different impression: she is variously seen as "coy," "arch, affected," "smug," "cocky," "cross and prissy," "hard and obstinate," "sulky," "ruthless," "mutinous," "mindless" and "absurd."

Part of the trouble must be that we never see her in her element (not that one would particularly wish to do so). When the Keep was "invaded" by evacuee mothers and their eighty babies, she was clearly heaven-sent; and Luke's observation that it must have been "tremendous fun" to be brought up by her could well be true. But the action of the novel limits her to contact with adults, so that her relentless soppiness is inappropriate, unwelcome and finally tedious.

Despite the fact that meeting Nanny Broome explains to Julia "quite a lot about Timothy," he is largely kept clear of her whimsy (though he does at one point call Julia his "holy one"). He is drawn sympathetically and wholly as an adult (it is the young man he supplants who appears child-like). Julia, too, makes her position clear at the outset by the commendable "firmness" of her reaction to the bridal bedchamber. Miss Allingham is gamely concerned to show all aspects of their intimacy, attempting to define both the physical and emotional tensions they sustain. But for all her insight and experience as a writer, she invariably becomes self-conscious in such a context, so that a basic unease characterizes their scenes together, even when a degree of conviction is achieved. Because they are lovers—and embattled lovers at that—some of the author's composure deserts her and she falls into over-emphasis. The reader is subjected to the full battery of endearments, sighs and breaks in the voice, the involuntary cruelties, the sudden panic, and the surges in the blood. Julia feels "on her tongue" the "poison" distilled by "love kept waiting." Timothy's cry is "as old as civilization," his appeal "the ultimate. . .as young as childhood and as old as the world." His sudden fear that he may never be certain of Julia's love makes him pull back from her "in terror" to ask "the last question of all" (as if he has only to utter for everything to vanish).

Their bizarre encounter with Barry towards the end of the novel has a similar heightened quality. Timothy reacts to the first horrific sight of the intruder by laughing it off "in the only way left to this century's youth, which has had its fill of terrors." Barry's unexpected vaunting of himself as a reading man proves so startling that "it almost touched off hysteria." Even in the context of so weird an encounter, such observations seem excessive.

Though the development of the action does not need it, the scene is clearly crucial, since Barry appears nowhere else, and the theme of each generation's responsibility for itself is brought into focus. It is significant that only Timothy and Julia confront their contemporary:

Barry's articulate, confessional mood is prompted by their closeness to him in years: "You're about my age, aren't you?" and he dismisses the idea that "the old generation is responsible for the next": "It's your own generation that lives with you, isn't it? Blaming the bloody old fools doesn't help."

Timothy's acceptance of the responsibility of Barry seems a clear response to this belief: "He's our pidgin." When Julia objects that he "can't feel responsible for him," his reply is direct and conclusive: "Why not? He's our age and I caught him." A curious kinship develops between Barry and Timothy, subtly underlining our awareness that both have a claim to the same identity. Practically, it emerges in Timothy's reluctance to incriminate Barry and in his recognition that Barry's identity "appears to be all he has." Conversely, Timothy sees an attempt to kill Basil as "the older generation's headache": "We're not in that at all."

Though it is not made an explicit theme until so late in the action, the idea of conflict between the generations is implicit from the beginning in the coincidence that the violated flat in Ebbfield houses an elderly couple. It is seen in the interference of Julia's father in his daughter's life and the failures of communication between Timothy and his elders; and even, obliquely, in the Kinnits' constant expiation of the guilt of former generations.

The distance between age and youth is emphasized not only by Barry: the older generation has much to say on the matter. Joe Stalkey is the only one actually to say "I don't know what the younger generation is coming to," but both Luke and Cornish express concern on the subject. Julia's age alone is sufficient to make Luke "gloomy" with thoughts of the "teenage world" and some of the "young thugs" he encounters in his professional life. He detects "a frightening streak of efficiency in modern mischief" in the vandalism at Ebbfield and the fire in Stalkey's office: "they're very clever, these modern kids. They know how to gang up, too, better even than we did." Cornish is contemptuous of Timothy and his contemporaries who know nothing of true slum conditions: "Your generation doesn't know what that means. You call yourselves 'sick' don't you? So do I."

The idea of a "sick" generation with its own distinguishing marks emerges as a part of the author's observation. Timothy and Julia are momentarily frightened when Barry brandishes a monstrous "paw furnished with mighty bloodstained talons," but their shock changes to amusement when he uses it for an "offbeat joke which to any other generation must be indescribably shocking." Earlier, Timothy is described as a product of "an off-beat age" in which "absurdity as an escape-mechanism had been in fashion for some time."

When Julia sees Campion as a "natural goon, born rather too early," the author implies a kinship between him and the younger generation, and it is noticeable that he trusts them without question, whereas Luke is suspicious even of Julia (only when her distress at Timothy's defection reminds him of his own loss—of Prunella, who has died in childbirth—does he emerge as "unreservedly on her side"). Campion has a sufficiently "strong streak of sensitive interest in his fellow men" to relate with ease to all generations, and his encounters in the novel show him more as visiting sage and family friend that detective. He takes Julia out to lunch, talks shop with Basil, consoles Mrs. Telpher, and rescues Timothy from the Stalkeys. Julia finds him "very easy to talk to"; Eustace clings to him as to "the only spar in an angry sea"; and Nanny Broome agrees to talk to Luke in a pub only "if Mr. Campion says it's all right."

He is brought into the case by his friendship with Julia's father whom he has known since their Cambridge days, and an invitation to Angevin "to see some ceramics" confirms his involvement—though he is hardly involved in any real sense, since his watching brief allows him only nominal participation. Timothy's identity emerges largely through his own efforts, and the murderer is named by an eye-witness. Campion's concern for Nanny Broome's safety seems excessive in the light of the almost random attack that is made on her. Even in his advisory capacity he seems occasionally ineffectual: though Eustace welcomes him with glad cries to a discussion of legal representation for Timothy, his contributions to the debate are negligible (indeed, he is most conspicuously seen as "effacing himself with his usual success"). Later, he offers even a crucial observation with characteristic diffidence: "Mr. Campion, who had taken no part in the proceedings and who had been forgotten by everybody, now ventured to intervene apologetically."

Even in his earlier days, he was always modest and unassuming, a subtle variation on the theme of the great detective, rather than a full, flamboyant development of it. Now he describes himself as "old-ladyish" and seems subdued by his unobtrusive role to a gentle, consoling wraith. Though Lugg is still at Bottle Street and the echoes of former days persist—the vigilance, the social address, the deceptively "gormless" appearance—Luke begins to doubt whether Campion is "not a bit too nice" to come adequately to terms with "modern efficiency" in crime: his approach in like "riding in a Rolls" and, by implication, more suited to a vanished way of life. But it has always been a feature of their relationship that Campion should go at least one better than Luke, and he does so again, here, by providing the motive for Miss Saxon's murder and the attempt on Basil immediately after Luke has dismissed the likelihood of there being one. Not for nothing does Joe Stalkey call him a "legend."

Chapter 14
Edward's Hour

The Mind Readers, first published in 1965, is the last novel Margery Allingham was able to complete before her premature death in 1966. It is an astonishing performance, looking confidently to the future and yet harking back to the high exuberance of the adventure novels written at the outset of her career—and even beyond them, to the boys' papers for which her father so assiduously wrote. Like those earliest stories, it is essentially an escapade, in which sinister powers battle for the possession of a treasure, while Campion and his henchmen strive to make it secure: it becomes a race among spies, with a triumphant denouement that leaves even Campion outdistanced. The whodunit element is once again negligible: though a suspected defector is murdered, the question of who killed him remains a minor mystery and is soon resolved.

The treasure is an invention, and its safety is very much a personal matter for Campion since it heavily involves the Fitton family: Amanda's niece, Helena, daughter of Mary and Guffy Randall; her American husband, Martin Ferris; their eight-year-old son, Sam; and Helena's nephew, Edward Longfox, a grandson of Amanda's brother, Hal. Edward is nearly twelve, and since his father is dead and his mother abroad, Campion and Amanda are effectively *in loco parentis*. In London, the action centers on St. Petersgate Square, and though Meg and Sam Drummock have moved on, Canon Avril, Miss Warburton and Mrs. Talisman survive to make their contribution to events.

Despite the presence of these and other old favorites, personalities seem less important than usual in Miss Allingham's novels. The book is memorable for no single character, probably because the main theme is naturally disruptive of human affairs and, so, fundamentally inhuman. The author retains her exact eye for an idiosyncrasy and

215

she offers many characteristic insights: but there is little of the loving elaboration of a personality that shows elsewhere as one of her greatest strengths. Not since *Traitor's Purse* has she seemed so little concerned with characterization. It is instructive that Lugg has no part in this adventure; and if the deplorable figure of Thos. T. Knapp is to some extent compensation, his presence is in no way a self-indulgence, since his practiced skills in professional eavesdropping fit him exactly for the role he plays.

Once the treasure is identified, in the fifth of twenty-three chapters, it becomes the focus of attention for everyone in the novel, and what has seemed a rather clotted accumulation of odd goings-on suddenly achieves a welcome degree of clarity and single-mindedness. At the outset we are given too much information in an indirect way, and the narrative is dense with carefully placed hints and allusions intended to alert and intrigue but just as likely, alas, to confuse. The complex opening chapter deliberately teases us with five separate beginnings to the story, "five stirrings heralding the main movement." Of these five, only one ultimately justifies itself in terms of excitement for the reader: the odd appearance of the End of the World Man in two separate parts of London in impossibly quick succession. The others recede as the action progresses, so that pointers to later developments are in danger of being overlaid by further accretions of fact and innuendo. The reader will need to be very alert to remember his first encounter with the white cat that haunts Avril's rectory; or to identify its master from the fact that he is said to be "ladylike"; or to appreciate the pun in Chapter 22 on a name occurring only in Chapter 1; or to detect the elusive echo of Canon Avril's initial distress at having indirectly caused good by indulging a weak impulse.

Perhaps because the essential story is a simple one, there is a proliferation of subordinate complications: not only the two prophets of doom and the "promenading" cat and its master, but a leakage of information from Godley's island research station, where Martin works; a libel action looming at the boys' school; and the disappearance of Sam's bag of "schoolboy junk." Because Helena is prevented from leaving the island to meet Sam and Edward at Liverpool Street, they are subjected to an attempt to kidnap them. Something approaching a subplot forms around alleged attempts at suicide by Martin and defection by his chief, Paggen Mayo, but even these are dovetailed neatly into the main structure. Most of the tributary mysteries are solved well before the end (though the exact nature of the contents of Sam's vanished bag is not made absolutely clear until the novel's final page). Even the murder of Mayo does not puzzle Campion for long.

Despite this, and despite a strong double commitment—to Edward and his discovery—Campion's performance here is one of his least distinguished. The attempted kidnapping prompts his return to Security "in a temporary, unpaid and senior capacity"; but he is largely out of his element—as who would not be—and like everyone else is finally upstaged by Edward. His quick identification of Mayo's killer hardly avails him, since he finds the knowledge "less than nothing because he did not know the man," and, more practically, since he almost becomes his next victim (at the end of a typical late-Allingham confrontation). However, he maintains his reputation for resource during the encounter; and though he is saved by the standard eleventh-hour intervention, the nature of the summons alerting his deliverer is refreshingly untraditional.

The old Campion continues to surface from time to time. On his way to make a report he feels regret for his "lost illusions" and wishes he were "seeking some colorful contact lurking, perhaps, in a cabman's shelter, or . . .half way down the emergency staircase of an underground station" (though current procedure proves sufficiently bizarre, requiring him to converse by phone with a woman agent addressed, by "romantic subterfuge," as "Dearest," and to exchange intelligence by way of an arch and allusive "flood of commonplaces"). Amanda is briefly reminded of "someone she had half forgotten; a pale blank-faced youngster whose continuous flippancy had masked an acutely sensitive intelligence"; his "light voice" for a moment is "so casual that those who knew it best would have been alarmed"; and he even falls back on his oldest trick of all: "Deliberately Mr. Campion sounded sulky and looked marvellously ineffectual." In the act of "signing" the murderer's van with a nail-file, he continues to suggest that he is "civilized and essentially harmless. . .his pale horn spectacles. . .making him appear owlish and rather helpless."

In the larger action that develops around him, Campion really is "helpless": though Mr. Knapp describes him as Edward's "guardian angel," Edward in fact looks after himself and his discovery, while Campion watches and wonders. He is an astonishingly resourceful and capable boy, calm and controlled even at the eye of the storm. He seems properly part of an eccentric family and is repeatedly described as odd and exceptionally mature for his age, "strange" and "thoughtful," "a funny little grig. . . with something. . .dangerous and grown-up" about him "something odd. . .a sort of austerity." He and Sam sit in their railway-carriage "like little old men engrossed by inner cares," and he alerts the constable at Liverpool Street in formal, authoritative tones "unmistakable in background and temper." One of his teachers wonders "if he had ever been different even in his perambulator." He shakes hands "gravely" and appears at a difficult moment "like some shy elderly person overtaken by an awkward social situation." His "week-end belongings" are severely practical and a letter to "The Boy's Technician" is awesomely competent.

He organizes his disappearance with typical thoroughness and determination, acting responsibly at a practical level—relaying messages to assure Amanda of his safety—and with a "dedicated" appearance that argues fiercely for the dignity of his enterprise: "he's behaving as if he considers he is on a mission." Even the hostile Commander at Scotland Yard concedes that " *he* seems to know what he's doing next."

Miss Allingham gives Edward a scientific achievement worthy of him: he has "succeeded in mechanising telepathy": he and Sam are the mind readers of the title. From trial and error at school, they have discovered "a scientific instrument which makes reception absolutely foolproof": "a small silvery cylinder, about half an inch long," a "transistor valve" containing the "new element" Nipponanium. Its official title is "Longfox's Instant Gen," but Edward calls it an "iggy tube" from its initials, "I.G." Edward's iggy tube is strapped across his jugular vein but Sam is young enough to wear his under the arm. With their devices in position, Edward and Sam receive other people's thoughts and effectively read their minds.

The author puts the boys' discovery spectacularly to work. It is at the root of the libel action and provides at least a part of the motive for Mayo's murder. The bogus chaperone is exposed at the station when the boys quite simply read her thoughts. Campion is saved from death by Sam's reception of signals both from himself and from his would-be killer. After Mayo has commandeered the devices, Edward's need to secure a replacement brings him ultimately to a finale grander by far than even he has envisaged.

Even before the novel begins, Miss Allingham declares her faith in the invention, by her dedication: "To my technical advisers. . .in the hope that I get this tale out before they do." She has never wanted for conviction in the presentation of her ideas and she embraces her "amazing concept" with total commitment. When she writes about "the fascination which the subject held" for Martin, she projects her own enthusiasm through him: for her, as for him, the "phenomenon of thought transference" is clearly a permanent challenge. (One is reminded of the seances on Mersea Island from which her first novel derived, over forty years before this one.) The endeavor to read minds is a part of man's history, something "men have been trying to do. . .since civilisation began," something "recorded ever since writing began"; its achievement will "alter the landscape of history" and may prove even more frightening than "the Bomb." For Amanda, the breakthrough is "a secret which the Earth is giving up. . . *another shot in the locker*," something enormously exciting with infinite potential. She sees it as "bursting out all over the place once it's started" and reacts with horror to the suggestion of interference and suppression and the wrong kind of control: "Once a key has been found and recognised in science it's like taking the Queen's shilling; the experience is on."

For Miss Allingham, indeed, "the experience is on"; and the attempt to make all this credible provides her creative imagination with an irresistible stimulus, to which she responds with contagious zest and copious invention. In particular, the technical side of the novel is admirably achieved—the author's "advisers" clearly served her well. She sets the boys' experiments against a background of seasoned adult research at the highest level. They do not conjure their iggy tubes out of the air, and Edward is reasonably reproachful of the Canon's apprehensions: "You didn't really think we were being witchy, did you? We do come of scientific families. We don't go in for magic!" Edward's letter ends with an acknowledgement of his debt to the research team, so that the adult world is finally not without honor in the achievement of the breakthrough.

The boys are alerted to the potential of Nipponanium when it begins to figure in experiments on Godley's island; and the iggy tube even "sounds. . .like an enormously simplified version" of Paggen Mayo's device. But Mayo's essential beliefs run counter to the boys' discovery: "the notion that the bloodstream is involved is right against his line of thinking." Though his establishment of ESP as a scientific fact depends on a pair of abnormal twins, he fails to take the hint offered by the men's mental deficiency and persists in the assumption that the brain must generate the impulse that is transferred: his new device is "applied to the head." Only Martin seems to have seen any hint of the truth: he is most excited to learn that the devices are "strapped on a pulse" rather than a "nerve centre," and claims to have been "bawled out by Paggen time and again for muttering something not unlike this."

When the iggy tube is worn by a sophisticated adult, the result is "a mind-shattering experience." Emotional signals and impressions are released "like a pack of wolves," in a "total chaos." It is interesting— and frustrating—that all five of the men who try the device—Luke, Avril, Mayo, the journalist "Peggie" Braithwaite and the TV presenter Giles Jury—are highly gifted men; and it is disappointing that the potential effects on, say, Mayo's subnormal guinea pigs are not explored. For Luke the experience is "agony," as "one emotion after another" chases through his mind; and Avril is impelled "to pull the thing away" as the "cacophony" floods over him.

But the boys are protected by their relative inexperience of life which gives them a capacity to isolate a response from the bombardment they receive: they have, in effect, "another gadget. . . built in": "The younger you are the fewer people you know, the fewer emotions you arouse and the fewer the facts of which you are aware." Edward is already less adept than Sam at operating the device because he is three years older; and he is properly "contemptuous" of a suggestion that a master might have trained them: "Masters would be useless!" because far too old.

Though the boys escape the adult "brainstorm," "experience of being shouted down by other people's casual thoughts" does leave its mark on them. Under the influence of his iggy tube, Sam undergoes a sufficiently startling change to prompt an alarmed letter from his headmaster; and Helena fears for a time that he has "forgotten how to use his head," so that he is briefly reduced to the therapy of sorting buttons. Even Edward is forced to concede that "the one bad thing about the iggy tube" is its inducement of "gen fatigue": "It did stop one thinking clearly."

Miss Allingham uses the boys' perceptions in a variety of ways, for effect, to solve a mystery, to show insight into personality. Sam has the lion's share and usually makes the most impact. It is he who precipitates the libel action and utters the most provocative remarks; he, too, who saves Campion and confirms beyond doubt Paggen Mayo's jealousy of his father: "All his thoughts and feelings go dithery when he sees you." Edward shares in the routing of the kidnapper, but his most spectacular performance is reserved for the denouement, when he receives and interprets relays from a friend in Paris.

The transmission from Paris establishes the validity of Longfox's Instant Gen for interested parties encountering it for the first time, but its more important function is to show the device living devastatingly up to its name. The prepared message sent by Edward's friend is projected only vaguely: it is quite overshadowed by the vivid involuntary message he was unaware he was sending. The shocked reaction of an unauthorized listener (subtly enhanced, perhaps, by her own position as an eavesdropper) enforces the point: "But it was his *secret*. . . That was the thing he *wasn't* telling." The "sort of horror" that she feels crystallizes the threat posed by the device, and serves as a climax to a series of earlier reactions—Miss Warburton's to the Canon's suggestion of "Popular Pocket Omniscience": "What a wicked idea!"; Avril's own observation that the iggy tubes are "bad manners—if nothing worse"; and Luke's bleak "vision of a dreadful over-intimate world in which every thought is absolutely communal."

Even without the iggy tube, the world of the novel is a grim enough place. The opening paragraphs present a picture of a revitalized London and look to a rosy future—but the narrative moves ironically on to introduce the End of the World Man! With characteristic resource, the author uses him not only as an outmoded Cassandra figure in a world where even the threat of "the Bomb" is "old hat," but as someone whose very persona is usurped in the interest of his country's enemies. This world is such that not even a prophet of doom can be trusted.

Informers, spies and schemers move against a background of bugging, power-seeking and complicated treachery, where double-dealing is standard and treble-dealing not unknown. There are spies on the island, in the school, on the station, in a teashop, in Fleet Street, and, briefly, even, in the Rectory kitchen. They themselves are often under observation: the name of the junior science master is "on the list of American doubtfuls," and as the would-be kidnapper takes to her heels a man "who had been loitering" sets off in pursuit. Privacy is under siege and the phone has become a weapon for the enemy. Technicians from Advance Wires, Mr. Knapp's firm, expertly bug the flat in Paris and effectively prevent communication with the Rectory. From housing Advance Wires Godley's island has the most comprehensive electronic resources but "no such thing as a reasonably reticent wire. . .let alone a private one." Edward's exchanges with his Parisian friend are relayed to a soundproof "monitoring theatre" on the island. Thos. himself is convinced that "the word 'private' is going plumb out of date. It's going to be an ole—fashioned concep'. . . .That's a prophecy" (and though he speaks from the standpoint of the oldest wire-tapper of them all, he, too, is aware of the new development: "No wires, no toobs, no frequencies, no beams. Nothing. Just 'ead to ruddy 'ead!") To survive is to be "compelled to take avoiding action"—like the cat-owner's resort to milk-bottles and the Book of Revelation; Miss Warburton's delivery of an excessive number of "clean surplices"; and Campion's use of "that safest of all telephone wires, the one belonging to a public callbox one has never used before and never intends using again." (On a less reliable line, the cozy exchanges with "Dearest" prove less than impregnable.)

The want of a private line on Godley's island epitomizes the numbing inhumanity of that "godforsaken" place, which, perhaps uniquely, combines with its total denial of privacy a bleak and daunting solitude. Images of desolation persist: Martin sees "no sign of life whatever" in "a scene of despair in a desolate world"; he and Sam "might have been alone in the world on the grey marsh"; their hut rises "dark and forlorn in the disconsolate scene"; and Campion is both overwhelmed by "the forlorn emptiness all round him" and aware that "he was scarcely more visible than a reed in the wide expanse of marsh and sky."

The island is destructive of human relations: Martin's marriage is threatened, Mayo's virtually destroyed. The men are there to work, the women because they are married to the men: they have no creative or rewarding occupation beyond the limitations this implies: "They try to pretend they're having a life." To Paggen Mayo women are simply adjuncts to men, their demands invariably irksome. He has no time for his wife, who is "desperately unhappy" as a result, and he sees Helena's concern to meet her son as irrelevant: having officially denied her transport, he reminds her that the island is "a research establishment, not a creche."

Helena's discontent is implied at the outset by Miss Warburton—"that marriage could founder if they drive him like that"—and her first words are a fanciful proposal to decorate and disguise the "converted army hut" in which she has to live. As her conversation with Martin develops, what are clearly familiar grievances rise to the surface and threaten to jolt them into a quarrel; but both are aware of the tensions between them and concerned to avoid a breach, and they are able to move from "hurt" and "anger" to a sudden awareness of "all the warmth and tenderness of their affection for each other." There is every hope for them, but none for the Mayos, even before his death puts an end to their shared misery. Both are rendered emotionally unstable by the pressures upon them, and what remains of their "most uncomfortable marriage" is inadequate to prevent both from being driven to extremes.

Fred Arnold, the barman and general factotum, is the other considerable figure on the island (we never actually meet the resident "great man," Professor Tabard, who heads the research project.) He

is established from the first as an enigma—"That's a strange guy"—
out of place on the island because of the very competence that makes
him such an asset to the community: he instructs and entertains Sam,
acts as butler for visiting VIP's, manages the canteen "as if it belonged
to the Ritz," and serves generally as "the only link. . .with normal
everyday life." Martin's remark "We're lucky to have him" immediately
implies that such luck should be suspect: and the point is made explicit
when Luke wonders why Arnold remains "down there" when, "with
his qualifications," he "could earn so much more anywhere else."

In the same way, when Helena describes him as "almost the only
ordinary normal person in the place," Luke at once assumes that
he must be "part of the security squad"; and "Dearest" soon confirms
that Arnold's responsibilities indeed extend beyond food and drink
for the island. Campion learns the full extent of his other commitments
too late for the information to be of use. Ironically, his earliest
reflections about the man suggest much of the truth about him: he
seems"an almost perfect example of . . .the communal manservant.
. .a peculiar type, not particularly happy, as if the hero's friend and
knave of classic story had been translated by a multiplicity of masters
into the loneliest of dogs, unattached and in business on his own."

The duality of the man's nature evidently fascinates the author,
and she shows him combining his two roles and also expressing the
same aspect of his personality in both areas of his life. His answers
to Campion's questions about Martin's supposed suicide bid are
perfectly correct, yet they illumine repeatedly the background of
contrivance and suspicion that characterizes the episode: information
is "adroitly delivered"; there is "no mistaking his emphasis"; his
"underlying amusement was intensified although he spoke most
respectfully." He is seen in two contexts as a "natural improviser
...stimulated rather than daunted by an unexpected difficulty": once
as "the indefatigable Fred Arnold, who could usually find a meal
for a friend in an emergency"; and once in an altogether more desperate
situation, when he needs a new weapon at short notice. By a final
irony, even his death reminds us of both sides of his life, since he
is killed by one of the tools of his more public trade.

In both his capacities, Fred Arnold is employed by Lord Ludor, a great communications mogul, who owns Advance Wires and finances Godley's research team. With infinitely more power than Arnold, he has much the same basic end: to exploit for his own purposes the unscrupulous world he helps to shape. Many of the people he employs are spies in one way or another: Arnold, the Advance Wires crew, "that celebrated 'fixer' 'Pa' Paling" (whose miscalculation in Chapter 1 does not come home to roost until Chapter 21). His investment in Godley's is intended to give him control over the invention "when it comes": so that he may "stifle it" should it prove a "threat to his business interests"; or wield it as a "secret weapon" in extending his empire; or use it, as Campion suggests, to move beyond "controlling vast quantities of people" to acquiring "complete power over the *individual.*" Having been "virtually omnipotent in his own particular empire," he sees the invention as his means to become "very nearly omniscient as well."

Although he is seen once as a comic ogre roaring in a fairy tale ("' *I want that boy,*' he said and might well have added 'Fee-Fi-Fo-Fum' Mr. Campion reflected, stung to laughter"), he is in general "as real and ugly as a busted atom," "a great big brutal demigod of whom everybody he comes into contact with soon becomes openly afraid." He is inhuman to the point where, like Jack Havoc, he seems more animal than man; but where Havoc was a tiger, Ludor is an ape, "an old male gorilla sitting on the top of his own dark tree" or achieving what he wants "by merely stamping towards it through the undergrowth." There is an "actual likeness between him" and the "life-size portrait of the fully-grown male gorilla" hanging in the "jungle fastness" of his mistress' apartment.

But though she fears Lord Ludor, Miss Allingham reserves her ultimate hatred for traitors, in particular for "the few who were natural traitors, the instinctive children of decay." She writes with contempt of the "small networks" of spies, nicknamed "Fungi. . .because they resembled patches of dry rot, their ever-growing tentacles streaming out from a parent eye," and she condemns the "filthy business" in which they engage, "as chill and stinking as dry rot itself." Campion's surprise at finding himself"emotionally involved in the safety of the invention" is contrasted with the cynicism of the man who tries to kill him, who scoffs at the idea that he, too, might "care who gets the invention": "Care? What are you? The Boys' Book of Heroes?" Because it "will be the death of" men like this, the "snakes in our society,"Campion suggests the invention be called the "St. Patrick," and he goes on to invoke "the old curse" already uttered against his enemy by an earlier victim of his treachery: "On your belly shall you go and dust shall you eat." When Campion reports the traitor's end, the author comments in deliberately emotional terms on what the country has gained by his death: "thus another patch of fungus in the oaken timbers of the old British warship was successfully sealed off for treatment." She seems to enforce the point by using an outmoded idiom in the vein scorned by the dead man.

At the end, both "the old British warship" and the invention are secure; one traitor is dead, the others disarmed; Campion is relieved, Lord Ludor outmaneuvered, and Edward triumphant. The outlook seems set fair, as Sam looks forward to his Ph.D.; Lord Ludor shows a human aspect in defeat; and Edward's sponsors profess a reassuring concern that each man's thoughts should continue to be his own preserve: "Men and women have a right to privacy that. . .will never. . .be violated." In addition, the unaccountable opening salvo of the novel is finally vindicated as the first indication of the concluding theme: that "the educated children. . .full of the future" will meet the demands made on them, by the invention or, by implication, by anything else.

Earlier doubts and fears are overridden by the pattern that emerges in the closing sequence: Amanda's fears of suppression, Luke's dread of a world with no secrets, Campion's worry as to which are "the right hands, which the wrong hands" to take charge. Luke's confession that he cannot "see *any* man" behind Edward is nearer the truth than he knows, less an admission of defeat than an indication that he needs to lower his sights a little, since there is no *man* there. As always, Campion is one step ahead: though out of his depth, he is not prevented from seeing the truth.

His perception derives, oddly enough, from Mr. Knapp, whose unending reminiscences are punctuated with the occasional stretch of sound sense. As he recalls the early days of wireless, Thos. begins to make the point: "Do you remember what we was like. . .when

Marconi first got going'?. . .Proper little wizards me and my lot was; in fac', we was the only part of the general public who understood it at all. Anybody over thirty was too thick to take it in." Later, he traces the developments in electronics during his lifetime, matching each stage to the man whose own maturity coincided with it: "Myself, I'm a Whisker man at heart. The Spark, he's born Toobs. Feeoh is a right Transistor type and we've got a youngster with a hooter for Light." His own experience shows him the pattern to justify his view that "Each noo step forwards has its generation of born technicians delivered with it. Along comes the idea, up comes the personnel, know-how built in." Because he has repeatedly seen it happen, he can accept with ease that it will happen again: "Now something else is coming. . .I can understand kids being important in it. You want a very fresh mind to understand a very fresh thing."

As even Edward has already allowed, Sam's mind is much the freshest of those involved, and it is he who, by right of juniority, is "in it from the start," not Lord Ludor, to whom the words are in fact applied. Sam and the invention will mature together, and Campion is right to believe that "any attempt of Lord Ludor's to control this thing is pathetic." Ludor himself appears to acknowledge something of the sort in the final exchange of the novel, between him and Sam; but though the boy politely acknowledges the offer of a job in ten years' time, he doubts the wisdom of Ludor's promise: "There's going to be a lot of change in the next ten years. You may not have anything for me to do." It is fitting that Sam should have the last word and that the novel should end with an outburst from Ludor that reduces him to the ranks of common humanity.

Chapter 15
Out With a Bang

Cargo of Eagles is the last of Margery Allingham's novels, published posthumously in 1968, two years after her death. Miss Allingham died before it was finished, but a reassuring note guarantees its authenticity: the "whole fabric" of the story "had been mapped out long before her death," and she specifically requested its completion by her husband and "partner for nearly forty years," Philip Youngman Carter, himself an accomplished writer. Although Edmund Crispin claimed in his review to be able to see the join, the book has the force and coherence of a unified whole, in no way diminished by the enforced collaboration. It is, in fact, vintage Allingham, a total success in her lighter vein, vivacious, various and enticingly mysterious. Zestful and fantastic like the earliest stories, it is also subtle and stylish like the later ones, combining detection with a treasure hunt and high spirits with the deftest control.

As so often before, the action moves between London and East Anglia, not Suffolk on this occasion, but Essex, in the coastal area beyond the author's real-life home in Tolleshunt D'Arcy. Saltey, like Mystery Mile, is "virtually an island," "on the road to nowhere" and "cut off by the saltings." It is approached through "a waste of worked out clay pits," now "turned into a wilderness," a "no man's land" with a "hair-raising" history. Its situation "on the end of an escape route" has for centuries dictated its role as "London's back door," "the funnel through which secret goods or people were smuggled in or out of East London." Its harbor, now, is "all that is left of the ancient bolthole, old London's eastern emergency exit."

For Mortimer Kelsey, a young American historian, Saltey is "a honey of a find," "full of good things." He is working on "a paper ...on London's approaches in the seventeenth and eighteenth centuries," and he finds in Saltey an embarrassment of riches: "If

I don't stick to my own period I'll be lost in a morass of information."
The "heyday" of the village "was probably pre-Saxon," and Morty
suspects "an early fortress. . .just waiting to be uncovered." Picturesque
names, "as ancient as anything in England," suggest a "dateless"
antiquity: the surname of a local farmer evokes the Green Man himself,
and the original name of the Demon Inn raises a similar echo. More
to Morty's purpose is a link with Mob's Hole, "a rakehelly dive"
established "in Wanstead about seventeen ten or so" (its existence
confirmed by "a fine, fruity account. . .in *The London Spy*").

Saltey, for Morty, is initially an "absurd place," "perfectly
enchanting in an off-beat sort of way" and with a population "almost
entirely vegetable." He questions whether "they think at all" and finds
their pretense of being "deeply and secretly wicked. . .naive and kind
of endearing." But increasing experience of Saltey undermines this
mistaken view and reminds him repeatedly of his "alien" status: he
is "very much a foreigner," an intruder in the village who can never
hope to understand its ways. He reaches a peak of disenchantment
when the arrival of a particularly vicious anonymous letter moves
him to curse "this godforsaken countryside with its sly venom and
its abominable secrets."

There is no pretense about Saltey's wickedness and nothing
"naive" or "endearing" about its people, who are more accurately
described as "smiling savages playing stupid," "pig ignorant and.
. .enjoying the fact." It is easy to draw up a crowded roster of potential
poison pens with the "roots of sin" in them. Trouble is inevitable
in such a "Contrary hole" with its long tradition of "native mischief—
the natural evil of the locality." Morty is warned against "Evil" and
a whole spiteful catalog of sin from the prayer book: "Envy, hatred,
malice and all uncharitableness."

For various reasons, Saltey's dislike of strangers is endemic and
the characteristic resentment of outsiders shows itself continually. The
locals are not so much "feudal" as "tribal," so surly and "suspicious"
that "they won't let you in the house if they can help it." Property
is all-important—"Their great interest is the contents of each other's
wills"—so that a bequest to a stranger raises "a fine old poison pen
storm" and prompts a chain of broken bottles across the approach
road. Under pressure from a full invasion, the "true inhabitants" lock

and bar their houses "as for a siege, offering no welcome to visitors."
At such times the village seems hostile, even sinister, "a secret place,
shrouded but still slyly awake."

The villagers obstruct authority as a matter of course, presenting
a united front against the police. "Saltey doesn't take kindly to the
law," and a wealthy farmer threatens any policeman who "puts so
much as a foot" on his land with "a backside full of lead." It is
futile for the police to investigate the poison pen campaign: "They'll
never get near it in a month of Sundays." The community reacts
as one to questioning, with a "dumb insolence" that yet maintains
a "grudging" minimal semblance of cooperation: there is "no loophole
in the facade, nothing to suggest conspiracy or even simple concealment
by omission."

Saltey offers only passive resistance to the police but meets more
active aggression head-on. When a group of city "tearaways" stirs
up trouble at the Demon, the men of Saltey welcome the chance to
settle old scores: "The resentment of the local men against the possessive
arrogance of invading strangers had reached the point of no return.
Each man sought out his opposite number, happily determined to
repay months of calculated insult." In an earlier confrontation, even
Morty crosses the line, applying first principles of Vere University's
"course on self-defence" to initiate a rout-though it is typical of Saltey
that he becomes not the hero of the hour but of "the minute before,"
his decisive lead quickly "forgotten."

The aggressors form a part of Saltey's alternative society, a
"caravan and tent lot" who "can mostly find a shed or a hut to doss
in if they don't want to go home." They are members of one of "the
wilder teenage gangs," "ton-up types" in "the ritual uniform of their
kind. . .tight blue faded jeans, decorative boots and leather coats,"
their hair in "scruffy ringlets," their eyes inscrutable behind "dark
glasses" that give them "a calculated anonymity with an underlying
note of menace."

Already the Mods and Rockers of the 1960's are a part of social
history, supplanted now by the Punk movement as they themselves
supplanted the Teds of the 1950s. Miss Allingham's gang are rockers,
"who by definition ride more powerful machines than mods and who
make a display of living dangerously." They are apt exemplars of

"the viciousness of modern youth," noisy and disruptive, "militant" and "menacing," often "as high as kites," "crazed with drugs or drink." They destroy the peace with transistors or firecrackers or the "insolent gunfire" of motor-bike engines. They dance naked on the sea-wall and establish "a rough-riding circuit of the inn regardless of property."

At times they are "actively" frightening, with a disturbing suggestion of violence held only casually in check. They favor "strong arm tactics" to impose their will and make their demands "with conscious truculence." Their behavior is "intentionally shocking," inducing "discomfort and unease" and "creating an atmosphere of dangerous uncertainty." Their storm-trooper garb obliterates sexual distinction and intensifies their aura of menace: for all their plaints about freedom, they affect a para-military "uniform. . .as rigid as a subaltern's at a Trooping."

To some extent the author sees them as part of a continuing tradition of aggressive license and explosive contempt for the restraints of conventional society. The point is repeatedly made that each era has its "tearaways," that "the ranks of disorder" are not a modern phenomenon. The Saturday of the Whit holiday is "one of those days which Ned Ward, the London Spy, would have recognized as belonging to his own age," and a group of extremist weekend invaders "might have come from a quattro cento harlequinade." Saltey's history is such that "the shenanigans" of the gang "don't seem half as modern as they might," and Morty's eyewitness account of an "occasional orgy" on the sea-wall is much in the spirit of his description of Mob's Hole. In particular, Doll Jensen, the "ringleader" of the gang, would have found her element in Ned Ward's London. Her vagrant life and aggressive sexuality establish her kinship with the whores and rogues who rode out of the city for "a barbecue and a punch-up": (the implicit parallel between two ages is confirmed by the author's modern usage in an eighteenth century context).

And yet the spirit of Ned Ward is, after all, lacking in these modern counterparts of his Queen Anne riff-raff. A positive note informs the brief passage from *The London Spy* that precedes the narrative, and a vigorous enjoyment characterizes the account of a progress to Wanstead. But the modern youths deny any such concept of communal delight: their view of life is negative and their pleasures are destructive.

Their idea of leisure activity is to "organize punch-ups at the coastal resorts mostly just for the heck of it"; they enjoy their "orgy" the more because Morty is unnerved by it; and they play darts in "truculent isolation," "giggling amongst themselves when one of the feathered needles went dangerously wide of its mark." What they take from the past they distort and debase: music is reduced to an "adenoidal moan," spraying the air "with a confetti of competing rhythms." What is already offensive becomes even more so: a catapult is refined into "a modern and vicious version of the ancient device"; and demonic masks transcend "echoes of the ancient pit" to achieve a shocking "modernity" of "mindless wickedness."

For all that he is near the gang in age, Morty is disconcerted by the defiant naked dance of which he is such a reluctant witness. Doll in particular disturbs him and he expresses a fear that he may be "growing old." Even when her sexual play for him confirms that they are of the same generation, he again feels "old" in comparison, and as their physical intimacy increases, their values increasingly diverge. Morty can only reject the gang's need to alleviate boredom by violence, even to the point of endangering such limited stability as they have: "There was a gap here which he could not bridge. The philosophy of life, if it could be defined by such a phrase, was beyond his grasp."

Doll and the gang show the author for the last time absorbing a social phenomenon into the fabric of one of her books: they are real and she presents them as they are. But a mystery novel is not a social document and she sets them deliberately in a traditional context; and though they are not subdued by their environment, neither do they challenge the essentially civilized tone of a typical Allingham entertainment. Mr. Campion has "a watching brief" and other old friends make characteristic contributions: Oates, now "older than God," but with his raconteur's flair intact, entertains friends and clients in the basement of a London club so reactionary as to be "on the direct route to embalmment"; and Lugg still "shoots the most magnificent line" in the raciest and least predictable of styles. Morty's romance with a woman doctor commands our sympathy throughout; and if its tensions are occasionally deeply felt they are no less convincing for being lightly stated.

For all its perversity, Saltey is Allingham territory, in its antiquity, in its secrets, in its seclusion. It has a stylish map, dating from 1758; a "grandiose" ghost town in its hinterland; and a colorful legend, buttressed by fancy cakes and a whimsical booklet. Its reporter is a daughter of the manor, relict for thirty years of Hugo Weatherby, Esquire; and its publican is a "genuine minor poet," who "shot up like a rocket and vanished," his early success apparently without sequel in an enigmatic lifetime of "silence."

Mrs. Weatherby is a particular triumph, a credible eccentric in the author's richest vein, lovingly observed and irresistibly tonic in effect. She holds her own with such seasoned charmers as Oates and Lugg, and her talk contains something of the best of both, combining Oates' exhaustive knowledge of his terrain with the bizarre eclecticism of Lugg's utterance. Indeed, her speeches derive more truly from life than Lugg's, so that they have a plausibility lacking at times in the baroque lingo he affects. Her conversational style embraces the odd rural metaphor, but leans most heavily on breezy cliches and antiquated slang. She gets "down to brass tacks" and argues "straight from the shoulder." A quarrel is "an up and a downer" and a lucky encounter a "right and a left straight off." A precautionary measure is a "jolly good wheeze" and a sudden departure "a moonlight flit." She suspects a neighbor "inclined to blow his top" of having "skedaddled"; and hopes that Morty will "see her pronto" since she can't "stay more than half a jiffy." After calling her office on "the blower," she deplores the grime that accumulates in telephone boxes—"Not enough grooming done to keep them tickety boo." Since it is "Too early for a snifter," she proposes "a chinwag" over coffee; later, she orders "a Harry pinkers" from the bar. In search of "the gen about who's really been kept in the cooler," she plans to "drop in at the Cop-shop."

She is "a tall thin woman" in her fifties, with "wild white hair" and "sharp intelligent eyes set above a nose which would have looked normal on an eagle." As gauche as a schoolgirl, she seems at times to be "carrying an invisible hockey stick," and she has "long since substituted a friendly heartiness for the feminine charm which eluded her." But despite her lack of conventional womanly appeal, Morty finds her attractive and "endearing": she is "autocratic" but in a "slap-happy" way that is "disarming."

Her manner is direct and "emphatic" and her voice holds "the unmistakable note of authority which long country breeding brings to women of gentle birth." She reacts to a suspicion of drug traffic in Saltey with the fierce concern of a squire's lady for her "hundred": distributing "dope" is a "dirty business" that must be blown "sky high": "I won't have it. . .It's got to be stopped." When, in her vehemence, she raps the table, Morty is "vividly reminded of his first schoolmistress."

She has a brisk way with inanimate objects, thumping the telephone, slamming her case onto the table, and kicking the support on her scooter. Her "large sensible shoes" are well adapted to the "slogging tread of a route-marcher" that she adopts for walking, and she swings "her shoulder bag as if it were a set of golf clubs." She wears "an outsize wrist watch" and quarters her territory on her "phut-phut," controlling it with such "impressive flair" that she can turn in the saddle at bends in the road to wave to a car behind.

Her insight into her neighbors is acute and unsparing and she assesses them with devastating candor: one is an "acid little runt with duck's disease," and another "a toothy vixen. . .with a mind like a cesspool." She describes herself in equally unflattering terms—as "an interfering old witch" with a face "like a dilapidated barn-owl." Perhaps because she regards curiosity as her own preserve, she disapproves of it in others, applauding a move to "keep out snoopers and nosy parkers," and deploring the need of Saltey's residents to "know their neighbour's business."

She clearly regards her own omnivorous curiosity as licensed by her profession: "I always tell 'em 'I only ask because I want to know' and that's how I earn my living." As a journalist, she is very much a professional, always on the alert for a potential story and resentful of casual intruders into her own specialist field: "too many people. . .cash in" on a fire: "they get a cut price and do honest journalists out of a job." She sees it as "all to the good" that a murder remains unsolved and looks forward to a decent number of arrests after a police raid. She hopes "the worst" of the "moonlight flit" she uncovers because a "disaster. . .would make tophole copy."

Mrs. Weatherby is the supreme example in the novel of the author's gift for high-spirited invention disciplined by intelligence, but there are many smaller details of "decorative embroidery" that briefly offer a similar pleasure: the ironing of the bootlaces at the Ottoman Hotel; the advertisement for "McNab's Dew of Kirckcudbright" at the Cap and Bells; the "Fertility Venus" exhumed near Saltey and now reposing in the "horror comic room" at the British Museum; the pub entertainer who vibrates "a pair of spoons. . .dexterously over every available section of his person"; Oates' recollection of an East End "snake farm"; and the "fabled collection of George III silver" at his London base. More significant factors are distinguished by the same vein of controlled creative fancy. The bottles strewn across the road have connoisseur labels; the local legend derives in fact from an inspired method of distracting attention from a batch of burnt cakes; the octogenarian cadging drinks from a corner at the Demon helped to launch the legend as a "miscreant" child; and the anonymous letters prove to be the latest in a series of works "with remarkable literary qualities." Even death in Saltey has a certain bizarre style. The village has wondered for twenty years about the undertaker found dead in one of his own coffins; the "ancient mariner" at the Demon is literally shaken to death, and a silver bullet kills the local solicitor in the house at the center of the poison pen storm.

Despite the gap of twenty years between the undertaker's death and those of the lawyer and the old man, all three stem from the same basic circumstance: the conveyance of a great treasure to Saltey soon after the war. The central excitement of the novel derives from the treasure and the race to locate and possess it. Most of the series of "Unexplained Incidents" appear to arise from a desire to protect the hoard or greed for so great a gain: the murders, the anonymous letters, the glass in the road, a calculated fire, and a whole string of assaults and break-ins.

If some of these circumstances suggest no more than anger at the perverse bequest of the house to a stranger, the majority point to a "reign of terror" in the style of two criminal veterans from Saltey's past, the notorious James Teague and "Target" Burrows, "the biggest villains for miles" in the years before the war. Neither has been seen for twenty years, Teague because he has been in prison, Burrows because he is thought to have "got clean away out of the country" and remained abroad. Now Teague is out of jail and already he has evaded the watch kept on newly released prisoners.

Both Teague and Burrows were irredeemably wicked men, vicious and destructive on a scale undreamed of by Miss Allingham's teenage toughs. Teague was "a natural killer with practical wartime experience," "a coldblooded adventurer," "so reckless that you could say he was mad." Burrows was less flamboyant, more brutish, "a shifty, foulmouthed bully," "sly" and "feckless" and so detested that "Every man would play Judas to him given the chance." But for all Teague's explosive instability and Burrows' "ugly reputation," their joint impact is muted by the distancing effect of twenty years. We are asked to take their wickedness on trust, rather as, earlier, we were expected to endorse the heroic qualities of Johnny Carados without ever having seen them.

In addition, both men are hung about with romantic trappings that further diminish them as dangerous killers in the Havoc mold and bring them into line as swash-buckling rogues in a more picaresque vein. Teague was "very colourful," "a violent, magnetic, unpredictable animal" whom no woman could resist, "one of those larger than life characters who resent any events which don't match up to their own idea of themselves"; and Burrows had a glass eye, over which he sometimes wore an eyepatch, like Long John Silver or the elder Douglas Fairbanks. Their criminal record enhances the theme: their prewar staple was smuggling, regarded in Saltey more "as a sport" than as a crime, and their crowning exploit was an actual pirate raid conducted "on the high seas." Comments by professional observers make the point explicit. Mrs. Weatherby remarks that smuggling "has a fine, romantic ring about it—once aboard the lugger, yo heave ho and all that kind of malarky"; and the local inspector jeers at the improbably "romantic" image of "The last of the Pirates. . . Dashing Jim Teague and One-Eyed Target." Appropriately for two such florid villains, both had bravura "trademarks. . .well known. . .in Saltey": Burrows announced his returns to the village by throwing stones to hit a weathercock; and Teague, believing that only a silver bullet could kill him, "used them himself in case anyone else had the same theory."

The silver bullet in the solicitor is only one of the "little bits of this and that" indicating that Teague and Burrows have come at last to collect their pirate hoard. The superior labels on the scattered bottles suggest the "parcel of booze" in the loot from the yacht they boarded; Morty is said to have been coshed by a man with "a black patch over one eye"; stones are again rattling against the weathercock; and the old codger is shaken to death soon after his public pronouncement of having "seen a ghost."

Mr. Campion, like everyone else, follows these signs to their logical conclusion, and the action is well advanced before he is forced to think again. But though he is fazed by appearances for far too long in a case with a pressing deadline, he commands respect even when on the wrong tack, and he has his usual small successes on the way— a "long shot" that rescues a kidnap victim; an insight into the poet's course during his "forgotten" years; and a devastating analysis of the anonymous letters. Even after his "downfall" there is still a shot in his locker, and he is able to counter "Elsie" Corkran's fears that they are "back to square one" with the hope that "one or two untidy threads" may yet lead "out of the labyrinth."

Corkran is about to retire as Head of Intelligence and has pressed Campion into service for the last time. In "extreme emergency," the Department has been denied official aid, so there is a score to settle as well as a crisis to resolve: Campion's mission is to meet the extremity but also to further Corkran's ambition to slip "a final fast one past the New Establishment." Both men know the history of the Saltey treasure and Campion intends not only to get to it first but to "misappropriate it" for "an excellent reason." As on former occasions he plays a lone hand, independent of the police and anxious, even, to deflect "official attention" from Saltey, since Teague, if caught, will "die with his secret." His aides are amateurs, whether new recruits like Morty and Mrs. Weatherby or old hands like Lugg and Oates, under no official allegiance since his retirement. Even at the end, the police are excluded, so that Campion may "compound a felony" and let the killer go free (ostensibly because Campion's responsibilities "are to the living, to the future," but actually because by then he has already commandeered the treasure).

For all his godlike resolve to allow the killer to evade punishment, Mr. Campion remains, as ever, the least assertive of men, modest and reflective, patient and benevolent, "a celebrated figure," but only "in his own apologetic way." His "careful veil of affable vacuity" is worn like a"second skin" and there is still the possibility that he may seem "negligible until...just too late." He speaks "gently" even when there is "no kindness in his tone," and his gripping exposition is delivered in a "diffident murmur." But he controls the final sequence with an assurance matching anything in his long career. From a hazy recollection of a photograph he identifies the cache, and by taking up the last of his "threads" he closes in at last on the killer. He provides a Biblical text as an exact forecast of the final scene, and with a fine sense of theater literally unmasks the murderer, stage-managing the subsequent revelations with a shrewd showmanship calculated to achieve exactly the effect he wants. It's a fine swan song, for Campion, of course, but more particularly for Miss Allingham: though his career is continued in two sequels by Youngman Carter, for her this was the end.

Margery Allingham:
A Checklist of Her
Books and Stories

A. Crime fiction: books

1. *The White Cottage Mystery*
Serialized in abridged form in 'The Daily Express' in 1927
First edition: Jarrolds, June 1928 (not dated)
Purple binding, orange lettering on spine and front cover
Dust-wrapper by Youngman Carter
New abridged edition, Chatto & Windus 1975, with a preface by
Joyce Allingham, who made the abridgement
Penguin 1978, in abridged text

2. *The Crime at Black Dudley*
First edition: Jarrolds, February 1929 (not dated)
Dust-wrapper by Youngman Carter
Penguin 1950: Uniform edition, Heinemann 1967
In: *The Margery Allingham Omnibus* (Penguin 1982)
Variant title: *The Black Dudley Murder*
First edition: Doubleday 1930
Two Amalgamated Press abridgements have this title:
(i) Thriller Library No. 15, 7. February. 1935
(ii) Bestseller Series No. 1, 1. July. 1936

3. *Mystery Mile*
First edition: Jarrolds, January 1930 (not dated)
Red binding, black lettering on spine
First U.S. edition: Doubleday 1930
Penguin 1950, abridged text from 1968
Uniform edition: Heinemann 1966
In: *Mr. Campion's Clowns* (Chatto & Windus 1967) and *The Margery Allingham Omnibus* (Penguin 1982), both in abridged text

4. *Look to the Lady*
First edition: Jarrolds, January 1931 (not dated)
Black binding, green lettering on spine

Dust-wrapper by Youngman Carter
Penguin 1950; Uniform edition: Heinemann 1966
In: *The Margery Allingham Omnibus* (Penguin 1982)
Variant title: *The Gyrth Chalice Mystery*
First edition: Doubleday 1931
Serialized in Union Jack Library with this title, 11. June—29. October 1932 In: *Three Cases for Mr. Campion* (Doubleday 1961)

5. *Police at the Funeral*
First edition: Heinemann, October 1931
Blue binding, yellow lettering on spine
Dust-wrapper by Youngman Carter, end-papers by Alan Gregory
First U.S. edition: Doubleday 1932
Penguin 1939; Uniform edition: Heineman 1964

6. *Sweet Danger*
First edition: Heineman, March 1933
Pale yellow binding, black lettering on red triangle on spine
Dust-wrapper by Youngman Carter.
End-papers and frontispiece by Alan Gregory
Penguin 1950; Uniform edition: Heinemann 1966
In: *Mr. Campion's Lady* (Chatto & Windus 1965)
Variant title: *Kingdom of Death*
First edition: Doubleday 1933
Bestseller Mystery No. 56, in abridged text
Variant title: *The Fear Sign*
First edition: MacFadden 1961

7. *The Mystery Man of Soho*
First edition: Amalgamated Press, 1. April. 1933
The Thriller No. 217, in newspaper format
Illustrated by A. Jones
Episode 4 of *Out of the Underworld* by Peter Brampton is also featured in this issue
In: *The Allingham Minibus* (Chatto & Windus 1973), with the variant title 'A Quarter of a Million'

8. *Death of a Ghost*
First edition: Heinemann, February 1934
Blue binding, silver lettering on spine
Dust-wrapper by Youngman Carter
End-papers by Alan Gregory
First U.S. edition: Doubleday 1934
Penguin 1942; Uniform edition: Heinemann 1964
In: *Crime and Mr. Campion* (Doubleday 1959)

9. *Flowers for the Judge*

First edition: Heinemann, February 1936
Red binding, gold lettering on spine
Dust-wrapper by Youngman Carter
End-papers by Alan Gregory
First U.S. edition: Doubleday 1936
Penguin 1944; Uniform edition: Heinemann 1964
In: *Crime and Mr. Campion (Doubleday 1959)*
Variant title: *Legacy in Blood*
First edition: Mercury 1949, in abridged text

10. *Mr. Campion: Criminologist*
First edition: Doubleday 1937
Black binding, orange lettering on spine
Dust-wrapper by Duggan
The first collection of Allingham stories, including *The Case of the Late Pig* and six stories

11. *Dancers in Mourning*
First edition: Heinemann, May 1937
Black binding, gold lettering on spine
Dust-wrapper by Youngman Carter, end-papers by Alan Gregory
First U.S. edition: Doubleday 1937
Penguin 1948; Uniform edition: Heinemann 1966
Number 32 in Jonathan series, in abridged text
In: *Crime and Mr. Campion* (Doubleday 1959) and *The Mysterious Mr. Campion* (Chatto & Windus 1963)
Variant title: *Who Killed Chloe?*
First edition: Avon 1943

12. *The Case of the Late Pig*
First edition: Hodder & Stoughton, May or June 1937
Published in a series called 'New-at-Ninepence', in wrappers
Cover is yellow, with title and an illustration in blue
Two unattributed illustrations precede the text
Penguin 1940; Uniform edition: Heinemann 1968
In: *Mr. Campion: Criminologist* (Doubleday 1937) and *The Mysterious Mr. Campion* (Chatto & Windus 1963)

13. *The Fashion in Shrouds*
First edition: Heinemann, June or July 1938
Green binding, gold lettering on spine
Dust-wrapper by Youngman Carter

First U.S. edition: Doubleday 1938
Penguin 1950; Uniform edition: Heinemann 1965
In: *Three Cases for Mr. Campion (Doubleday 1961)* and *Mr. Campion's Lady* (Chatto
& Windus 1965), the latter in abridged text

14. *Mr. Campion and Others*
First edition: Heinemann, March 1939 (not dated)
Green binding, gold lettering on spine
Dust-wrapper by Youngman Carter
Penguin 1950, with variant contents
Uniform edition: Heinemann 1967, with original contents
The second collection of Allingham stories, including fourteen stories

15. *Black Plumes*
Serialized in Collier's Magazine in 1940
First edition: Doubleday, November 1940
Yellow binding, black lettering and design on spine
First British edition: Heinemann, November 1940
Fawn binding, black lettering on spine
Dust-wrapper by Youngman Carter
Penguin 1950; Uniform edition: Heinemann 1965
Bestseller Mystery No. 33, in abridged text

16. *Traitor's Purse*
First edition: Heinemann, February 1941
Orange binding, black lettering on spine
Dust-wrapper by C.W. Bacon
First U.S. edition: Doubleday 1941
Penguin 1950; Uniform edition: Heinemann 1965
In: *Three Cases for Mr. Campion* (Doubleday 1961) and *Mr. Campion's Lady* (Chatto
& Windus 1965)
Variant title: *The Sabotage Murder Mystery*
First edition: Avon 1942

17. *Coroner's Pidgin*
First edition: Heinemann, March 1945
Black binding, silver lettering on spine
Dust-wrapper is unattributed
Penguin 1950; Uniform edition: Heinemann 1965
In: *Mr. Campion's Clowns* (Chatto & Windus 1967), in abridged text
Variant title: *Pearls before Swine*
First edition: Doubleday 1945
(This edition has a different final sentence from the British)

18. *Wanted: Someone Innocent*
First edition: Stamford House 1946

Published as Pony Book No. 56, in wrappers
Pictorial cover is unattributed
The third collection of Allingham stories, including the titular novella and three stories
19. *The Case Book of Mr. Campion*
First edition: Spivak 1947
Published as Mercury Mystery No. 12, in orange wrappers
Introduction by Ellery Queen
Cover design by Salter
The fourth collection of Allingham stories, including seven stories

20. *More Work for the Undertaker*
First edition: Heinemann 1948 (actually February 1949)
Black binding, with silver lettering on spine
Dust-wrapper and end-papers are unattributed
First U.S. edition: Doubleday 1949
Penguin 1952; Uniform edition: Heinemann 1964
In: *Mr. Campion's Clowns* (Chatto & Windus 1967), in abridged text

21. *Deadly Duo*
First edition: Doubleday 1949
Black binding, white lettering on spine
Dust-wrapper is unattributed
The first book is Allingham novellas, including *Wanted: Someone Innocent* and *Last Act*
Variant title: *Take Two at Bedtime*
First edition: World's Work, August or September 1950
Blue binding, black lettering on spine
Dust-wrapper by James E. McConnell
Penguin 1959; Uniform edition: Heinemann 1965

22. *Mr. Campion and Others*
First edition: Penguin 1950
Penguin No. 762, green and white wrappers
The fifth collection of Allingham stories, omitting six stories from the 1939 edition and adding five different ones

23. *The Tiger in the Smoke*
First edition: Chatto & Windus, 30. June. 1952
Red binding, gold lettering on spine
Dust-wrapper by Youngman Carter
First U.S. edition: Doubleday 1952
Penguin 1957
Heinemann Educational Books (1966), in abridged text
In: *The Mysterious Mr. Campion* (Chatto & Windus 1963)

24. *No Love Lost*
First edition: World's Work, 30. November. 1954
Green binding, black lettering on spine
Dust-wrapper is unattributed
First U.S. edition: Doubleday 1954
Penguin 1959; Uniform edition: Heinemann 1965
The second book of Allingham novellas, including *The Patient at Peacocks Hall* and *Safer than Love*

25. *The Beckoning Lady*
First edition: Chatto & Windus, 25. April 1955
Blue binding, gold lettering on spine
Dust-wrapper by Youngman Carter
Penguin 1960
Variant title: *The Estate of the Beckoning Lady*
First edition: Doubleday 1955

26. *Hide My Eyes*
Serialized in abridged form in 'Suspense', August/September 1958
First edition: Chatto & Windus, 24. September. 1958
Orange binding, gold lettering on spine
Dust-wrapper by Youngman Carter
Penguin 1960
Reader's Digest Condensed Books Vol. 22 (1960) includes an abridged text
Variant title: *Tether's End*
First edition: Doubleday 1958
Variant title: *Ten Were Missing*
First edition: Dell, October 1961

27. *Crime and Mr. Campion*
First edition: Doubleday 1959
The first U.S. omnibus, containing: *Death of a Ghost, Flowers for the Judge* and *Dancers in Mourning*

28. *Three Cases for Mr. Campion*
First edition: Doubleday 1961
Black binding, gold lettering on spine
Dust-wrapper by Sydney Butchkes
The second U.S. omnibus, containing: *The Fashion in Shrouds, Traitor's Purse* and *The Gyrth Chalice Mystery*

29. *The China Governess*
First edition: Doubleday 1962
Red binding, gold lettering on spine
Dust-wrapper by Saul Lambert
First British edition: Chatto & Windus, May 1963

Sage-green binding, gold lettering on spine, title against a mauve background in a gold frame
Dust-wrapper by Youngman Carter
Penguin 1965

30. *The Mysterious Mr. Campion*
First edition: Chatto & Windus, October 1963
Red binding, gold lettering on spine
Dust-wrapper by Youngman Carter
The first British omnibus, containing: *The Case of the Late Pig, Dancers in Mourning, The Tiger in the Smoke* and 'On Christmas Day in the Morning', with an author's introduction, 'Mystery Writer in the Box'

31. *The Mind Readers*
First edition: Morrow, June 1965
Dark mauve binding, black spine with silver lettering
Dust-wrapper by Paul Bacon
First British edition: Chatto & Windus, October 1965
Black binding, gold lettering on spine
Dust-wrapper by Youngman Carter
Penguin 1968

32. *Mr. Campion's Lady*
First edition: Chatto & Windus, October or November 1965
Red binding, gold lettering on spine
Dust-wrapper by Youngman Carter
The second British omnibus, containing *Sweet Danger, The Fashion in Shrouds* (revised by the author), *Traitor's Purse* and 'Word in Season', with an author's preface

33. *Mr. Campion's Clowns*
First edition: Chatto & Windus, September 1967
Red binding, gold lettering on spine
Dust-wrapper by Youngman Carter
The third British omnibus, containing abridged texts of *Mystery Mile, Coroner's Pidgin* and *More Work for the Undertaker*, with a biographical foreword by Youngman Carter

34. *Cargo of Eagles*
First edition: Chatto & Windus 1968
Mauve binding, gold lettering on spine
Dust-wrapper by Youngman Carter
First U.S. edition: Morrow 1968
Penguin 1969
Completed by Youngman Carter after the author's death

35. *The Allingham Casebook*
First edition: Chatto & Windus, May 1969

Light brown binding, gold lettering on spine
Dust-wrapper by Youngman Carter
First U.S. edition: Morrow 1969
The sixth collection of Allingham stories, containing eighteen stories

36. *The Allingham Minibus*
First edition: Chatto & Windus, February 1973
Mauve binding, gold lettering on spine
Dust-wrapper after an unattributed illustration in 'The Daily Express'
First U.S. edition: Morrow 1973
The seventh collection of Allingham stories, containing eighteen stories

37. *The Margery Allingham Omnibus*
First edition: Penguin 1982Wrappers, with pictorial cover by George Hardie
The fourth British omnibus, containing *The Crime at Black Dudley, Mystery Mile*
(in abridged text) and *Look to the Lady*

B. Crime fiction: stories

Stories are listed alphabetically according to title. Precedence is given to the collected
title where the story features in a collection, and to the alphabetical title where the
story is uncollected but has at least one variant. Ghost stories are included in this
section.

Key: **MCC/MR. CAMPION CRIMINOLOGIST; MCOH/MR. CAMPION & OTHERS**
(Heinemann); WSI/WANTED SOMEONE INNOCENT; CMC/CASE BOOK OF MR.
CAMPION; MCOP/MR. CAMPION & OTHERS (Penguin); AC/THE ALLINGHAM
CASEBOOK; AM/THE ALLINGHAM MINIBUS

1. The Barbarian (in AM)
2. Bird Thou Never Wert (in AM)
3. The Border-line Case (in MCC, MCOH, AC)
4. The Case is Altered (uncollected)
5. The Case of the Frenchman's Gloves (in MCOH)
aka Frenchmen Wear Gloves and The Frenchman's Gloves (in MCOP)
6. The Case of the Hat Trick (in MCOH)
aka The Magic Hat (in CMC) and The Hat Trick (in MCOP)
7. The Case of the Longer View (in MCOH)
aka The Crimson Letters (in CMC) and The Longer View (in MCOP)
8. The Case of the Man with the Sack (in MCC)
aka The Man with the Sack (in AM)
9. The Case of the Name on the Wrapper (in MCOH)
aka The Name on the Wrapper (in MCOP)
10. The Case of the Old Man in the Window (in MCC, MCOH)
aka The Old Man in the Window (in MCOP)
11. The Case of the Pro and the Con (in MCC)

aka The Pro and the Con (in AC)

12. The Case of the Question Mark (in MCOH, CMC)

aka The Question Mark (in MCOP)

13. The Case of the White Elephant (in MCC, MCOH)

aka The White Elephant (in MCOP)

14. The Case of the Widow (in MCC, MCOH)

aka The Widow (in MCOP)

15. The Chocolate Dog (uncollected)

aka The Dog Day and Here Today

16. The Correspondents (in AM)

17. The Curious Affair on Nut Row (uncollected)

aka Father of All Fish and The Man with the Cuckoo Clock

18. The Danger Point (in MCOP)

19. The Definite Article (in CMC, MCOP)

20. Evidence in Camera (in AC)

21. Face Value (in AC)

22. He Preferred Them Sad (in AM)

23. He Was Asking After You (in WSI, AM)

24. Is There a Doctor in the House? (in AC)

aka The Doctor and the Silver Plate, Felony at Mr. Mevagissy's and The Great London Jewel Robbery

25. It Didn't Work Out (in MCOH)

26. Joke Over (in AC)

aka the Man Who Utterly Vanished

27. The Kernel of Truth (uncollected)

28. The Lie-about (in AC)

29. Little Miss Know-all (in AC)

aka The Neatest Trick of the Month

30. The Lying-in-State (in AC)

aka It's All Part of the Service and The Lying-in-State Affair

31. A Matter of Form (in CMC, MCOP)

32. The Meaning of the Act (in CMC, MCOP)

33. The Mind's Eye Mystery (in AC)

aka Catching at Straws and Open Verdict

34. Mr. Campion's Lucky Day (in AM)

aka Dead Man's Evidence

35. Mr. Yansen's Gift (uncollected)

aka The Wind Glass

36. The Mistress in the House (in MCOH)

37. Mum Knows Best (in AC)

aka Mother Knows Best

38. On Christmas Day in the Morning (in *The Mysterious Mr. Campion*)

39. One Morning They'll Hang Him (in AC)

40. The Perfect Butler (in MCOH, AM)

41. A Proper Mystery (uncollected)

42. The Psychologist (in AC)

aka The End of the Rope, Money to Burn and For Love or Money
43. Publicity (in MCOH, AM)
44. A quarter of a Million (in AM)
aka The Mystery Man of Soho (see Section A, no. 7)
45. Safe as Houses (in CMC, MCOP)
46. The Same to Us (in AM)
47. The Secret (in AM)
48. The Sexton's Wife (in WSI, AM)
49. She Heard It on the Radio (in AM)
50. The Snapdragon and the C.I.D. (in AC)
aka Murder Under the Mistletoe
51. Tall Story (in AC)
52. They Never Get Caught (in MCOH, AC)
53. Three is a Lucky Number (in AC)
aka Bluebeard's Bathtub, Bubble Bath No. 3 and Murder Under the Surface
54. 'Tis Not Hereafter (in WSI, AM)
55. The Unseen Door (in AM)
56. The Villa Marie Celeste (in AC)
aka Family Affair
57. The Wink (in AM)

Variant titles with numerical references

Bluebeard's Bathtub (53); Bubble Bath No. 3 (53); Catching at Straws (33); The Crimson Letters (7); Dead Man's Evidence (34); The Doctor and the Silver Plate (24); The Dog Day (15); The End of the Rope (42); Family Affair (56); Father of All Fish (17); Felony at Mr. Mevagissy's (24); For Love or Money (42); Frenchmen Wear Gloves (5); The Great London Jewel Robbery (24); Here Today (15); It's All Part of the Service (30); The Lying-in-State Affair (30); The Magic Hat (6); The Man Who Utterly Vanished (26); The Man with the Cuckoo Clock (17); Money to Burn (42); Mother Knows Best (37); Murder Under the Mistletoe (50); Murder Under the Surface (53); The Mystery Man of Soho (44); The Neatest Trick of the Month (29); Open Verdict (33); The Wind Glass (35).

C. *Novels as Maxwell March*
1. *Other Man's Danger*
First edition: Collins 1933
Variant title: The Man of Dangerous Secrets
First edition: Doubleday 1933
2. *Rogues' Holiday*
First edition: Collins 1935
Dust wrapper by Youngman Carter
First U.S. edition: Doubledy 1935
3. *The Shadow in the House*
First edition: Collins Crime Club 1936
First U.S. edition: Doubleday 1936

D. *Other Books*

1. *Blackkerchief Dick*
First edition: Hodder & Stoughton 1923
First U.S. edition: Doubleday 1923
Romantic adventure novel set in the 17th century

2. *Water in a Sieve*
First edition: Samuel French 1925
One-act play with incidental music by Donald Ford
No. 2 of French's Plays for Juvenile Performers
Performed at Earlham Hall, Forest Gate, London on 3. October. 1924

3. *The Oaken Heart*
First edition: Michael Joseph 1941
First U.S. edition: Doubleday 1941
Re-issued with illustrations by Youngman Carter, Hutchinson 1959
Wartime autobiography

4. *Dance of the Years*
First edition: Michael Joseph 1943
Variant title: *The Galantrys*
First edition: Little, Brown 1943
Mainstream 'saga' novel

E. *20 Other stories*

1. The Beauty King (uncollected)
2. The Day of the Demon (uncollected)
3. The Funny—Faced Horse (uncollected)
aka Sweet and Low
4. Happy Christmas (uncollected)
5. Jubilee for Two (uncollected)
6. The Pioneers (in *The Allingham Casebook*)
7. Word in Season (in *Mr. Campion's Lady*)

F. Unpublished work

1. *Dido and Aeneas*
Verse play performed at St. George's Hall in London c. 1922

2. Without Being Naturally qualified

Early play written in the '20s

3. *Green Corn*
Mainstream novel about youth in the '20s, written after *Blackkerchief Dick*

4. Room to Let
Radio crime-play broadcast by the BBC in 1947

5. *The Relay*
Non-fiction book about the care of the old, written 1964
6. *Stories:*
The Black Tent (crime story)
Once in a Lifetime
The Studied Insult
The Wisdom of Esdras (ghost story)

Commentary

I have examined all British first editions except *The Crime at Black Dudley*, of which I've been unable to find a copy.

The dates of most American editions are taken from published sources. All the information about Penguin and Uniform editions derives from the books but my knowledge of American paperback variants and abridgements is almost entirely second-hand. Of the books that appeared first (or only) in the U.S.A. I've seen *Mr. Campion: Criminologist, Black Plumes, Wanted: Someone Innocent, Case Book of Mr. Campion, Deadly Duo, Three Cases for Mr. Campion, The China Governess* and *The Mind Readers*.

I've listed abridgements because it's interesting, and perhaps instructive, to see how many there are.

Three books were published in 1937. I've put *Mr. Campion: Criminologist* first because it certainly ante-dates the U.S. edition of *Dancers in Mourning*. It doesn't necessarily follow that it also ante-dates the British edition, but that's what I've assumed. *Dancers in Mourning* appears to have been published just before *The Case of the Late Pig*, since the British Library dates the former 31. May. 1937 and the latter 9. June. 1937: but the *English Catalogue of Books* dates both to May 1937.

The Fashion in Shrouds is dated 29. June. 1938 in the British Library and the *English Catalogue* puts it in July 1938.

The British Library has two firsts of *Black Plumes*, the American, dated 1. November. 1940, and the British, dated 26. November. 1940. On this somewhat slender evidence I've assumed that the Doubleday edition is the true first.

Take Two at Bedtime is dated 2. August. 1950 by the British Library but the *English Catalogue* gives September 1950.

It is possible that the Doubleday edition of *No Love Lost* is the true first, since the British edition appeared so late in the year. I believe there's no doubt about *The Mind Readers*, since the American first

252

in the British Library is dated 10. June. 1965 and the British is dated 12. October. 1965. In addition, the dust-wrapper of the Chatto edition quotes American reviews. *Mr. Campion's Lady* appeared shortly after *The Mind Readers*, which is described as 'just published' on its wrapper: thus, it came out later in October or some time in November.

Albert Campion does not appear in *The White Cottage Mystery, The Mystery Man of Soho, Black Plumes, Wanted: Someone Innocent, Deadly Duo* and *No Love Lost*. Otherwise, he features in all the novels and omnibus volumes and in all the stories in *Mr. Campion: Criminologist, The Case Book of Mr. Campion* and the Penguin *Mr. Campion and Others*. In the other three story collections, there is an admixture of non-series stories.

CPSIA information can be obtained at www.ICGtesting.com
Printed in the USA
LVOW13s2309240414

383187LV00002B/223/P

9 780879 723804